ST. CHARLES COU...

85 0004896

W9-CMO-776

Money and European Union

Money and European Union

Stephen Frank Overturf

St. Martin's Press
New York

SCCCC - LIBRARY
4601 Mid Rivers Mall Drive
St. Peters, MO 63376
WITHDRAWN

MONEY AND EUROPEAN UNION
Copyright © Stephen Frank Overturf, 1997
All rights reserved. Printed in the United States of America. No part of this book may be used
or reproduced in any manner whatsoever without written permission except in the case of brief
quotations embodied in critical articles or reviews. For information, address St. Martin's Press,
Scholarly and Reference Division, 175 Fifth Avenue, New York, N.Y. 10010

ISBN 0-312-17301-6

Library of Congress Cataloging-in-Publication Data

Overturf, S.F. (Stephen Frank)
   Money and European Union / Stephen Overturf.
      p.   cm.
   Includes bibliographical references and index.
   ISBN 0-312-17307-6
   1. Money—European Union countries.   2. Monetary unions—European
Union countries.   3. Monetary policy—European union countries.
4. Money—law and legislation—European Union countries.   I. Title.
HG925.094   1997
332.4'94—dc21   96-53464
                                                                                       CIP

First published in July, 1997

Typeset by Letra Libre

10 9 8 7 6 5 4 3 2 1

To Patti

Contents

Introduction

Europe is integrating around money; that is the core thesis of this work. This view seems well supported by the available evidence and appears robust in spite of important, continuing questions about the future of monetary integration in Europe. The purpose of this book is to examine this thesis in some detail, and in the process, attempt to explain why it is that many of the states of the European Union have agreed to sacrifice to a European central bank one of the most important manifestations of what it means to be sovereign—the ability to identify and create money independently. An understanding of this movement toward economic and monetary union (EMU) in Europe becomes much easier with a full appreciation of its history, economics, and politics, for if there is any subject that benefits from an interdisciplinary approach, it is this. In fact, it may be impossible to understand the nature and progress toward EMU without such a broadly-based vision. Hence, an integrative approach can bring the interested observer into a fuller reading of this critically important development in Europe, as well as make more accessible a movement that to many seems too complicated and abstract to fathom. That is not to say that an understanding of EMU is exactly easy, however, and one purpose of this work is to guide the intelligent reader through some of the complexity surrounding the topic and encourage a fuller appreciation of the public debate and private concerns surrounding EMU.

In that effort, attention is paid to the underlying forces that have created and maintained the momentum toward monetary union, in spite of seemingly overwhelming obstacles. In this way I try to provide a long-term vision, a core of thought around which the news and daily occurrences surrounding EMU can be put into perspective. The reader ought to find ample reward for approaching what is, after all, a very exciting topic.

The structure of the book is intended, then, to make it accessible and useful for a variety of readers. In being systematic in structure, fully referenced, and objective in approach and tone, it is intended to serve an academic audience. On the other hand, by providing an explicit thesis, and, at many junctures throughout, being willing to draw conclusions as well as attempting to distill some of the overtly technical material into an approachable form, my hope is that the more general reader can find this book rewarding. If this work serves to bring a broad spectrum of people somewhat closer together in a more complete understanding and appreciation of the full nature of EMU, whether they embrace it or not, this book will have served its purpose well.

The book begins with a broadly historical view of the progress toward EMU and in each chapter I seek to draw conclusions pertinent to a more complete and current understanding of the integration movement. Chapter 1 begins with the first significant attempt toward EMU, the Werner Report, and its aftermath. Chapters 2 and 3 examine the establishment and experience with the European Monetary System. Chapters 4 and 5 establish the basis for, and structure of, a most important document in the history of monetary integration: the Delors Report. Chapters 6 and 7 do the same for the Maastricht Treaty, while chapter 8 presents and analyzes the ratification and exchange crises that followed upon the signing of the treaty. Chapter 9 looks more closely at the economics of monetary union, attempting to bridge some of the gaps between the ways economists and the public approach such questions. In chapter 10 I look to political thought to help further an understanding of why states might wish to bring themselves closer together in this way. Finally, in chapter 11, in essay form I provide a synopsis, taking evidence and conclusions from the historical, economic, and political analyses of the prior chapters to inform my thesis on the nature of money and European Union. For easy reference, three appendices provide the texts of the more important documents in the monetary integration process, the Werner Report (Appendix 1), the Delors Report (Appendix 2), and pertinent selections from the Maastricht Treaty (Appendix 3).

This book would have been impossible without the help of many friends and colleagues, and they are due a great deal of gratitude. For providing excellent working conditions and moral and financial support, thanks are due to: Niels Thygesen and the Economics Institute of the University of Copenhagen; Douglas Ferguson and the Ferguson Chair of International Economics at Whittier College; and to Willard and Betty Beling and Norman Fertig of the Borchard Foundation. I was able to take semester leave with the help of Richard Millman and Whittier College at the Château de la Bretesche—a site without parallel—allowing me to complete a work begun earlier in different, but no less amenable, surroundings at the institute. Several colleagues provided wonderful help on all or parts of the book (or prior works upon which it is based), and they include David Aaron, David Dixon, Kathryn Fortá, Craig Johnson, Matthias Kaelberer, Hugo Kaufmann, Jerry Laiblin, Doug Leigh, Maureen Nerio, Longépé Norbert, Erling Olsen, Carolyn Rhodes, Antonin Rusak, J. Robert Schaetzel, Friedrich Sell, Niels Thygesen,

Kim Thomas, Horst Ungerer, James Walsh, Paul Welfens, Gregory Woirol, my editor Karen Wolny, Hans Wrage, and Joseph Zanetta. Sandra Auman and Elizabeth Winters of the Delegation of the European Commission in Washington were especially helpful with the cover design. Special thanks are reserved for Patti, without whom it would have been impossible, and certainly much less fun.

ONE

The Early Modern History of European Monetary Integration

L ate in 1990 an intergovernmental conference of the European Community began to consider the steps necessary to achieve a single currency for Europe. Agreement at Maastricht in December 1991 followed, with new treaty language on economic and monetary union, and completion of the transition to such an end by 1999 at the latest. Even at that time, prior to final treaty ratification and what would eventually happen in transition, Europe had moved on to a higher plane of economic and political integration, closer to a United States of Europe, than would have seemed imaginable only two decades earlier. Yet, imagined it was, for it was in the Werner Report of 1970 that the concept of economic and monetary union (EMU) for Europe received its clearest definition as an ideal, that is, as a method to achieve political integration. This chapter examines what might be termed the early modern history of the movement toward monetary integration in Europe, from the Treaty of Rome (1957) through the experience with the exchange-rate system called the snake. Several conclusions follow from this past experience to help one understand the nature of this central form of economic integration.

Any conclusions must include a strongly revealed preference among the European states for stability of exchange rates, even if a virtual locking of rates has not always seemed desirable. The further movement toward integration implied by monetary union takes a conformity of national interests around such an objective. Whether or not monetary crises help or hinder such a movement is almost moot; what is clear is that increased and increasing capital mobility has called into question the ability of states to retain full control over their own monetary policies. This may make it easier to adopt the kind of coordination of policies necessary to be able to fix exchange rates, and even to consider taking the next step of moving monetary policy to the European level by adopting a common currency.

Treaty of Rome

Any examination of the recent progress toward economic and monetary union in Europe must necessarily begin with the 1957 Treaty of Rome. Whereas the document leading to the establishment of the European Economic Community (EEC) spoke decisively on the nature of the free flow of goods, services, and factors that would constitute a true common market,[1] it contained only vague, or tangential references to the common economic policies that are inherent in the concept of EMU. Hitiris and Fervoyianni (1983), for example, refer to the "imprecise" language of the treaty on these points, while Bloomfield (1973, p. l) finds the language "sketchy" and the "commitments ambiguous."

The external economic conditions of the late 1950s certainly contributed to the lack of any felt need to be more precise in delineating movement toward monetary union. Such a union is desirable, at least partially, for the stability it would bring, and the Bretton Woods system of international monetary management created at the end of the second world war had been largely successful in forging a high level of stability at the international level. In fact, it could be argued that a good degree of the stability associated with integration was already created for Europe through the United States dollar, in the gold-dollar exchange standard that was Bretton Woods. As long as economic policy in the United States was consistent with the system in not creating too much international liquidity—in the form of dollars as the key postwar currency—confidence in the system provided for continuing relatively fixed exchange rates between countries, allowing them to fluctuate only 1 percent on either side of their given values in terms of dollars. In truth, the rebuilding of Europe necessitated so significant an access to the United States capital and goods markets that a dollar shortage, or gap, was the perennial European concern, leading these states in the late 1950s to willingly run surpluses in order to accumulate dollar reserves.

In addition, Tsoukalis (1977) finds that the political setting was likewise not amenable to further expansion beyond that already achieved in the consensus to establish the Common Market. Indeed the future of the EEC as such was in doubt, with continuing debate on what would later be called the "widening" of the market into a broader free trade area, including the United Kingdom. Care was taken not to jeopardize the consensus that had generated the EEC, so that this experiment in leading to a political unification of Europe through economic integration would not be lost in an organization with more simple economic aims. This political motivation must not be undervalued. The postwar euphoria that had led to a myriad of proposals for the political unification of Europe, in order to avoid yet another military catastrophe in the name of divergent nation-states pursuing their own interests, had produced many fine pronouncements, but no concrete results. It was the vision, indeed many Europeans have called it the inspiration, of Jean Monnet, often called the "father of Europe," and Robert Schuman, French foreign minister, that the bringing together of the "Six,"[2] but most especially of West Germany and France, into an economic union would naturally lead to the desired political union. The historical precedent of the *Zollverein,* literally the customs union that eventually forged the basis of the modern German state in the previous century, has always been a powerful example of this process, and at the time the Treaty of Rome was viewed by those in Europe largely in these terms. Likewise, any threat to the EEC was viewed as a threat to an eventual United States of Europe, and it is for this reason that there was such care taken in not moving too fast too soon. The additional political problem during the late 1950s was that Germany was generally in favor of liberal, that is free-market, economic solutions to economic problems, and hesitated to allow for excessive governmental, not to mention supranational, intervention into the natural functioning of the economy.

That there was such conscious restraint by the drafters of the Rome Treaty (1957) seems clear enough from the language of the treaty itself. It is true that part one, Article 2 establishes the goal of "progressively approximating the economic policies of Member States, to promote [among others] . . . an increase in stability. . . ." Similarly, Article 3 looks to "the application of procedures which shall make it possible to co-ordinate the economic policies of Member States and to remedy disequilibria in their balance of payments."

Nevertheless, nothing specific could be construed to infringe upon the sovereignty of the members in their control over their own economic policies. Title I deals with economic policy, and Article 103 states that "Member States shall consider their policy relating to economic trends as a matter of common interest." To this point, however, they need only "consult with each other" on the actions to be implemented. The Council may, upon a proposal from the Commission, decide on "measures appropriate," but only "by means of a unanimous vote." The rest of the title deals with balance of payments (chap. 2, Articles 104–109) and commercial policy (chap. 3). The articles concerned with the balance of payments come closest to establishing the need for common policy, but here again the language is important. Article 104, for example, has each member state pursuing "the economic policy necessary to ensure the equilibrium of its balance of payments and to maintain confidence in its currency, while ensuring a high level of employment and the stability of the level of prices." In spite of such a tall order, there is the implication of need for intra–EEC policy action, and, indeed, Article 105 specifies that "in order to facilitate the achievement of the objectives stated in Article 104, Member States shall co-ordinate their economic policies." The only specific, however, to this end is the setting up of a Monetary Committee to "keep under review the monetary and financial situation of Member States." The remainder of the chapter speaks to the elimination of exchange controls (Article 106), the fact that rates of exchange are "a matter of common interest," especially with regard to competitiveness (Article 107), the granting of mutual assistance to deal with a state's extraordinary balance of payments crisis (Article 108), and the limited use of protective measures, again by a state facing severe balance-of-payments problems.

Reinforcing the notion of conscious restraint is the lack of any explicit reference—perhaps especially in the context of Article 107—to fixed rates of exchange. Although the argument is that Bretton Woods would have made such a reference redundant, the fact remains that a state was nonetheless free in its sovereign power to alter its own exchange rate, except to the extent that it appeared clearly that the member state was engaging in a competitive devaluation. Even then the result was that the Commission could "authorize" other member states to do what they could have been able to do in any case. It is at this juncture that the mild nature of the treaty emerges, reflecting the desire to not go too far in hindering the members from full and complete control over their own economic policies. As Swann (1988, p. 176) puts it, "The conclusion we can draw is that the EEC did not envisage a centralized control over macro-economic management." Likewise, Peters (1982, p. 2), finds that the treaty "contains virtually no obligation that might disturb the freedom for manoeuvre of those member states that remain firmly attached to the principle of national sovereignty in monetary matters."

This lack of specificity in the Treaty of Rome has, to this day, meant that further movement toward integration in the economic and monetary policy spheres has had to rely upon a coincidence of interests of the member states, and an ability to translate that coincidence into the specific form of policies and institutions developed from the beginning. Indeed, it was only with the basis of the European Monetary System as a prior and established institution that a rudimentary base structure for EMU developed. While the rationale of the drafters of the Treaty of Rome to not be more specific in this regard is understandable, it has made the process that much harder. This is nowhere clearer than in the events that developed in the 1960s and 1970s; for example, the difficulties encountered in establishing a stable exchange-rate system, and in moving toward monetary union.

Toward the Werner Report

In the late 1950s and early 1960s several proposals, chronicled well in Tsoukalis (1977), emerged on the monetary front. These were not embraced by all members, for various reasons, and hence came to nothing. The relatively stable international markets and continuing EEC surpluses lend some credence to the old notion that in European monetary affairs it takes a crisis to thrust the Community onto a higher level of integration. Indeed the revaluations of the German Deutschmark (DM) and the Dutch guilder, in response to the especially large surpluses in Germany and the Netherlands, provided part of the impetus for the Commission's Action Program (of 1962) for the second stage.[3] The other form of crisis, in a sense, was the application by the British for accession into the Community. Tsoukalis (1977, p. 57) refers to Miriam Camps' proposition that one purpose of the Action Program was "to guard against the loss of momentum in the process of integration, as a consequence of a possible British entry."

The Action Program, EEC Commission (1962), itself suggested a high level of economic planning at the EEC level, including a committee of governors of member central banks; a common monetary policy with "fixed rates of exchange between Member States with very narrow limits on the variation allowed;" a European reserve currency; a "confrontation" of national budgets; and a continuation of the liberalization of capital movements. It was a significant document in providing an agenda for future movement toward EMU that would be echoed in the Werner and Delors Reports much later.

The theory that crisis gives impetus toward greater integration snags on this particular example, however, for the reaction to the Action Program was frosty, with the German negative reaction being the strongest. German liberal attitudes, coupled with fear of jeopardizing Atlantic economic and political ties, explains part of this response. Fear of generating inflation through an uncontrolled European monetary organization, a perennial German argument, probably explains the rest. France's, that is de Gaulle's, veto of the British application in January 1963, subsequently insured that little movement on the plan would occur.

The Council did enact several of the institutional suggestions of the 1962 plan in April and May 1964, probably in reaction to the Italian inflation and balance-of-payments crisis in 1963 and early 1964. The recognized need for greater coordination resulted in the establishment of the Committee of Governors of the Central Banks of the EEC, designed for prior consultation on monetary and exchange rate changes, as well as of a Budgetary Policy Committee and a Medium-term Economic Policy Committee.

The following four years, 1964 to 1968, have been called the "years of indifference," in which "no significant action was taken to promote monetary integration," Bloomfield (1973, p. 6). In spite of the Commission drawing the attention of the members to diverging economic trends, and the increasing importance of these trends as the integration process of the Community progressed, there was little, or no, reaction. The reasons must include, first, in spite of increasing United States inflation rates that held alarming implications for the continuance of Bretton Woods, a level of complacency and sense of stability engendered by continuing European payment surpluses. Second, de Gaulle's unwillingness to give up even a shred of French sovereignty to the EEC also meant that, politically, any proposal for further movement toward EMU was most certainly foredoomed.[4] The establishment of the Luxembourg Compromise in 1966, which essentially accepted unanimity in EEC decision making in return for France's continued association, is indicative of the fact that the Community was in these years more mired in a process of surviving as a common market than in taking the next steps toward economic union. Third, Tsoukalis (1977), emphasizes what he calls the "agricultural mythology." Because agricultural prices were now set at the Community level in units of account that were translated into farm prices within the various states by using the existing exchange rates, under the rules of the Common Agricultural Policy (CAP) any change in the exchange rates would yield either increases in farm income and EEC subsidies in the case of devaluation, or reduced farm incomes and reduced subsidies in the case of revaluation.[5] In either case there was a political problem, in the latter internally for a country with its own farm sector, in the former externally with one's EEC partners. For this reason, and during these years, changes in exchange parities appeared tantamount to unthinkable, especially if CAP was to survive as one of the few examples (other than the customs union) of European integration, and so, as Tsoukalis (1977, p. 62) puts it: "There was a widespread belief that de facto monetary union had already been achieved."

This level of complacency was shattered when several crises at the end of the decade demonstrated that the Bretton Woods System was in serious trouble and that intra-European exchange rates were not necessarily immutable. After these crises the idea of monetary stability based upon a fixed exchange-rate system through the dollar was seriously questioned in Europe. Splitting of the gold market into two tiers and the 1967 U.K. devaluation provided ample evidence of the former, while the first serious EEC crisis was French, a payments crisis following the student revolts in May of 1968 and subsequent wage increases. Belief in a DM appreciation and French franc devaluation, reflecting divergent inflation rates in both countries, led to corresponding speculative capital flows, which both countries attempted to stem through the use of exchange controls. France's reluctance to devalue has traditionally been associated with the psychological importance, that is the prestige, of its unit of account; whereas the Germans, in spite of heavy external pressure, at this time seemed most concerned about the impact of revaluation on powerful internal export and farm interests. These were more political than economic interactions, and both countries were forced finally to acquiesce, with France devaluing by 11.1 percent in August of 1969, and Germany revaluing by 9.3 percent in October of the same year, but not before the serious level of concern with the stability of the international monetary system and the lack of any real level of EEC coordination led to renewed interest in EMU.

The most significant result of these concerns at the time, although not well accepted at first, was the first Barre Plan of February 1969. The plan, or report, consisted of two sets of proposals, each of which had been made before, separately, but together they contributed what Kruse (1980, p. 25) called "a coherent whole, complementing and reinforcing each other." The proposals were intended as responses to the failure of the EEC states to coordinate policies and support each other in the immediately preceding crisis. To this end the first Barre Plan suggested first a more complete level of coordination and consultation (or "concertation") of economic policies prior to decision making, in contradistinction to past practice, and second, a level of mutual financial assistance to allow members to borrow from each other in exchange crises, as a complement to other forms of international aid.

Again, Kruse (1980) suggested that the Barre Plan was more backward- than forward-looking, was designed to deal with a particular perceived problem, and that its intent was to ensure the continuation of the previously achieved customs union and CAP through preservation of fixed exchange rates. It was, nevertheless, as Kruse also pointed out, "the Community's first attempt to formulate a systematic, coherent approach to monetary union," and it served as a catalyst to the focusing of thought on economic and monetary union as the next step in European integration. An interesting tactic in the report was to stress that unless further actions of an integrative nature were taken there would be the threat of losing much of what had already been gained through the customs union, whereas if these actions were taken it would further the economic welfare of all. This notion of the carrot and the stick will be seen to be common to other subsequent proposals dealing with greater monetary integration.

While the first Barre Report was initially not well received, continuing speculative flows during early 1969 caused much of the opposition to evaporate. In July 1969 the Council adopted a decision in direct response to the recommendations of the report whereby prior consultations were to occur on every form of economic policy that might have an "important" impact on the other states.[6]

These were the conditions that were facing the Europeans at the end of 1969: alarming developments on the international monetary front that spilled over into the intra–EC exchange markets, enhanced through an increasing degree of interdependence and diverging economic conditions. There was serious concern over the future of the customs union and CAP that led to a much more open attitude toward movement on the monetary front. The transition period seen by the Treaty of Rome was over, and it seemed an appropriate time for a new thrust toward unification. The Hague Summit of December 1969 was the result.

The Werner Report

The Hague Summit was important in the history of European integration. Charles de Gaulle had resigned in April 1969, and the French under Georges Pompidou showed much more inclination toward integration, including expansion through British entry. French attitudes were also influenced by the economic value to them of the continuance of CAP. The Germans were more receptive to monetary integration given the threats to the union, including potential protective actions against the rapidly growing EEC markets for German goods, as well as the concern over continued international monetary stability under Atlantic cooperation. The other four states followed along in the initiatives. They were, and are, more open economies, "extremely vulnerable" to events in the larger countries, and EMU "offered them an opportunity to exercise an influence on those events" (Swann, 1988, p. 179).

The question of British entry was intertwined with the EMU discussions, with the Germans emphasizing that those who feared growing German economic strength ought to embrace the proposal for enlargement. This would not be the last time a German government would use the growing power of that state as a rationale for potentially dissipating its own influence through an integrative move, but, in this case, it was not a crucial argument in that French opposition to British entry had already disintegrated.

In this way it appeared at the Hague that there was the coincidence of constellations that simultaneously inclined all of the member states toward greater integration, based upon their own economic and political self interest and the need to respond to a clear crisis. Thus resulted the "Spirit of the Hague." It is an interesting question whether this coincidence is what must occur before the governments can come together to consider a higher plane of unity. Events after the Hague, of course, demonstrated that even this is not always enough to bring it to fulfillment.

In spite of some apparent difference in French and German views that surfaced at the summit, the Council was called upon to draft a plan leading to EMU. The final communiqué of the conference mentions specifically the first Barre Report as a "basis" for the plan to come from the Council, which should be "a plan by stages." In addition, it states that the "development of monetary cooperation should be based on the harmonization of economic policies," and that the states agree "that the possibility should be examined of setting up a European reserve fund, to which a common economic and monetary policy would lead."

Also inherent in the language of the communiqué is explicit recognition of the implications of these moves for eventual political union. The document emphasizes "preparing the way for a united Europe," and the desire by the members to "reaffirm their faith in the political objects which give to the Community its whole meaning and significance, the determination to carry the enterprise through to its conclusion, and their confidence in the final success of their efforts." Indeed, the Ministers of Foreign Affairs at the Hague were called upon "to study the best way of realizing progress in the field of political unification." These words are important for two reasons. First, they established the need to move toward political unification in tandem with economic and monetary union. This was to be echoed some twenty years later in the Delors Report. Secondly, they directly addressed what has been something of an intellectual conceit for decades; that the development of the EEC, and also EMU, is intended as an economic mechanism in some way to "fool" the Europeans implicitly into accepting political union. The argument in this extreme form almost presumes that the sovereign governments of Europe are unprepared for the task of understanding the implications of their acts, and, as though that does not do enough disservice, it ignores a more continuing and honest theme among the "Europeans." This is that economic integration certainly will make more apparent some of the benefits of greater unity, but unity must be entered into openly, knowingly, and enthusiastically by all members in order for it to survive and thrive.

After the Hague Summit the fact began to surface that agreement on EMU was based upon conflicting ideas of what was entailed. Two plans for EMU that were presented in the first few months of 1970 underlined the differences: the Schiller Plan, presented by the German government and endorsed by Italy and the Netherlands, and a second Barre Plan, presented by the Commission and supported generally by France, Belgium, and Luxembourg.

The Schiller Plan has been identified with the "economists." Its authors felt that economic policy coordination must come before any attempt to fix exchange rates. In this view it is the disparity in economic conditions, most especially inflation rates, that provides the market pressure to alter rates, so that full and complete coordination of policy at the Community level, and in Community institutions, would be a necessary precursor to fixing exchange rates. Fixed exchange rates, and perhaps a common currency, would and could only come at the end of a process of increasing policy coordination.

The Schiller Plan saw four stages. First there would be increased consultation on economic and monetary policies to a level of coordination, and the establishment of short-term assistance. In the second stage coordination would be enhanced to the extent necessary to see national economic trends merge, and this would also see some economic decisions taken by the Council. In the third stage a degree of supranational economic control, including a Community central bank, would come into being, along with the fixing of exchange rates and pooling of reserves, as well as the establishment of a free capital market. The fourth phase would yield a common currency and complete economic control exercised by Community institutions, reporting to the European Parliament.

Two other aspects of the Schiller Plan are important, in retrospect. It is at this juncture that the concept is introduced of the Community central bank having an independence from political control, resembling the Federal Reserve System in the United States and the Bundesbank in Germany. Price stability was to be a prime objective. Also, it is at this point that member states were seen to need to "commit themselves at the outset" to the entire plan, and "in full awareness that it would in time entail the transfer of authority over economic policy to central organizations" (Kruse, 1980, p. 62).

The "monetarists" were the other, opposing, group, and their views were, although not entirely, represented by the second Barre Plan. They argued for the need to establish, first, the most apparent and visible evidence of greater unity, the fixing of exchange rates, that would demonstrate EMU. Swann (1988, pp. 181–2) quotes Coffey and Presley in reference to the monetarists as "categorically" rejecting fluctuating exchange rates as a matter of principle, it being "preferable to irrevocably fix the exchange rates as soon as possible."

Only the first stage of the Barre Plan is described in any detail, with its establishing fixed rates, reducing fluctuations around the parities, and pooling of reserves to assist in the endeavor, the latter through a European Monetary Cooperation Fund (EMCF). Also, and not necessarily in concert with monetarist views, it also implied decision making at the Community level and harmonization of taxes.

Herein lies a scholarly controversy regarding the "economists" and "monetarists." Some maintain that the views of the two groups are mutually exclusive. Kruse (1980, p. 68), for example, describes the contrast between the two positions as "striking," noting that the "Schiller Plan describes the final stage in great detail, explores the political and institutional implications of EMU, and presents the route to be followed all the way to the achievement of the ultimate goal; the Barre Plan is vague on the precise attributes of the final stage, skirts the political and institutional questions, and specifies only the measures to be taken during the first stage." Also, the Barre Plan is more keen on establishing new institutional structures early on than is the Schiller Plan. The sense of this view of mutual exclusivity is that there were two warring camps that had identified their positions in such a way as to be in essentially diametric opposition to one another.

The other view is that these plans differed simply on means and not ends. In other words, they consisted of different strategies to a common goal. Swann (1988, p. 180) puts it that the "two schools differed not in terms of the ultimate objective to be achieved but over the path that should be followed in order to achieve the objective." That is, one may explain the seemingly perverse "monetarist" insistence of fixing exchange rates first in that such a move would force any policy coordination needed for maintenance of the fixed rates and thus avoid the possibility of endless debates between the states over the proper policy. In the same vein, Tsoukalis (1977, p. 92) felt that the "controversy was only about the strategy to be adopted during the transition period in order to reach a harmonization of policy preferences." There was, according to this view, a full understanding by the monetarists that if one attempts to fix exchange rates before coordinating monetary policies, the different growth rates of money between any two member countries would soon surface in differential inflation rates and lead to a balance-of-payments crisis and pressure to adjust parities. Recognition of this problem would, from the start, oblige governments to engage in those policies necessary to keep the parities fixed. In this way, there would be the "concertation" needed to fully move onto the desired EMU at a later stage, and, in fact, this could be a superior method by which to achieve such union rather than attempting to fix, say, monetary growth rates from the beginning.

What occurred next historically allows for some reinforcement of both of these positions. Due to the contradictory nature of the two plans, and the strength of the adherents to each, a committee was established early in 1970 (under Pierre Werner, the Prime Minister and Finance Minister of Luxembourg) to attempt to resolve the conflict of opinion and establish a plan for EMU acceptable to all. The Werner Committee was clearly chosen with this compromise objective in mind, rather than, say, to choose one plan over another based upon the utilization of objectively and independently applied logic.

Reinforcing the opinion that the monetarists differed from the economists only over means and not ends, the committee very early on agreed on the nature of EMU. It would entail, as eventually spelled out in the final Werner Report (1970), and included here as Appendix 1, "total and irreversible mutual convertibility free from fluctuations in rates and with immutable parity rates, or preferably they will be replaced by a sole Community currency," a centralized control over money and credit, a unified capital market, strong control over public financing at the Community level, and increased regional and structural policies. Moreover, the language of the report makes it very clear that there will be a transfer of sovereignty from the states to the Community. Specifically, the report establishes the need for the transfer of powers to a "centre of decision for economic policy" and a Community system of central banks. "These transfers of responsibility . . . represent a process of fundamental political significance which implies the progressive development of political cooperation." In case this was still unclear, the report goes on to emphasize that EMU "thus appears as a leaven for the development of political union which in the long run it will be unable to do without." In fact, it goes on even further to note the need to simultaneously transfer parliamentary power from the state to the Community level, that is, to a European Parliament.

Again, the fact that the Werner Committee was able to agree on this definition of EMU, and all that it entailed politically, is evidence that the economist-monetarist debate was simply one over means to a common end. It set down on paper and received unanimous support for a vision of a type and level of consensual integration among strong, sovereign, nation-states with few parallels in history. This decisive language remains a powerful clarion for those in Europe who believe in integration.

The other side of the coin, of course, is that in practice there was no agreement within the Werner Committee on how to achieve these goals. The committee very soon split into the same two camps represented under the names "economist" and "monetarist." In fact, even the goals spelled out above were considered minimalist with regard to what could be achieved, representing only those necessary to the free flow of goods, services, people, and capital. The real question is how seriously even these goals were taken by those who agreed to them. If they were all viewed as necessary and desirable would there have continued such an intense level of debate and disagreement when it came to establishing the actual steps that might or might not be taken to achieve them? Why fight so strongly for example, as a monetarist might, against greater coordination of monetary and economic policies if this were to be the eventual and desired outcome of the process; and if it were seriously accepted as important by all those participating? The proposition must be considered that some of the goals enumerated above were valued highly, but that there was a lower level of priority placed on others. Without accepting this view, again, it is difficult to understand the intensity of the debate.

Specifically, it can be argued that the monetarists, in general, or rather the French in particular, felt very strongly about fixed exchange rates, and the need to establish them as the first priority for monetary action, both in importance and in time. This was because of their connection with the continuance of a CAP that benefitted France, as well as with an independent stance, or "monetary personality," of Europe versus the dollar. Such an attitude could well explain France's insistence upon the need for a system of mutual aid to maintain fixed rates while also being very reluctant to give up any sovereign control over policy setting to the Community.[7]

Likewise, the German (or economist) position was strongly opposed to establishing fixed rates until and unless there were greater coordination of policies. They saw little importance in a "monetary personality" that made a political statement opposed to dependence in an Atlantic setting (in fact, just the opposite). As well, they were certainly not interested in setting up mutual aid facilities that could encourage countries to continue to run lax monetary policies, unhindered from the need to disinflate by the ease of balance-of-payments financing coming from otherwise "responsible" European states, such as West Germany. In this view, the only option, in an increasingly interdependent system, would be to give up to a higher level independent economic policies so as to establish the base conditions upon which fixed rates, and eventually a common currency, might be built. Such a transfer would have the promise of not only insuring the continued growth in trade but also in controlling inflation.

In sum, it seems that the debate was due not so much to a difference in strategy as it was to different ends, representing the different economic and political objectives of the states involved. In any case, the positions were so entrenched that when it came to deciding upon specific action at the first stage there was no agreement, the French insisting upon fixing rates (without coordination), and the Germans insisting upon coordination (without first fixing rates). The deadlock continued through May 1970 when an interim report from the committee established only a "minimal" level of agreement. The consensus, to the extent that it really was one, was achieved only in the final description of EMU (as represented above), and that union could be attained by 1980. The debate continued, was shunted briefly back to the Council with no success, and then back to the Werner Committee, where neither group was willing to yield. Finally, compromise was reached whereby the basis for eventual movement in the monetary sphere would be outlined as the first stage, while the nature of the other stages would, of necessity since there had been no agreement, remain undefined. Together with the already accepted description of the final necessary elements of EMU, it constituted the document that was filed as the final Werner Report of October 1970.

Again, without establishing that prior coordination of economic and monetary policies is to occur, or is even useful, it was possible for the monetarists to accept under the first stage that the "reinforcement of the coordination of economic policies during the first stage seems one of the principal measures to be taken," but "this can only be applied progressively." Likewise, it was possible for the economists to accept "from the start of the first stage, by way of experiment, the central banks acting in concert will limit de facto the fluctuations in the rates of exchange between their currencies. . . ."[8] This compromise was termed "parallelism," or moving on both fronts simultaneously, but it does bear further emphasis that in reality neither side did finally agree to desert their position, except in a very minor way. It was not clear whether movement to the next stage would be either in the area of policy coordination or exchange rate pegging.

Nevertheless, the Werner Report was, and is, an important document. The description of the final nature of EMU, as noted above, continues to serve as the accepted vision for this area of European integration. The need to create recognition, and full acceptance, of the transference of powers explicit in the EMU definition by altering the Treaty of Rome is established in the report. The type of institutions necessary to achieve this purpose, specifically a "centre for decision for economic policy" and "a Community system for the central banks," the latter on a Federal Reserve System model, is outlined. The concept of stages, although mandated in the directions to the committee, and not evidencing a great degree of precision, is nonetheless present. The notion of constraint on national economic policies, including budgets, financing of deficits, the alignment of indirect taxes, and, of course, monetary policy, is there, as is the need to abolish "obstacles to capital movements, in particular residual exchange control regulations, and a coordination of policies as regards financial markets." Finally, the Werner Report recognizes the need for a European monetary fund, first in the form of an institution for monetary cooperation (to coordinate funds for mutual support) and, eventually, to keep and manage Community reserves.

The impact of the Werner Report on Europe is hard to overemphasize. A reading of the report in tandem with the later Delors Report (1989), which effectively set the agenda for the intergovernmental conference and eventual Maastricht agreements, reveals just how much the latter document owes to the intellectual influence of the former. The similarities between the two documents are striking. Indeed, the similarities trigger speculation on the eventual fate of the later thrust toward economic and monetary union as compared to that of the initiative some two decades earlier. One of the similarities between the two reports is the imprecision of definition of the stages, although the Delors Report compares rather more favorably on this score. It must be said that there is still a good deal of imprecision. In the earlier report the imprecision was represented by a lack of ability to agree on process as well as a fundamental disagreement on ends. It is at least possible to sense the same degree of disagreement inherent in the Delors Report, although, of course, it does not emanate from the consensus-building process as had the earlier report.

Events of the Early 1970s

It is instructive to examine the fate of the Werner Report given the (at least perceived) parallel with the more recent initiative on EMU. The filing of the report resulted in further debate within the Council on the value of the document. Yet again, reinforcing the view on means versus ends, the French government, with significant internal turmoil, decided to oppose the description of the final objective of EMU as contained in the report. There was such strong opposition, especially by the Gaullists, to any transfer of sovereignty to an EEC supranational body that France simply refused to accept the previously agreed upon definition of EMU, and insisted upon proceeding only on the very limited steps outlined under the studied compromise reached for the first stage. The "Spirit of the Hague," which really meant a coming together around a common concept of EMU, including by France under Pompidou, had disappeared.[9] France refused to consider any binding agreement on final transfer of powers, a revision of the Rome Treaty, the creation of new economic and monetary institutions, or new powers for the European Parliament.

Finally, a compromise was reached in early 1971, whereby it was resolved to establish EMU by the end of the decade, and although generally following the Werner sense of the final objectives and first stage, it significantly watered down the language on transfer of powers, treaty revisions, and new institutions. If greater coordination had not been achieved by the end of five years, the exchange rate elements of the first stage would be abandoned. This latter clause was included at the insistence of Germany, and was the basis for their willingness to go ahead with a plan now heavily "monetarist," or French, in spirit. Going ahead in this case meant primarily the experiment to limit exchange rate fluctuations, albeit coupled with commitment on regional aid, the balance-of-payments support and consultation procedures suggested in the first Barre Report.

Agreement around the Werner Report occurred only after a full realization of the political implications of seriously moving on toward EMU had caused one powerful Community state to essentially force an emasculation of the plan to the lowest level of agreement, and temporary agreement at that. Specifically, the agreement was that the margins of fluctuation between the exchange rates of the Community members in June 1971 were to be narrowed to 6 percent on either side of par, from the prior 75 percent.[10] This has been called a tunnel within the IMF tunnel, since the limits to fluctuation, or "bands," create a tunnel within which rates may effectively move.

As it happened, this plan never went into effect because of the coincidence of a major international monetary crisis in May, in which the deteriorating balance of payments of, and reduction of interest rates in, the United States led to heavy speculation and flow of capital abroad, much of it toward the DM. The response within the EEC could not be called the high point of coordinated decision making. The countries could not agree on an appropriate response, and so they went their own ways. Germany felt it would have been best to jointly float the Community currencies against the dollar, and suggested this. France was adamantly opposed to this, insisting instead that it was up to the United States to take the political statement of weakness that it considered devaluation of the dollar and suggested the use of exchange controls until that could be effected. Since such controls were antithetical to liberal ideals, the Germans, joined by the Dutch, floated their currencies against both the dollar and the other Community currencies. At this, the French instituted stronger exchange controls and refused any further talk on, or implementation of, EMU, and the entire project was put on hold until December 1971. Thus directly after at least a form of agreement, the concept of EMU had significantly and rapidly retrogressed.

A further dollar crisis of August 1971 led to President Nixon's closing of the gold window and instituting other measures designed to improve the United States' balance of payments. Again there was no agreement in the EEC, and Belgium and Luxembourg joined the Dutch in a joint float while Germany and Italy floated independently. Kruse (1980, p. 94) says that, at this time, "the divergent actions of the member states meant that the Community was considerably further from the goal of fixed and immutable exchange rates than it was before the EMU project was launched."

As 1971 progressed the two sides, controls versus individual floating, gradually came together with dissatisfaction with both antidotes to the heavy capital inflows coming to Europe. The Germans felt that floating had not effectively reestablished equilibrium, but instead had driven the exchange rate too high, while the French found they were unable to control flows through regulation, and they were concerned over the effects of other EEC currency floats on the CAP. The Community thus agreed on the need for movement back to fixed rates, but which would entail some realignment of the old rates. A joint Community position was formed, and was presented to the United States, from which a compromise was reached, first with President Nixon in the Azores, and then more formally at the Smithsonian Institution in December 1971. There was a realignment of exchange rates, with the dollar taking most of its downward adjustment against the other currencies (9 percent) by an explicit devaluation. The French franc was not appreciated. The return to "fixed" rates was to be effected by increasing the fluctuation margin to 2.25 percent (from one percent) on either side of the dollar.

This last part of the agreement, intended to allow for some breathing room on the need to intervene, nevertheless meant that the "tunnel" had significantly widened, and that any two European currencies could diverge from one another by no less than 9 percent. The pricing system under CAP, as well as the now tattered concept of EMU, would not allow for this. So, there was finally again a level of agreement reached when it was decided to limit rates to 2.25 percent among each other, and allow this narrower band to float within the wider International Monetary Fund (IMF) bands. This is the famous "snake in the tunnel," describing the appearance of the movement of the EEC rates on a time graph against the dollar.

It turns out that the dollar crisis, although initially resulting in disunity, finally brought the governments together in March 1972 with their common perception of the importance of greater fixity for them all within a European setting, independent of the United States. The agreement also included provisions for short-term credit,[11] and would apply to the prospective new entrants as well, that is, to the United Kingdom, Denmark, Norway, and Ireland. This appeared to be a renewed commitment to economic and monetary integration, especially when viewed in terms of, or perhaps because of, a collapsing international monetary system. Still, of course, it contained no political or extensive institutional changes, and so was not what one could call a large commitment.

The Snake

The history of the exchange-rate system called "the snake" as an example of European unity is checkered. Almost immediately, in June 1972, the pound dropped out, under considerable speculative pressure after a turn from balance-of-payments surplus into deficit, and was allowed to float. Ireland and Denmark were next, although Denmark soon reentered the arrangement. Early in the next year, specifically in February 1973, Italy left the system and allowed its currency to float. France left in January 1974, reentered during July 1975, and left for good in March 1976. By that time Norway had decided against membership, but decided to stay in the snake. Sweden had entered the arrangement in March 1973, but left it in August 1977. So, by 1977 the membership had been reduced to West Germany, Denmark, the Netherlands, Belgium, Luxembourg, and Norway. It was a system that contained not all of the members, including three of the larger ones, and was not even coincidental with the Community. It was best described as a group of countries whose economies were strongly influenced by West Germany, and so could be considered something of a "DM zone."

In addition, by February 1973 the international monetary system had deteriorated to such an extent that the tunnel had "exploded." The United States' balance of payments had continued to deteriorate in 1972 and early 1973 so extensively that the speculative pressure against the dollar was intense. Exchange controls in Europe had little net impact on the enormous inflows of capital, so there was little choice but to allow for appreciation against the dollar. There was opposition to a joint float, and its implications for the prior system of fixed rates, so the United States, although at this time in favor of floating, agreed to a 10 percent devaluation.[12] This, however, failed to quell the speculation, which intensified at an even greater rate than before, and, failing to acquiesce to another devaluation of a dollar that was not considered overvalued, the Community finally opted for a joint float. Bretton Woods was now dead. This was actually viewed as a type of victory for EMU because the snake had survived the turmoil. However, it was a victory with many casualties, for the snake had begun to shrink to become less than a Community institution. It was becoming clearer as time progressed that there was not the political will to maintain this symbol of union at the cost of domestic economic priorities, which took precedence to such an extent that it was increasingly difficult for members not obviously linked closely in trade to the DM to stay in the system.

The oil crisis that began in late 1973 only tended to exacerbate the differential economic trends of the several countries, not to cause them. Kruse (1980) is especially persuasive on this point, noting that the countries involved had about the same level of dependency upon oil, and the impact was very similar on their balances of payments. Whereas Germany responded to the crisis by continuing low demand growth, France responded by continuing its previously high utilization rate. This only placed further pressure on the snake, with France, as noted, pulling out in 1974.

In the meantime, the proposals by the Commission on further movement toward EMU by taking (relatively mild) steps toward economic policy convergence, pooling of reserves, and increasing short run balance of payments aid, ran into the same problem as before of the countries having irreconcilable views on policy coordination and institutions. The core disagreements that had been hidden after the Werner Report had not gone away, and, therefore, needed addressing for there to be essential movement on EMU. The lack of convergence of economic policies had put enormous strains on the snake, and now, with the rejection of the Commission's proposals, there was no chance for overcoming this obstacle. EMU could not continue, with countries not yet willing to give up their own domestic concerns to the higher objective.

The departure of the franc from the system underlined this fact. Under pressure from the exchange markets France chose, in January 1974, to float. It might have continued to support its currency with the use of reserves and institute the kind of economic policies that would bring, especially, its expected inflation rate closer in line with the rest of the snake members. It would not do that, nor would it devalue and remain within the system, since it was felt that the level of devaluation would have had to have been too great to restore equilibrium, at least in the minds of the market. It is significant that adherence to the system was not of great enough importance to the French authorities so that at least some attempt was made to maintain momentum toward EMU. As it was, the franc withdrew from the snake, although, as noted above, it was to reenter in 1975 and then leave again, turning the institution into a very different animal. Decisions were now formally made only by the participating members, and it was clear the thrust toward EMU through the symbolism of the snake had been lost.

It is true that the discussions on the movement toward the "second" stage of EMU had led to the establishment of a European Monetary Cooperation Fund in 1973 and movement on setting up a Regional Fund (March 1975), but the former had turned out to be a fund only in the most narrow sense of the word. Any consideration of pooling of reserves, or turning the institution into much more than one to facilitate the short-term credit network in an accounting sense, was not forthcoming. In fact, it has been emphasized that there was even a degree of symbolism in that the system actually was run through the Bank of International Settlements (BIS) in Switzerland, although there was at least an office with a nameplate in Luxembourg.

By October 1974 it was recognized that the process had stalled, and that even though there was still some level of commitment to the ideal, no date was set for its attainment. Thus at the end of 1974, and in spite of France's brief reentry and exit, the concept of monetary union was considered by most to be far from a serious possibility for Europe, and yet, the concept of the European Monetary System was not so very far off.

Conclusion

An historical account of the progress toward EMU from the Treaty of Rome to the mid-1970s is helpful in gauging the source and development of trends and concepts that can be expected to influence developments in the future. It is difficult to imagine the present state of affairs, or to construct a view of the future, without such a thorough examination of history. This is especially so with a topic that has been driven as much by political (and even personal) as economic considerations. Several notions surface from the preceding that seem important in analyzing the progress toward monetary integration in Europe.

First, progress toward EMU has occurred at times when countries saw their individual interests, again either political or economic, to be coincidental with such a movement. Although the pronouncements at the Hague Summit, indeed the entire "Spirit of Hague," may have been based upon differing and vague views of the meaning and implication of EMU, and that there is some evidence of greater seriousness of intention among some than others, it nevertheless seems that for a moment EMU did appear to hold promise for more benefits than costs for all of the members of the Community.

The events of the early 1970s, on the other hand, suggest that progress is simply not possible when members hold diverging views concerning their individual interests. Again, the record is persuasive that the lack of progress toward EMU, building upon the Hague Summit, and subsequent approval of at least part of the Werner Report, was not caused by deteriorating international monetary conditions and the oil crisis, but rather by differing national objectives regarding macroeconomic variables. These differences were too fundamental to be either glossed over through diplomatic language or avoided altogether by emphasizing areas of agreement. In the end the economists' assertion that lack of economic policy coordination would foredoom any premature attempt at fixing exchange rates proved correct.

Indeed, the second conclusion to come from the experience of these years is this: Coordination of economic policies is necessary, if hardly sufficient, to any attempt to fix exchange rates. This is especially true of the monetary policies that lead to diverging rates of inflation, balance-of-payments difficulties, and pressure on exchange rates. What was brought home to the world, as well as to the Europeans, in this period is the degree to which market expectations of differing economic trends can place immediate and overwhelming pressure through the exchange markets on exchange rates.

The third point follows directly from the second. The increased and increasing degree of international capital mobility cannot, in the final analysis, be countered by governments using either intervention with reserves, as the flows are too large, or by exchange controls. The gradual recognition of these facts, especially by the French who have had less of an ideological aversion to controls than, say, the Germans, was apparent during this time. It explains, for example, the final coming together on a joint Community policy after the disagreement over how to react to the exchange crisis of 1971.

The full implication of this third point, however, may not be entirely appreciated by states, for it is that national governments have lost a significant amount of their ability to control their own monetary policies. Indeed, the debate should be on how to design and coordinate joint monetary and, possibly, other economic policies. In many ways, after Maastricht, this is what the concern over EMU constituted. It is clear from the earlier period, however, that unless there is finally a serious willingness to sacrifice a good deal of what has traditionally been considered part of the very definition of national sovereignty, that is the control over economic policies, to a supranational body, then monetary stability of the type being sought in Europe is unlikely. One cannot simply define a fixed rate system and, again, not support it with joint policies. It appears as if "intergovernmental" consultation, in other words, is inadequate to the task, and supranationalism, or a federal structure, is the only real alternative.

This raises the fifth point, on the desirability of fixed rates within Europe. Economists employ the concept of "revealed preference" to suggest that the best evidence of real desires lies with actions. Although the snake, in the manner described above, could certainly be called a failure to the end of EMU, from another perspective it emphasized the desire by at least the original Six, and later the Nine (including Denmark and Ireland, but with the always possible exception of the United Kingdom) to continue to reach for ways to establish structure between exchange rates. Optimum currency area theory may be appealed to in order to explain the degree to which the countries were drawn together, often almost in spite of themselves as evidenced by their diverging policies, to a form of greater fixity. The brief French reentry into the snake in 1975 is a case in point. The rapid recognition by the Europeans in late 1971 of the undesirable impact of floating on their economies is another. This innate force may, of course, form the basis for eventual success of EMU over reluctance by some states to part with their sovereignty.

The next point belies the sixth, for it establishes that pure fixed rates were not the real objective of the period, but rather, relatively fixed rates were. It is instructive that the "first stage" of the Werner Report called for a narrowing of margins, and not their elimination. Is it that zero margins around par are considered desirable but undefendable in an increasing mobile environment, or that there are other advantages? It is also important to note that at no time was there serious consideration of fixing rates without allowing for parity changes, even with coordination. Certainly, the Werner Report saw irrevocably fixed rates in the last stage, but the actual experience over these years was a willingness to accept a great degree of flexibility. It was a fixed (with margins) but adjustable rate system that broke down, not a system of irrevocably fixed rates.

The seventh point is that during the debate over the Werner Report there was great reluctance to take budgetary responsibilities away from the national governments. Most of the sovereignty issues were fought over monetary policy and monetary policy institutions, in which less need was felt for removing public expenditure and tax policy from national control.

Next, there is a theory prevalent in this field that crises precipitate movement toward greater integration. The evidence here is mixed. Working for the theory is the perceived breakup of the Bretton Woods system, which led to the agreements at the Hague, the eventual joint stand in December 1971, and even the establishment of the snake as a reaction to increased instability. There is also the long quiescent period from 1964 through 1968 when no movement was made in spite of continued pleas from the Commission. Working against the theory is that the oil crisis, even if it was not the cause of the dissolution of the snake, hardly brought the countries together, in terms of joint-policy reaction or increased resolve to maintain the only outward symbol of EMU. France abandoned the snake with aplomb in 1974, as Italy and the United Kingdom had done before in the face of payment crises. It may be easier to establish that crises make it easier to establish institutions when those institutions are otherwise desirable. That is, unless greater cohesion and integration are seen as fruitful in the long run, it is difficult to imagine European states accepting, other than just as temporary expedients, policies that are not seen as fostering the long-term welfare of their citizens.

Finally, as something of a corollary to the above, it also can be said that even for states who otherwise view greater cohesion and integration as desirable, unless the conditions of integration are considered acceptable, there may be a strong barrier to agreement. This point applies a fortiori to the Germans, for whom price stability and an independent central bank dedicated to its maintenance, was, and is, at the core of their concept of responsible economic management. They have been consistent in holding this view, and they will accept nothing less.

TWO

Creation of the EMS

B y the end of 1974 what had been clear at the beginning of the year was officially recognized: EMU had failed. The experiences of the early 1970s seemed to lead the Community further away rather than closer to the achievement of greater union by the 1980 deadline. In addition, the conditions during the mid-1970s did not promise quick regeneration of a spirit leading to monetary integration.

Nevertheless, by the end of the decade there would be in place a new institution, the European Monetary System (EMS), that would serve as a most important base along the way toward greater union. In the process there was to be a greater understanding of the critical nature of the German-French alliance, the relative lack of influence provided by the British, and the increasing strength of Germany; the last perhaps especially in providing for Europe, if not the world, a powerful macroeconomic model for growth centered around low inflation.

Years of Malaise (1974–1977)

The snake during these years, as noted in the previous chapter, was decreasingly a full Community organization, and increasingly a DM-zone. The second French withdrawal in 1976 significantly reinforced this fact. Although there was, of course, nothing inherently wrong with Norwegian and Swedish membership, it must be said that this too confirmed the notion.[1]

The differing economic conditions of the member states also did not seem propitious for a renewed interest in EMU. West Germany was very strong, in fact, it had become a world class economic and monetary power, the latter represented by a DM that was increasingly being used as a reserve asset. The Benelux countries were less strong, as certainly was Denmark with its high unemployment rate, but all of the DM-zone northern European countries were decidedly superior to France, at least in terms of inflation rates and balance of payments. At least French output was high, a condition not shared by Britain, which also had a high inflation rate. Italy's inflation was high as well, while Ireland was, of course, very poor. As it was this very divergence in economic performance that had condemned the snake to failure likewise insured little additional forward movement on EMU during these years.

As well, it must be mentioned that there seemed to be a lack of political will to move forward. Certainly most observers feel that the failure of the EMU experiment in the 1970s, as represented by economic divergence, had its roots, nonetheless, in the lack of political commitment to Europe that could have made it easier to induce convergence of economic trends. The Tindemans Report, referred to below, spoke of lack of political consensus, while Ludlow (1982, Chapter 1) links this closely with a political leadership that was either unwilling or unable to bring the Community together. The Germans were strong enough, but were timorous of accepting a role in which they might be viewed as yet again attempting to establish power and control over Europe. The British were, as always, saddled with an ambivalent attitude toward Europe both in its geographical sense and in movements toward greater integration. The peculiar aspect of British national character that can be described as "insular" (owing a good deal to literal geographic isolation), coupled with former imperial power, tended to establish a wider world-view (greater say, than simply Europe) and important connections with former (English-speaking) colonies around the globe, including the United States. It is arguable that insularity and a wider world-view also reinforced a British aloofness, a superiority, from the rest of Europe. These tendencies, although difficult to quantify, certainly have meant difficulty in Britain's accepting a serious leadership role within Europe. In addition, however, there was not the strength of leadership at home by either party, and especially by Labour after 1974. Finally, the French, under Giscard d'Estaing from 1974, were unable to seriously consider Europe while the Gaullists were still such a strong force, emphasizing, as their prior leader had, both the need for independence of France and an attitude toward the EC that could only be generously described as self-interested.

Bringing the economics and politics together, there existed in these years also quite differing attitudes concerning the appropriate economic policies that governments ought to employ in order to deal with economic problems. It is facile but it also does not do too much violence to describe two schools of thought. One, of course, is Keynesian, which in its simplest form is relatively more concerned with short-term performance of real variables, such as output and employment, and is willing to use both monetary and fiscal policies to maximize these. Inflation is less of a concern.[2] This view generally correlated well with those of the French and Italians during these years, and explains in some ways the curious intellectual delinking of exchange rate stability (needed for trade) and policy convergence (undesirable if constrictive) characteristic of the ill-named "monetarists." The in many ways more seriously "monetarist" view of the Germans and the Dutch follows more Chicago-school thought, which emphasizes the importance of controlling monetary emission at all costs, in order to allow for the internal stability necessary for growth, growth that in the long run will insure both greater output and employment than could ever be achieved by short-run policy changes. As can be seen, these differing economic philosophies were not only crucial to some of the "monetarist-economist" inconsistencies inherent in the Werner Report compromise and subsequent failure of the EMU attempt, but also in the failure of governments to come together in agreement over common aims.

Several reports were filed during these years which, if anything, reinforce the descriptive power of the word malaise. The Tindemans Report was commissioned at the same Paris summit of 1974 where the unattainability of EMU by 1980 was recognized, and essentially tabled. The report, filed in 1975, as above, noted the lack of political consensus, and established that although EMU was needed for uniting Europe, common monetary and fiscal policies were unlikely to come about, because, as quoted in Kruse (1980, p. 239): " . . . there is not sufficient mutual faith to permit the transfer to common controlling bodies of the powers which they would of necessity have to be given." In these circumstances about all that could be done was a gradualist approach of making adjustments to present institutional arrangements, such as the snake and methods of consultation, rather than another major thrust. It also mentioned a parallel currency as potentially helpful in creating an asset that might eventually replace national currencies. This echoed a similar idea of a group of prominent economists, proposed in 1975 as the "All Saints' Day Manifesto." The currency was to have been called the "Europa," and intended for private use.

The Duisenberg Plan came from the Dutch in 1976 and, in this same spirit, tried to establish minimalist methods of reintegrating the non-snake members into a system. "Target zones" were to be set up for the exchange rates of these countries, and, although there was no necessity to intervene in case of rate divergence, there were methods encouraging consultation and convergence of policies. Mutual aid was to be extended for this purpose. Although generally well received, the non-snake governments, after having taken political flak for more or less recently dropping out of the snake, were reticent to link up yet again with the DM, even in such a loosely defined way.

Jenkins' Initiative

It is within this economic and political context of malaise that what occurred next was in a way extraordinary. Roy Jenkins, as president of the

Commission, made a proposal that was to lead to the establishment of the European Monetary System (EMS), an institution without whose existence it would be difficult to image the Delors Report and the Maastricht Treaty.

The incentive behind the proposal was clear enough. Jenkins, as something of an outsider to what even the most fervent supporters of Europe admit have been periods of inertia in Brussels, wished to make some institutional headway toward greater integration, and to do so in a fashion that might speak to the then high unemployment rates, high and varying inflation rates, and most especially to the unequal distribution of income within Europe. His first thoughts on income redistribution were not well received, if for no other reason that in coming from a declining Britain it looked too self-interested. So, in the second half of 1977, he changed the assault to a debate on monetary union, in order to focus attention on all three issues simultaneously. Strategically, the concern with inflation would appeal to the West Germans, so that it would not necessarily be ruled out immediately, while at the same time the French, British, and Italian governments were concerned with methods to bring down their own individual inflation rates.

Another auspicious coincidence was that the Belgians had assumed the presidency of the Council, and were eager to see that the Tindemans Report was no longer simply ignored. With Jenkins' good wishes, therefore, they proposed a greater level of cooperation on monetary and fiscal policies, an increase in balance-of-payments mutual aid as well as a tightening of the conditions for such aid, reinforced by structural aid to the weaker economies. The intent, as with the Duisenberg Plan, was not to eliminate the snake, but to reinforce it in such a way as to bring the non-snake EC members back into the system. The initiative was needed to hold down "the instinctive resurgence of nationalist tendencies which still have their poisonous charms," as quoted in Ludlow (1982, p. 45).

With this support then, progress on the monetary front became the prime objective of the Jenkins' presidency for the next months, and, with the help of Michael Emerson, a member of the Jenkins cabinet, he gave a now famous speech in Florence in October 1977. The speech asked for greater movement toward union, of which monetary union was an important component. It chose neither the economist nor the monetarist approach over the other, but found them complementary, in terms of ends (monetarist) and means (economist). It also did not attack the value of the national state, but rather drew a distinction between functions that could best be performed at the Community level, leaving to states those that could best be performed there. In this way unification could come about from better results, and not simply from some vague view of pan-Europeanism. Specifically, this meant a more decentralized monetary union, with just enough transfer of power and resources to allow it to function well. The economic benefits he saw, again not otherwise attainable, included (1) seigniorage benefits from issuing a world class currency; (2) a lower rate of inflation for all members; (3) reduced unemployment; and (4) an evening out of regional imbalances. Politically, the "successful creation of a European monetary union would take Europe over a political threshold," from Ludlow (1982, p. 49). This concept of a federation with a minimum of activities necessary for functioning, and yet strong enough to carry real, tangible benefits to the states involved, is an important inspiration in the political acceptance of greater integration. It is an idea that is echoed later in the concept of "subsidiarity" in the Delors Report, the Working Report that followed upon it, and the Maastricht Treaty.

Another speech by Jenkins in Bonn not only reinforced the Florence themes, but implicitly recognized what would be a natural German reluctance to be tied monetarily to other states; hence it was more purely political in nature and emphasized the necessity of convincing the Germans if anything were to happen. The speech appealed to German pride, in drawing a parallel to the possible configuration of monetary union modeled on the successful German federal structure. It also, however, appealed directly to German self-interest, in suggesting that a European structure could allow Germany to escape continuing pressure from the outside to act as a "locomotive" to pull the world out of recession.

This last concept requires a bit of explanation. The dollar had been falling dramatically with the United States' policy of expansion, and the U.S. balance of payments was increasingly in deficit. As opposed to contracting spending, the United States felt rather that the Germans should expand, thus taking pressure off the dollar and allowing for full growth. The Germans, of course, were worried about such an increase in demand, especially through increases in the money supply, on internal, that is, price stability. Reinforcing the pressure from the United States, however, were other European states that felt constrained to adopt perhaps overly restrictive policies in spite of their own concern over inflation, for fear that expansion by any single country would trigger a depreciation in their currency and hence further inflation. The carrot, in other words, that was held out to Germany was that of monetary coordination within Europe as an alternative to worldwide pressure to become the locomotive.

In spite of some of the more positive forces and strategic advantages, this plan met with heavily negative response, including within Jenkins' own Commission and especially by the Germans, who felt that economic conditions were not right, and that the political will was still not there.

Nevertheless, the notion fell of fertile ground with Valéry Giscard d'Estaing, who had always entertained such ideas, but had never been able to voice them over the opposition of the Gaullists. Helmut Schmidt also was at first tentative, but then intrigued by the concept, and for exactly the political and strategic reasons offered by Jenkins. The result was that the European Council in December of 1977 not only did not kill the idea, but "reaffirmed its attachment to the objective of EMU," and requested a "thorough study" of the Jenkins Plan. This was the "fair wind" to Copenhagen.

Given the generally negative reaction in Germany to further overtures toward EMU, the positive response by Schmidt deserves further reflection. A good part of his openness to the initiative must stem from his concern about the nature of the new Carter administration in Washington. There were problems with the implications of the U.S. human rights initiatives on delicate relations between Western Europe and the Soviet Union, as well as the negative U.S. stance on nuclear energy impinging on significant prior German commercial and public investment. As well, the dollar crisis cannot be overemphasized. Between June 1977 and March 1978 the dollar had dropped by some 13 percent versus the DM, the budget deficit had trebled, and the Carter administration seemed both uninterested in and then incapable of handling it. This was the first serious crisis since the official freeing of exchange rates in 1973, and the cavalier approach to it taken by the United States was not encouraging.

The German attempt to look for a "European solution" was even stronger than an assessment of weakness or stupidity of the Americans. It hinged on the fact that the flight from the dollar was extensively toward the DM, which was then forced up further against the currencies of its major trading partners. This speculative pressure away from equilibrium, in the eyes of the Germans, could only hurt exports and the further strength and growth of their industrial sector. European views on flexible exchange rates resulting in equilibrium rates have never been as sanguine as those on the other side of the Atlantic, including, as established in chapter 1, the very first experience in the autumn of 1971. Again, add to this the international pressure on Germany to reflate as a locomotive to bring the world along through the effects of greater German imports on trading nations' gross domestic products (GDPs), and one begins to see Schmidt's attraction to a plan that could put Germany out of the spotlight and also promise a degree of stability and continued export growth, at least within Europe. Finally, Schmidt was politically strong at home, and he had room to maneuver against otherwise strong domestic forces.

Once he had accepted the movement on monetary integration that was to become the EMS, Schmidt sought out and received the backing of Giscard d'Estaing who, also politically strong by early 1978, felt that monetary union offered an excellent chance to emulate German industrial success by tying in with German monetary views through such a system. For his part, Schmidt was reluctant to go on this road by himself, and so the two men forged a bond that was, and still is, rare in postwar international politics. As subsequent events demonstrated, when a French leader joined his German counterpart in pressing for greater integration within Europe, it held a good chance for success, in spite of great reluctance elsewhere. Again reflecting back upon a decade earlier with the Werner Report, when France took up the objective, and Germany saw it in its interest to not (at least immediately) demur, movement would follow. This conclusion, on the possibilities inherent when French and German leaders agree, is even on its surface quite simplistic and ignores in application a spectrum of other economic and political influences, both in other countries and in France and Germany themselves (always including the attitudes of the Bundesbank). It might be tentatively and possibly more convincingly stated in the negative. In other words, without strong, even assertive, revealed preferences by the French and German leaders, movement in this sphere is unlikely. The chances of "backing into" integration are weak, at best.

Swann stated that "there can be no doubt that the reason for the creation of the EMS was the destabilizing effects of foreign currency movements, in particular those of the dollar," and mentioned an important cause behind the movement as exchange rate "overshooting," or better, movement away from long-term equilibrium in terms of relative prices noted above (1988, p. 190). He quoted an influential person in the EMS movement, Jacques van Ypersele, advisor to the Belgian prime minister and chairman of the EC's Monetary Committee, as suggesting that such disequilibrium movements were negative on output both for the appreciating countries (depressing profits and export activity, in Germany for example), and to the depreciating countries (inflationary pressures causing undue restrictive policies). Swann also noted that "the motivation behind the EMS was therefore significantly different from that which inspired the EMU" (1988, p. 190). The idea of a crisis forging a coincidence of opinion on the value of fixed rates in a floating system is, of course, correct. Indirectly, the same force of a threat to the continuance of international monetary stability applied—represented earlier by the breakup of the system of fixed exchange rates that was Bretton Woods—and that was instrumental in establishing the snake. In fact, the two episodes together demonstrate how external attacks on the stability of the international monetary system, and hence intra-European exchange rates, can force the countries toward consideration of some form of monetary integration. In this sense, the experience of the late 1970s reinforces the theory of institutional movement which emphasizes the role of crisis.

Copenhagen

The meeting of the European Council on April 7–8, 1978 under the Danish presidency outside Copenhagen was a watershed even in the rich history of monetary integration. There were many interchanges in preparation for the meeting, including an attempt to bring the British, under Prime Minister James Callaghan, into a monetary scheme. For various political and philosophical reasons this was impossible, but at least there was solidarity to the notion among Schmidt, Giscard d'Estaing, and Jenkins.

The Copenhagen meeting itself is famous for having been almost theatrically orchestrated by Schmidt and Giscard d'Estaing. Only the heads of government were present for the show, which saw the French president divide the world into three zones: North America (dominated by the United States), Asia (Japan), and Europe. Given the uncertainties in the world it would be well if the countries in the latter group could work together to lessen potential shocks, using something more than the snake. The German chancellor reinforced this view with expressed concern over the influence of American policies (under Carter), especially overissue of dollars, on continuing international monetary stability. The plan they presented after dinner was the embryo of the EMS, with the reestablishment of greater fixity of rates among all Community countries, a pooling of reserves, an expanded use for the old European Unit of Account (EUA) (becoming a new reserve asset), and the creation of a European Monetary Fund (EMF). In time, the EUA could become a single European currency.

Except for the British, the reception was not unfavorable, undoubtedly because of the evident strength of the political commitment presented by the leaders of France and Germany. In other words, here was a chance to overcome what had always been the ultimate roadblock to progress before—reluctance by one of the two major states to move forward. It must have occurred to those present, as well, that Schmidt in particular was taking a stand with regard to the traditional concerns of his country that could only be described as statesmanlike. Again, the presentation of ideas was quite a performance, and Copenhagen continues to be associated with the highest ideals of European monetary, if not political, integration.

After Copenhagen a secret study group was set up with French, German, and British (later to drop out) representation. This group devised a plan for the EMS independently, but it was certainly not unaware of the discussions that were simultaneously taking place within the established committee structure. What emerged from this interim period, from Copenhagen in April to the summit at Bremen in July of 1978, was a series of ideas which seemed to command consensus on the nature of the new system for a "zone of monetary stability" in Europe. First, the snake was to continue, at the insistence of Germany, Denmark and the Benelux countries. Second, at the broader Community level, and including all currencies, there was, as the discussions proceeded, a willingness to establish exchange rate stability even before resolving economic, especially inflationary divergences. This bow to the monetarist position was taken for symbolic as well as technical reasons, it being presumed that the commitment would engender the kind of policies which would insure exchange rate stability. Third, there was a strong but not necessarily universally shared view that a weighted index of currencies be used as either a base for the new system, or at least a supplement to the snake. The French were especially strong on this issue as it would introduce "symmetry" into the system. The bilateral parity grid of the snake, in other words, only put pressure on the weakest of any diverging countries to adjust its policies, but the weighted average would potentially focus on divergence of a single strong currency, such as that of Germany, and force that country to "adjust" by increasing monetary emission and inflation, up to the general Community level. Fourth, there was a felt need for an expansion of an existing institution, the European Monetary Cooperation Fund (EMCF), created by at least a temporarily pooling of reserves, that did not rely upon repayment in dollars. Fifth, as noted above, there was seen to be a greater role for the EUA as a means of settlement. It was at this time that the renaming of this unit as the ECU, both an acronym for European Currency Unit and the name of an old French coin, took place. Sixth, even greater credit facilities were needed, and those in existence needed modification. Finally, the system was not to be locked tight, but rather would allow for exchange rate changes when needed. That is to say, it was to be a fixed but adjustable system.

Bremen and Brussels

It was around these notions that the Bremen Summit took place, in what had become an entirely different atmosphere than even a few months before. It was again an atmosphere of optimism, a view to what could be accomplished, similar to that at the Hague almost 10 years before. The communiqué issued out of Bremen called upon the finance ministers and the "competent Community bodies" to draft the provisions necessary for the system to be approved in Brussels by December 1978, including "concurrent studies" of the actions needed to aid the lesser-developed EC states. The annex describing the system established it as "at least as strict as the 'Snake,'" with changes in exchange rates "subject to mutual consent," and the ECU to "be at the center of the system." A deposit of 20 percent of member states' gold and dollars, as well as member currencies, would provide the pooling of reserves necessary to create the ECU as a serious base for the creation and distribution of ECUs among central banks. This was to become a true EMF, not just an EMCF, after two years. Finally, "a system of closer monetary cooperation [would] only be successful if participating countries [would] pursue policies conducive to greater stability at home and abroad; this applies to the deficit and surplus countries alike." The latter was intended as a strong statement of "symmetry."

After Bremen the difficulties began to arise. A broad spectrum of German opinion, including within the Bundesbank, was not at all in agreement over the symmetry issue, since it meant almost certain German inflation. In this light, putting the ECU, as a weighted average of Community currencies, at the center of the system became a concern. Certainly the psychological impact was recognized, but if symmetry meant an engine for inflation, most Germans wanted none of it, and preferred to stick to the bilateral snake arrangement. The British were even more disenchanted with the entire plan, and essentially opted out early on. They took a more global view, seeing stability as an international (IMF) rather than a European (EMS) issue. This is perhaps understandable given the large amount of non-EC trade then still conducted by Britain. Ludlow (1982) also points to the length of time it took the British to recognize the strength and implications of the political commitment on the continent to the idea. Prime Minister Callaghan's comments in parliamentary debate, on the other hand, seem to explicitly recognize the political implications of the plan. He saw it as facing "a decision whether [a country] wished to remain poor and independent or whether it was willing to sacrifice some powers and be more prosperous" (p. 144). Finally, Italy and Ireland insisted upon regional aid as part of the definition of the system, and Italy wished for broader exchange rate margins as an alternative.

The decisions that were taken by the committees between Bremen and Brussels were based upon these disagreements. The German view on the ECU as the center of the EMS held sway, and, instead of currencies and intervention limits being defined only in terms of ECU (the French wish), there were central rates, but with a parity grid (like the snake) superimposed on the system. The fact of the matter is that the French lost this fight, in no small measure because there were technical flaws in the definition of the system as defined around the ECU. The final outcome was a compromise proposed by the Belgians, again using the two-tier system, that allowed for the presumption to act if a currency hit 75 percent of its adjusted divergence against the ECU, with changes every five years in the ECU weights. The ECU then could reasonably be said to be at the center of system, although of course not as strongly as if there were no snake mechanism, and the EMS could likewise be said to be more than a snake of a different color. In a similar example of compromise, Germany's concern about the future of permanently vesting reserves with a central authority led to the deposit of 20 percent of gold and dollar reserves as short-term swaps only in the EMCF. It would become an EMF only when these became permanently vested with the new institution. It was also agreed at this time to give Italy a band of fluctuation of 6 percent, versus 2.25 percent for the others, and the credit facilities were increased in size. The only obvious negative was that the concurrent revision of the amount of regional aid seemed hopelessly deadlocked, reflecting fairly accurately the attitude of the richer states toward such aid.

The external conditions cooperated at this time also for easy acceptance of the EMS: there was another dollar crisis. This great downward pressure on the dollar finally led to adequate U.S. policy changes and a revaluation of the DM, as it had with the snake. What it also did was to reinforce the importance of the EMS negotiations and the stability that was being sought by and within the system. Here again, external crisis seemed helpful in fostering agreement.

But yet again, it was not enough, in sympathy with the theory that any breakdown in the Paris-Bonn axis can fatally threaten final movement. It appeared that this would happen in the eleventh hour, as France deadlocked the Brussels meeting in early December 1978 by insisting on bringing in issues related to CAP, clearly to assuage French farmers near the time of French elections. France also opposed regional funding increases, and reinforced the possible breakdown of the talks by having Italy and Ireland withdraw. It had all progressed far enough that these were only minor irritants, and the system was begun, a little later, on March 13, 1979. All joined all aspects of the system except for Britain, which was officially included in the EMS and the definition of the ECU, but not in the exchange rate mechanism (ERM), that was, nevertheless, at the heart of the system.[3] Ireland then joined the EMS, implying a break in the historic link of the punt with sterling. Although they had received a bit of regional aid in order to help their entry, this was small recompense indeed compared to the risk of appreciation and subsequent impact on exports with their major trading partner. As it turned out, however, the punt in practice depreciated against the pound, trade became more diversified toward other EC countries, and Ireland had been to some extent released from its ties to a slow-growth, inflationary country, as in Harrop (1989).

The British decision finally to not fully join had been based partially on British insularity and perhaps broader world view. Specifically, however, there was concern, as there had been with the original establishment of the Community, that the enterprise would fail. If it did not fail, then there was the prospect of the United Kingdom losing the ability to alter its exchange rate if, as had certainly been true in the past, wage demands forced inflation above productivity growth rates. In this case deflationary policies would have been necessary. As it was, the level of acrimony introduced by the British into the EMS debate, in an obvious attempt to subvert the outcome, and joining only as a "half-way home," engendered considerable political ill-will.

Conclusion

Several conclusions may be drawn from the important negotiations and formal establishment of the EMS. First is the critical nature of the French-German alliance. If cooperation is strong enough at the head-of-government level, it appears that movement is possible, if not probable. Without it, nothing is likely to happen. Second, the facts of the case speak to the relative importance of Britain in decision making. The other states have been more than willing to go ahead without the British, and, in spite of the indistinct association worked up for Britain, actually have done so. Some of the negative negotiating tactics used after the decision had been taken by Britain to not fully participate may have even enhanced the chance for success. More than ten years later attitudes toward similar tactics seemed to move a larger number of states closer to EMU at the Rome Summit in October 1990. Third, is the increasing strength of Germany. The fact of Jenkins' making such a special and well-developed plea to German self-interest speaks to their power.[4] Finally, there was beginning to be an appreciation that the strength of Germany not only made it a political power with which to reckon, but also an economic power to emulate. That is, the policy debate based upon conflicting economic philosophies had begun to subtly shift at this time to a greater appreciation of the long-run benefits of policy, especially monetary policy, restraints. It was the beginning of an acceptance in Europe of the futility of expansionary policies of influencing more than short-run unemployment, and this at the potential sacrifice of long-run growth. The 1980s would see more and more of a lining up behind this German model of successful macroeconomic management, but it was represented early on in the establishment of the EMS, a mechanism destined to help in fighting inflation by establishing a zone of monetary stability. Germany and the DM were to be the model and the anchor, respectively, in that objective.

THREE

Development of the European Monetary System

From the beginning the objectives of the European Monetary System (EMS) were two-fold. First, the fixed-but-adjustable exchange rates based upon the augmented snake model were intended to reduce exchange-rate volatility in a flexible-rate world, and lessen the impact of international fluctuations on the large and growing intra-European trade flows. In addition, the willingness by the members to "fix" exchange rates prior to policy convergence was intended as a strategy to induce such convergence and, therefore, create consistent and lower inflation rates (Thygesen, 1988). The debate over symmetry shows that the objectives were not fully shared by all, perhaps especially by the French, in spite of the fact that the inflation of the 1970s had certainly been felt by all.

Nevertheless, by the end of the 1980s the EMS would be viewed as having worked—and even worked well—in bringing the member countries together around common monetary and economic ends. Even though the sense of success may have led to a premature fixing of exchange rates in a system not fully capable of supporting such a move, the EMS provided the basis for further union on the monetary front.

EMS Description

As noted in the last chapter the EMS included as its most important part the exchange-rate mechanism (ERM) which, in turn, was composed of two parts. First was the bilateral parity grid, which operated much like the snake in setting bilateral exchange rates. The EMS, however, established exchange rates somewhat artificially through "central rates" in terms of ECUs, that were allowed to fluctuate weakest to strongest by 2.25 percent, or 6 percent for any country that desired to have a wider margin. Most of the nine original members[1] opted for 2.25-percent margins, except for Italy which entered at 6 percent, again remembering that the United Kingdom had decided not to participate in the ERM. When weak currency countries hit the margin they were obligated to act by buying up enough of their own currency and, if necessary, borrowing currency of the stronger country to maintain the margin. Again, the bilateral parity grid was designed to work just like the old snake, and the ECU was central to the pairing of currencies only through their joint definition in terms of ECUs.[2] The amount of borrowed currency, however, was also denominated in ECUs.

It was originally intended that central banks not keep large amounts of other Community currencies for intervention purposes, as in Ungerer, et al. (1983), but this policy proved to be impractical. Several central banks held large reserves of DM. A good deal of intervention had also been in dollars rather than Community currencies, and had occurred increasingly prior to a currency reaching the margins, where intervention was compulsory. Since the use of other Community currencies required the permission of the other central banks, it had, even in the case of previously accumulated DM, say, frequently been convenient to use the dollar.

The need for intramarginal intervention requires some explanation. Whereas originally it was thought that use of the full-rate band would serve as a form of shock absorber for exchange-market conditions, central banks frequently and increasingly found the need to keep well within the official limits. One reason was to reduce potential speculative momentum before it became established in the market. Another, perhaps even more important, reason was that central banks increasingly wished to tie their currencies and, by implication, their monetary policies to that of the Bundesbank. In this way a clear signal was to be sent to market participants, especially wage earners, of the determination of the government to keep down inflation, since the attitude of the Germans in this regard was well known. What that meant for intramarginal intervention was that as the participating currency began to decline in value there was immediate purchase of it on the exchange market (through the use of foreign-exchange reserves) in order to demonstrate that the money supply was not being allowed to grow excessively. The DM in this way acted as a "nominal anchor" for the monetary policies of other ERM countries, and, as indicated, most intervention became intramarginal in nature, in comparison with the experience of the first years of the EMS.

If a country found itself at or near the margin it could change its exchange rate, either by devaluing or revaluing as the case may be. This "realignment" within the system was required, however, to have been accompanied by consultations with the participating central banks, with any resulting change being by "mutual agreement," in the words of the original resolution. In this way the system was viewed as incorporating both structure and flexibility, and rules and discretion, making it a "fixed but adjustable" system.

In addition, and still concerning the ERM, the "divergence indicator" was, after intense debate, superimposed upon the bilateral parity grid, the intention being to introduce greater symmetry of policy response into the mechanism. Each currency, therefore, had a defined "central rate" in terms of ECU, and also clear margins beyond which it would not move without certain actions taking place. The margins were the same as those that applied to the grid, that is 2.25 or 6 percent, and were adjusted downwards according to the weight the currency itself bore in the construction of the ECU. Heuristically this may be understood to be necessary since a currency cannot depreciate or appreciate against itself. A true representation of a depreciation of the DM against the other currencies of the ERM must compensate for the amount the DM plays in the composition of the ECU.[3] In reality a "threshold of divergence" was defined as three-quarters of the maximum spread, which was to be the signal light, warning that action was necessary.

The actions that were "presumed" to occur, in the language of the Belgian compromise, would include either intervention into the exchange markets, a change in domestic economic—especially monetary—policies, or a change in the central rate. Since a strong currency could hit its own threshold as easily as a weak currency could hit the other side of its own threshold, there was the hope that the stronger country might feel as much pressure to inflate as the country with the weaker currency might be forced to deflate. Symmetry would be the result, encouraging, most optimistically, greater policy and inflation convergence, or, ironically, a sacrifice of inflationary discipline, depending upon one's point of view.

The ECU was introduced in 1979 with the beginning of the EMS, and was to have played a central role. It was at the beginning equivalent to the old European Unit of Account (EUA) used under the snake, and included sterling in the weighting of currencies in its composition even though the United Kingdom was not a member of the ERM. This, what is referred to by Swann (1988) as a "currency cocktail," included weights for each currency based upon the issuing country's share of the total EU GDP, its share of total trade (exports), and its "size."[4] The original March 13, 1979 weighting gave the DM a 33-percent share, the French franc a 20-percent share, and so on, down to the Irish punt at slightly above 1 percent. Because the ECU was actually defined as a basket of currencies, that is, it was composed of defined quantities of the constituent currencies, the weights could change over time as individual currencies strengthened or weakened. It was, therefore, decided to review the weighting any time one currency changed by 25 percent or more, or, in any case, every five years. This was first done in 1984, when the Greek drachma was added to the ECU, at slightly more than a 1-percent weight. The subsequent change in 1989 added the Spanish peseta and the Portuguese escudo.

The ECU was to serve several functions as a central feature of the working of the EMS. In addition, it was to be, as the EUA was before it, the unit of account by which Community activities were measured. Thus, the EC budget was to be denominated in ECUs, and farm prices were established in ECUs under the CAP. Finally, it was recognized that the basket might be attractive for non-official, or private, uses. In terms of the first of these functions, it was, of course, hoped that as the EMS developed, and the EMCF became the EMF, that the ECU "[would] then have to play its full role as a reserve instrument and a means of settlement."[5]

The working of the exchange rate mechanism, most especially the bilateral grid, required adequate funding in order to insure adequate support of the relatively fixed rates, as well as the perception of the market that there was sufficient backing to withstand speculative pressure. At the margins this automatic line of defense (subject to limits) was to be the "very short-term financing facility" (VSTF), previously in existence but expanded in size and the pay-back period extended from 30 to 45 days. This, and the short-term monetary support (STMS) scheme, also already in existence but expanded in 1979, were run by the central banks through the EMCF. In 1988 an EC Council medium-term financial assistance facility (MTFA) merged with a Community loan mechanism first established in 1975 to provide funds for longer periods, two to five years, on the basis of balance-of-payments difficulties. Each facility was subject to greater levels of "conditionality," meaning that the demonstration of the adoption of appropriate economic policies as the time for repayment was lengthened. As mentioned earlier, the EMCF was to help establish the ECU as a reserve asset, issued in exchange for 20 percent of member central banks'—that is EMS central banks'—gold and dollar assets, and used for the VSTF and STMS schemes. These were not to be permanent deposits, but rather rolling 90-day "swaps" (gold and dollars temporarily exchanged for ECUs); exchanges that could, of course, be regularly renewed through time. When they were to become permanent, two years after the establishment of the EMS, the EMCF was to become a full-fledged EMF.

Institutional Development

Greece's entry to the EC in 1981 was not coincidental with that high-inflation country entering the ERM, although it did join the EMS. Spain and Portugal entered the Community in 1986, although both waited until later to join the ERM (Spain in 1989 and Portugal in 1992, both at the 6-percent band). Italy dropped its voluntary margins from 6 to 2.25 percent, and Britain in October 1990 decided upon entry into the ERM, although both later felt forced out in 1992. The latter experience of currency speculation eventually forcing a widening of the margins, was important, and will be examined in greater detail.

The British case of protracted debate at the time of the establishment of the EMS and beyond is especially interesting given the size of the country and the historic and continued importance of the pound sterling. The reluctance of the Labour government to allow for anything more than a British half-way house of initial membership has been given reference already. The subsequent reluctance of Thatcher governments during the 1980s to allow ERM participation for sterling needs more explanation given that the Conservatives had not had quite the same history of division over EC participation that had characterized Labour. Several reasons were important. First, there was a much stronger and longer intellectual sympathy with the view, not so prevalent on the continent, that the market was the best determinant of the equilibrium exchange rate, and any system that would interfere with this price-setting was ill-designed. Second, a central tenet of British economic anti-inflation policy during the first part of the decade was control over the money supply, using monetary rather than exchange-rate targets, as in Harrop (1989). This meant that the kind of intervention necessary to support a given exchange rate could jeopardize the achievement of the targeted monetary growth rate, and hence either the target or the continuance of the fixed rate. Ungerer et al. (1986, p. 4) quotes Loehnis (1985) as suggesting that ERM participation "would involve in unfavorable circumstances greater interest rate volatility and perhaps more frequent realignments than many of its advocates admit." A third point is that the stability of the pound was not to be assumed, in that its value was tied more closely to petroleum than those of other ERM countries, the United Kingdom being a large producer of oil. A related point was that, like the DM, the pound was still a significant reserve currency whose value was subject to considerable external shifts, thus potentially affecting its value within the system, as had happened to the DM often in the past. Finally, the structure of trade in the United Kingdom was less closely aligned with other EC countries than for a country like West Germany.

As the decade progressed, these arguments gradually lost credibility. Economists attracted by the intellectual arguments behind freely fluctuating exchange rates increasingly found dissatisfaction with the way they worked in practice.[6] In addition, by mid-decade money had ceased to be the sole target in Britain, partly for technical reasons, and was supplemented by greater attention to interest and exchange rates. This considerably weakened the argument related to maintaining a stable monetary growth rate. In fact, Britain attempted to "shadow" the DM, and maintain a secret target zone for the exchange rate after the Group of Five meeting in Paris in 1987, according to Harrop (1989). The petro-currency argument, likewise, was becoming less important over time,[7] as was the role of the pound as a reserve currency, ironically losing position to the DM. Finally, there became "a high degree of economic convergence between the United Kingdom and the Federal Republic of Germany, the most important economy among the present ERM participants, a convergence that would facilitate U.K. participation," as noted in Ungerer et al. (1986, p. 4).

In addition, some potential major benefits were seen to accompany ERM membership. It would restore the monetary link with Ireland that was lost when that country went with Europe in 1979. Interest rates would not need to be so high, as an extra risk premium to holders of sterling, that is if exchange-rate stability was desired, by committing the currency to such a link institutionally through the EMS. This would be a signal to market participants of the desire of the government in this regard. Along the same line, ERM participation would strengthen government and market participant, especially wage earner, discipline in maintaining low inflation.

An extra incentive was the need, as part of the first stage toward monetary union—as voiced in the Delors Report—to have full ERM participation by July 1990, with exceptions for the very weak countries. By the summer of 1990, in spite of losing a chancellor of the exchequer over the issue, Prime Minister Thatcher was saying Britain would enter "when the time was right." This appeared to be the case in October of the same year. The new chancellor reinforced the nature of the ERM commitment in helping to convince labor of the need for restraint, an argument that had been heard and heeded in the 1980s in France. Nevertheless, the old question of sacrifice in autonomy of control of monetary policy had hardly disappeared with British entry.

Exchange-Rate Mechanism

An important institutional development of the EMS that occurred during the 1980s was the dominance of the bilateral parity grid as the effective mechanism of exchange-rate control, and the relative unimportance of the divergence indicator, in spite of all the effort that had gone into the indicator's design and acceptance. Ungerer et al. (1986, p. 5) notes that "the indicator has never been fully able, as its proponents had hoped, to assume the role of linking exchange rate developments to an increasing convergence of economic policy, for example by triggering restrictive measures in the case of a weak currency or expansionary measures in the case of a strong currency."

There are several reasons for this development, again remembering that France at least considered this part of the system as what made it truly distinctive from the snake, and hence justified it as a new system. One reason was a technical flaw with the design of the indicator which would, in certain circumstances,[8] allow for the margins in the parity grid to be reached before the threshold of divergence acted as an "early" warning for the need for concern and action. Another technical problem was that by not clearly identifying a "partner" country for intervention, since the indicator only specifies single-currency divergence, another country could be involuntarily forced into borrowing or loaning its currency. Perhaps more important, however, was that convergence was promoted not necessarily toward a low level of monetary growth and inflation, but—by putting pressure on strong currency countries to inflate—toward some undesired average level.[9] This was hardly acceptable in a Europe that was searching for a mechanism of achieving distinctly lower levels of inflation. It was clear that the bilateral parity grid, with a strong and low inflation-prone DM as the nominal anchor of the system, could produce just such a salutary result. In other words, asymmetry in the ERM actually became desirable as a mechanism to bring down inflation. Any country running a money-supply growth rate too divergent from that of West Germany would find, if not sooner due to market speculation of a potential devaluation, lower interest rates at home than abroad that would trigger a flow of funds and move the exchange rate toward the margin. Restrictive action was necessary to bring interest and exchange rates into line, thus insuring a break in the temporarily easy policy. Again, it was this very constraint that was desired by governments after the excessive inflation of the 1970s, and which sealed the fate of the divergence indicator as a serious option within the ERM of the EMS.

European Currency Unit

Reflection on the history of the ECU can help inform the role of an eventual common European currency. The institutional development of this nascent currency may, because of the effective separation of the two functions, be easily divided into public and private use.

In its official function, that is, as a means of settlement and reserve asset, the ECU never did acquire the prominence its creators intended. It did not work especially well as a means of settlement between central banks, say, in association with exchange-rate interventions, for at least two reasons. First, as noted above, most interventions took place at the intramarginal level, well before the automatic mechanism of the financing facilities came into play, so they had not been much used. Second, the temporary nature of the very existence of the ECU—created and maintained by the central banks only by revolving swaps of gold and dollars for ECUs through the EMCF—meant a level of uncertainty by banks in their value if they had to be repaid at a later date. Net holdings above the swap arrangements never got above 10 percent of the total amount of official ECUs invested. For these reasons, plus the fact that official ECUs could not be used directly for intervention in the exchange markets to support currencies,[10] the ECU was never embraced as an important reserve asset by the ERM central banks. A step in this direction by making the gold and dollar deposits permanent, that is by turning the EMCF into an EMF, did not happen, despite the 1979 two-year deadline.

If one couples this continuance of official institutional infancy for the "currency" with the recognition that the ECU was really not necessary for maintaining the bilateral parity grid, and that the divergence indicator had never been used as expected, one can see why some suggested that "at bottom the EMS has almost no direct relationship with the ECU and eventually can function without it," as in Padoa-Schioppa (1989, p. 198).

There turned out to be, however, a relatively healthy market for private ECUs. Currency per se was never issued,[11] but bank deposits (and travelers checks and credit cards) certainly were, as were bonds and other debt obligations. Even futures and options markets were established. Banks could create ECUs for depositors by crediting them to an account, and then "bundling" the equivalent amount of (weighted) EMS country currencies. The amounts involved were often significant, although in total still well behind other major currencies. Statistics quoted in Lomax (1989), for example, show the ECU dominated by the dollar, yen, DM, and sterling as currency of denomination in Eurobond issues, at about 4 percent of the total.

There was also a small amount of trade invoicing, see Jozzo (1989), and at least one major French company kept its accounts in ECUs. The numbers here were small, however, with invoicing at less than 1 percent of total trade even for those countries, such as Italy, where it ostensibly had been embraced. Of course, a major feature of the attractiveness of the ECU for these purposes was that it was a basket currency, and could be used to spread exchange risk, at least among major European currencies. On this Masera (1987) found the ECU, in simulations, to be a part, and often a big part, of the efficient portfolio for investors in different countries.[12] In order to create a currency portfolio similar to the ECU, private agents would have had to engage in many more transactions, each involving discrete changes, than they would have by using the ECU. It was thus efficient from an administrative and transactions cost aspect as well. It is a question of economies of scale; once the basket was defined and accepted by the marketplace, banks could create ECUs in great quantity for both assets and liabilities, without the need to "unbundle" them, except in some instances for any net positions.

Another part of the attractiveness of the ECU was that it took advantage of the higher interest rates paid by some weaker ERM currency countries in order to keep capital from leaving and forcing realignment, and yet also took advantage of the exchange stability between currencies fostered by the system. This meant that "savers living in strong currency countries [would] receive a higher interest rate in ECUs (though they may have [had] to accept some depreciation against their own currency)," while savers "living in weaker currency countries and investing in ECUs [would] be protected more against losses by depreciation," as noted by Harrop (1989, p. 139).

Also, the relative lack of control by national authorities of ECUs certainly added to their allure. Reporting of income and positions was more lax, as was the potential and real application of any exchange controls by national governments. It was partly for this reason that it was well into the 1980s before the West German government was anything but reluctant to allow for their widespread use, the other reason being a fear of losing control over money creation.

Finally, although the ECU may not have been necessary for the ERM, the converse may not have been true. Padoa-Schioppa (1985, p. 37) emphasized early on, in 1981, that it was the institutional nature of the ERM that would lend the ECU a much greater level of credibility as a basket currency, than, for example, the special drawing right (SDR) of the IMF. The ERM was set up in the public rather than in the private interest. The currencies of the ECU were linked in a specific way through the ERM rules and procedures, the ECU was "the monetary expression of an integrated economic area, of a genuine common market [and was] backed by the infrastructure of a public authority." Padoa-Schioppa (1989, p. 198) added in a 1987 conference on the ECU, "I think nothing would have happened in the private ECU market without something happening on the official side." The fact that the EC institutions had actively encouraged the private use of ECUs, including issuing EC debt obligations in the unit, had not hurt their cause.

The question of attractiveness of the private unit is interesting also in terms of institutional development. The position had been taken that the entry of the United Kingdom into the ERM would have made the ECU more attractive to private investors, in that it added an extra level of stability to the unit that was lacking when sterling, part of the ECU basket, was allowed a greater level of fluctuation. Indeed there is evidence that the large depreciation of the pound, and the resultant negative influence on the value of the ECU, surprised many market participants (including the Japanese) who had expected a greater level of stability, triggering a downturn in ECU-denominated instruments in 1986.[13]

A very different view is also tenable. It holds that much of the value of the ECU in the past had been due to market imperfections, including exchange controls and thin markets in instruments in some of the minor currencies. With capital controls being lifted and financial integration continuing apace in advance of the single market, there would seem to have been less need of such an asset. If one were searching for a high rate of return within the ERM one could simply buy into the currency itself, as suggested by Christie (1989). The value of diversification may also have become less important the more successful countries became in achieving policy convergence. If, in this case, exchange-rate changes would be less of a threat, and if interest rates would move more closely together as policies converge, an asset like the ECU would lose much of its value. The purchase or sale of a financial instrument in any of the ERM currencies would therefore be adequate, and there would be little need for ECUs in an optimal portfolio.

There was indeed a good deal of slowing down of asset creation in ECUs during the very late 1980s and early 1990s. Some of the slowdown must surely be ascribed to the perceived stability of the system, at least up until 1992, as in Tsoukalis (1993).[14] Nevertheless, this was hardly due as much to serious policy convergence as it was to what might be called a premature fixing of the EMS in advance of EMU.

Without contradiction, it can also be concluded from the private ECU experience that there would at least be a significant market for assets created in a common currency. The currency in that case would obviously have full institutional support behind it, as the ECU did not. Moreover, although there would be no need to diversify around several defunct currencies, there would nevertheless be a huge market encompassing the entire group of countries included in the European currency. This would apply even more forcefully if the common currency could be expected to have certain qualities associated with it, such as a reputation for price stability. In that case it would attract investors and borrowers not only from within the currency union, but also from well beyond to a quality currency. The fact that the ECU market for assets became as large as it did carries profound implications for the power of a serious common currency.

Basle-Nyborg

Another important technical innovation in the cooperation of states participating in the system was the Basle-Nyborg agreements of 1987, which extended very short-term financing to intramarginal intervention, improved the sharing of the intervention burden, increased Community surveillance of the markets, and encouraged the use of more tools, including interest rate changes, in the management of exchange rates. It also established an increase in short-term credits, an extension of the repayment period, and at least the opportunity to use more ECUs (rather than mainly DMs) in repayment of positions. The new innovations seemed to work quite effectively in defusing a crisis in late 1987, leading to the maintenance of the established ERM rates under no little pressure in the exchange markets.

What is perhaps more important, however, is the spirit of compromise that characterized Basle-Nyborg. The Basle-Nyborg agreements were the result of a successful negotiation between the two major players, France and Germany. Here France got what it wanted in an increased commitment by the Germans to support exchange-rate stability within the parity grid, through the explicit ability of states to use member currencies and the credit facilities to finance intramarginal interventions. After Basle-Nyborg there would be a presumption that a country would allow the use of its own currency in these cases, and by implication, that included the DM. Germany, on the other hand, fixed the general recommendation on the books that there should be greater monetary policy coordination as well as greater use of interest rate policy in maintaining exchange rates, see Gros and Thygesen (1992).

Economic Results: Exchange-Rate Variance

The goals of the EMS when it was founded were twofold; more or less summed up in the concept of a "zone of monetary stability in Europe." Although this phrase could be open to interpretation, the reasons, indeed pillars, behind the establishment of the system were not; they were to reduce exchange-rate variability and to reduce inflation rates, and perhaps bring the latter closer together for the participating countries. On the one hand it is appropriate that assessments of the success of the system have focused especially closely on these two economic results. However, there has been the problem of how to apply effective measures so as to be able to objectively decide on success or failure of such a policy or system. This is not so much a problem of choice of proper variables, although of course that enters, but rather the structure that ought to be applied in the assessment.[15] One may, for example, compare current with past performance. This is a simple and clear-cut procedure, but certainly one that can do some violence to the question of causality. Another procedure is to compare actual results with what could or might have occurred. A typical method is to compare performance with others who were not subject to the policy or system. Although this is conceptually appealing, it is tantamount to history in the conditional, because it suggests that if the policy or system had not been in place the results would necessarily have been more like those in the control group. This is often subjective and open to controversy because conditions may or may not have been similar in the other group. An extension of this idea is to compare present with past performance, each compared to equilibrium values. The definition of equilibrium here embodies a good degree of conditionality to it as well, and again opens the procedure to question.

With these caveats, it is possible to examine the experience of exchange-rate variability among the member countries of the ERM and the EMS. An extensive study was prepared by Ungerer et al. (1983) which, after employing components of the above procedures, drew the conclusion (p. 9) that "in sum, it appears that the exchange rate variability of the EMS currencies has diminished since the introduction of the system." An even more extensive analysis, based on three additional years of experience as well as an extension of methodology (Ungerer et al., 1986), generally confirmed the previous conclusions. It appeared to be the case, even for the early years of the EMS, that exchange-rate variability had been reduced, irrespective of the measure used, and whether one used nominal or real exchange rate variability as the criterion, or whether one compared variability with the past experience of ERM countries, or versus non-ERM currencies.

A reduction in nominal exchange-rate variance would be considered an important result if one were concerned that such a mechanism would force countries to converge, via the discipline of the nominal exchange rate, to lower inflation. Ungerer et al. (1986, p. 18), for example, report a drop in variance from the pre-EMS (before 1979) period to the EMS period, with a "particularly pronounced" drop after 1983, and called the statistical significance of the drop "a strong result." Non-ERM nominal exchange-rate variability generally increased at this time.

A reduction in real exchange-rate variability would be important from the need to measure exchange rate risk, that is, exchange-rate changes not necessary to correct for underlying inflationary trends. Again, Ungerer et al. (1986, p. 19) reported "for the ERM currencies real exchange rate variability against their own group fell for all currencies by all three measures [of variability], which is a strikingly uniform result." Also here, the post–1983 period added to the level of stability; and again non-ERM real rate variability increased.

Subsequent studies based upon the same methodology and updating the variables,[16] at least through the assaults on the system in 1992 and 1993, have confirmed the early statement of Ungerer et al. (1986, p. 20) that "the clear diminution of exchange rate variability within the system, together with the absence of such a trend elsewhere, is certainly consistent with the view that the system has been successful in contributing to exchange rate stability among participating countries."[17]

A somewhat different approach is based upon the notion that unanticipated, or "conditional," disturbances in exchange rates cause the real problem. Such studies measure both anticipated and unanticipated, or total, variability. Again, the question of how the market effectively predicts the exchange rate raises the specter of agreement on measurement,[18] but these studies have, nevertheless, found, as did Artis and Taylor (1988, p. 198), that "there is a significant reduction in the conditional variance of exchange-rate innovations for the ERM currencies . . . and signs of a significant rise in the conditional variance of U.S. dollar exchange-rate innovation." By almost any measure, therefore, it may be said that the EMS, or better the ERM, evidently reduced exchange-rate variance among its members.

A deeper issue arises when one begins to ask the question of the importance of the exchange-rate variance reductions on the well-being of the citizens of the ERM countries. Has there been a real impact of the EMS on the welfare, including income and employment, of the member countries? Although an empirical question, it is a first step in defining what to measure, requiring a clear notion of how a fixed but adjustable exchange-rate system can be expected to transmit real benefits.

One possible benefit of a reduced variance of exchange rates could be a reduction in uncertainty and risk of engaging in international trade. This, according to the theory of comparative advantage (still accepted as valid albeit with some recently developed theoretical caveats), should improve income and growth. The avoidance of exchange risk, however, is possible with the use of hedging through the forward exchange markets, where one can contract to purchase or sell currency at a future date at an already established price. For this reason the debate has tended to narrow to the expected effect of floating exchange rates on the transactions costs involved with trading currencies (most especially the bid-ask spreads). This influence would affect both those traders and potential traders who do and those who do not hedge. An important question here is whether the generalized floating that has characterized the broader international monetary system since the demise of the Bretton Woods system in 1973 has affected world trade. These measures are also counterfactual and complicated, and at this point it must be said that the jury is still out. Most of the earlier studies on the effect of increased exchange-rate variability on world trade flows, for example, did not find a significant impact. See Thursby and Thursby (1985) for a summary of the empirical evidence on that point, plus additional work on the evidence of exchange-rate variability on international trade. Somewhat later work, however, using more sophisticated techniques, suggests at least the possibility of a negative causal link, as in Thursby and Thursby (1987) and Cushman (1986 and 1988). Probably because of these mixed results even those who are or were supporters of the EMS do not claim many benefits from this aspect of the system. Thygesen (1988, p. 12), for example, notes that the "contribution that a reduction in the short term variability of exchange rates can make to the creation of trade among the participants is probably in itself modest."

Still there may be a benefit from what is, after all, a demonstrable and well-accepted result of the system. One view, as outlined in Overturf (1989), is that reduced exchange-rate volatility can help avoid a longer term misallocation of resources when it comes time for private firms to decide to produce either goods that do or can enter into the international markets (tradeables, such as automobiles), or good or services that are not involved in trade (nontradeables).

A second area of potential gain, one not necessarily addressed by the measures of reduced short-run variance of exchange rates, is the avoidance of longer term "misalignments" of exchange rates. Williamson (1983) and others have argued that floating, far from the hope of establishing equilibrium in the exchange markets, has resulted in rates that diverge for very long periods away from the fundamental bases of equilibrium. One important measure of the latter is purchasing power parity (PPP), the concept that in order to insure competitiveness for one's goods on the international markets the exchange rate needs to change, at least in the middle-to-long run, to reflect the relative rates of inflation between countries. Although it was thought early on that floating would increase PPP, it now seems clear, with more experience, that this has not been the case.

Yet again the appropriate measure of equilibrium provides for a significant source of disagreement, so that this area of empirical research is open to no little controversy. In terms of the EMS the question, however, is an important one, for at heart what it suggests is that if real exchange rates are misaligned in a flexible rate system for long periods of time, there is less cost involved with joining a fixed, but adjustable, system. Moreover, although certainly a polar case which deserves more attention below, EMU itself becomes somewhat more attractive.

In the first years of the EMS, especially from 1979 through 1983, there were such frequent "realignments" within the system, in response to differential underlying inflation rates, that the question of longer term misalignment could hardly be said to apply. In general, the participating countries did not suffer a loss in competitiveness because they were allowed to devalue in relation to the degree of relative inflation experienced. There were seven realignments from the beginning of the system until March 21, 1983, including two each in the years 1979, 1981, and 1982. In general it can be said that the Deutschmark and Dutch guilder were revalued, while the French franc and the Italian lira were devalued. A common source of tension within the snake had been the external weakness of the dollar, causing differential, often large, capital flows into the DM, rather than into other EC currencies. This had tended to force revaluation of the DM versus neighbor currencies. Such an explanation is not useful for the 1979–83 period, however, for this was a time of dollar strength. Instead it was the differential inflation rates of the weaker ERM currencies that forced their devaluation, and, of course, German policy had insured consistently low inflation rates in that country.

At about this time, however, that is 1982–83, several countries began to reassess their macroeconomic policies, and make an explicit choice for price stability, based upon the German model. The Danes, for example, with the coming to power of a Liberal-Conservative government in October 1982 switched from a policy of using the EMS as a "crawling peg," that is allowing for periodic devaluations to adjust for intervening inflation, to a nominal exchange-rate commitment and the anti-inflationary policies that go with it. The French, likewise, in March 1983 adopted an austerity program along with the EMS realignment, and more or less formally committed themselves to the German anchor. Italy and Ireland had also somewhat less dramatic shifts at this time, evidenced by their acceptance of devaluations not fully adequate to cover intervening inflation, this resulting in a real appreciation of their currencies within the system. These policy changes had all been taken as representing a very different phase of the EMS, where it was being actively used by the member states in an attempt to control inflation.

This regime shift was especially interesting for the way it seems to have effectively proven that the drafters of the EMS, and indeed the "monetarists" of more than a decade earlier, had not been entirely incorrect in their notion that the institutionalization of greater exchange-rate fixity could lead to the coordination of policies necessary to maintain the rates themselves. Two points are worth making here, however. The first is that this is as much a political as an economic question. Commitment to the fixed exchange-rate system was to be used as a political device to encourage price actors, most especially firms and labor unions in their role as wage and price setters, in order to exercise discipline.[19] The record is that these countries became convinced that the German model was the best one to emulate. Germany had established not only the otherwise desirable trait of low inflation to show for its discipline, but had demonstrated well to the world that this could be coincidental, if not instrumental, in maintaining high growth rates. It was this coming together, not around an economic theory, but around a concrete example of success, that encouraged these Europeans to abandon more expansive demand management policies. It was a step in a direction that was to take the British another seven years to follow.

From 1983 until 1987 there were to be four more devaluations. The adjustment in Italian policy was hardly complete, and the July 1985 realignment was, in essence, simply an 8-percent devaluation of the lira. The only component of the August 1986 realignment was a similar 8-percent devaluation of the Irish punt. The April 1986 and January 1987 realignments involved more currencies, again with the DM and the Dutch guilder revaluing as before 1983, but the nature of these changes was very different. The dollar had peaked in value in February 1985, and the events subsequent to the Plaza Accord of September 1985 by the Group of Five convinced the world of their desire to lower the value of the dollar. This external asymmetric shock to the EMS was caused by speculation against a declining dollar falling more heavily on the DM than the other ERM currencies.[20] Thus the 1986–87 realignments may be interpreted as not affecting the notion of post–1983 as a different EMS regime than before.

There was not to be another realignment in the EMS between January 1987 and the ERM crisis of 1992.[21] This had its own political consequences, which will be examined below, but here it bears mention in that it only reinforced a risk that the ERM had become an agent for the misalignment of its members' exchange rates. As rates become more rigid there is the possibility that differential inflation rates can create longer term divergences from PPP. Indeed, early on in this history, Thygesen (1988, p. 12), writing in 1987, in commenting on Artis and Taylor (1988), worried that the apparent "real depreciation of some currencies (DM, Dutch guilder and Belgian franc) [had] persisted along with real appreciation of the remaining currencies, though the speed of building up such misalignments [had] been reduced. While the standard of reference here is less clear, and the interpretation of what are sustainable imbalances is somewhat arbitrary, the residual lack of convergence is worrying."

Nevertheless, direct measures of misalignment had not found these to be an inherent problem of the system, at least before 1987. De Grauwe and Verfaille (1988) directly calculated PPP rates, corrected for productivity changes, and drew the conclusion that, although misalignments were present in the ERM, they were smaller than those of non-ERM countries. Using longer data series (as well as cointegration techniques), extending to December 1988, MacDonald and Taylor (1990) came to similar conclusions.

Inflation and Monetary Policy Convergence

It is impressive that through the EMS a zone of exchange-rate stability, including stability at both the shorter- (volatility) and longer-term (misalignment) levels was established. There is no mystery as to how these results were achieved. The results bear upon the nature of the second pillar upon which the EMS was built: inflation reduction and convergence. The record is clear. From the commitments made in the early 1980s inflation rates dropped considerably, and converged around significantly lower levels. EMS inflation, as measured by the private consumption deflator, fell from 3.7 percent in 1979 to 2.3 percent in 1986, while deviations from the mean dropped almost in half during the same period, as reported in Russo and Tullio (1988). This price performance did not appear to improve significantly until after 1983, however, reinforcing the notion of a change in country attitudes at about that time.

In fact, studies covering mainly the earlier years of the decade do not seem to show much result in terms of inflation reduction and convergence. This is especially true when one compares results with non-ERM countries during the same period. About all that can be drawn from this analysis is that most of the countries in the world were engaged in deflation at this time, and there is no clear evidence of any special impact of the EMS on European incentives.[22] The same point holds true for an examination of monetary policy convergence as well. However, after 1983 there became clear evidence of increased monetary policy and inflation convergence around significantly lower levels, when compared to non-ERM countries.[23]

This raises the question of whether it was the system itself that generated these positive results, or was the system something of an artificial appendage that was only needed to encourage states of the benefits of lower rates of inflation. Collins (1988) seemed to argue for the latter, generating empirical results that did not allow for a separate EMS effect on inflation.[24] She also drew a distinction between the establishment of the EMS and subsequent performance based upon how the EMS functioned in practice. This latter is a good point, for it suggests that the system had evolved into one that encouraged and aided disinflation among the members, and that it had taken some time to do so.

The French case is especially interesting because it interjects political elements into an understanding of what would become the way in which the system would actually function, as opposed to the ideal of its original design. The Socialist government of Mitterand found early on, in 1981, 1982, and 1983, that expansionary policies could not be run without a rapid negative response from the financial markets. Lack of confidence in the Socialist macroeconomic policies was demonstrated in stock prices and capital outflows. Similar events in the 1970s had led to France's dropping out of the snake rather than sacrificing old-style (Keynesian) demand management policies. Here market pressures led to continuance within the ERM, albeit with devaluations in all three years, but accompanied by increasingly restrictive measures, the last one of which, in 1983, was particularly noteworthy for restoring confidence. Could the French have restored confidence and applied such restrictive measures without the EMS? Sachs and Wyplosz (1986, pp. 29) felt that the external pressure was important, "since there

[was] good reason to believe that French commitments to the EMS tipped the balance towards austerity." Unlike the snake which, as noted earlier, France had been willing cavalierly to desert, "membership of the EMS [had] been invested with enormous political importance at the very highest levels of government," and that leaving the EMS would be tantamount to abandoning the EC and the cause of European integration. In deciding whether the EMS made a difference, or indeed whether exchange-rate commitment could build national policies, the "example of the Socialist turnaround in March 1983 suggest[ed] that an international agreement [could] help to tip the balance towards domestic restraint."

Italy seems to have gone through a similar political learning period, as outlined in Giavazzi and Giovannini (1988), as had Denmark, culminating in its 1982 commitment to the system. This would mean reduced monetary growth rates—with an eye on lower and converging inflation rates—closer to those of West Germany, and a commitment not to seek devaluations that would even make up intervening differential inflation. The potential cost of this would mean real exchange-rate appreciation, a loss of competitiveness in European markets, and potential losses of output and employment.

The important point is that France, Italy, and Denmark, as the Benelux countries had done earlier, willingly subjugated their domestic policies to the constraints of German monetary policy through the ERM of the EMS. Their rationale, again, must be considered to have been as much political as it was economic. The economic model of the strong German state has been mentioned, but that is really only part of the story, since countries could simply have announced their intention to follow the German lead.

It has now been generally accepted that after 1983 the EMS functioned as a mechanism to positively affect market expectations of the credibility of the central banks in their resolve to disinflate. The cost of disinflation will be lower in terms of lost output and increased unemployment if market participants believe that inflation is dropping, and will not be increased again by the authorities, and hence they can be encouraged to accept, say, lower nominal wage increases than otherwise. Countries establish their credibility through the discipline of the system, the incentive to keep exchange rates constant and the costs they would bear within the system if they were to inflate, thereby tying their own hands from any subsequent chance to reinflate. In this way many countries borrowed West Germany's reputation by tying themselves to the economic policies of the Bundesbank. Melitz (1988) took the institutional-political story one step further by suggesting that it is not only in achieving these ends at lower cost (ideally maintaining employment and output by affecting expectations through credibility), but that without the EMS France would have been unable to get an adequate level of credibility to do this in the first place. His contention was based upon the polit-

WITHDRAWN

ical independence of the Bundesbank and the then lack of political independence of the Bank of France, which needed to place as much priority on
the next French election as adhering to price stability. It took the institutional commitment of France, in other words, to convince participants that
they were, and had to be, serious in their policymaking. Coupled with this
was the above-noted implication of not following the rules for continued
participation in an increasingly integrated Europe, as well as memories of
the negative results of pulling out of the snake.

Contiguous to this view, then, is that there were three things that made
West Germany appropriate as the leader, or anchor, to which the other
countries were willing to tie themselves. The first was, as noted, a history of
policymaking that had resulted in excellent macroeconomic results, including long-term growth. The second was an independent central bank (although there were constraints placed upon this independence). Finally,
there was the well-understood (some would say pathological) fear of inflation that insured continuance of price stability as an objective. This fear
came from the dire consequences of hyper-inflation experienced between
the two world wars.[25]

Game theory has frequently been applied to the policy area of the EMS,
and a natural question in modeling the system is how did Germany benefit?
It is appropriate to suggest credibility gains for other countries, but the EMS
seemed fraught with risks that go to the heart of its policy priorities for Germany. The ERM, in other words, could force Germany to unwillingly inflate if it were forced to extensively underwrite exchange rate intervention
among the weaker currency countries. This would be no idle threat, of
course, and it was part of the great institutional reluctance surmounted by
Helmut Schmidt that helped construct the system in the first place. Two
possibilities suggest themselves. One is that the DM had for over three
decades been increasingly the target for capital outflows from other international currencies, especially the dollar, in times of international tension.
Such an external demand was bound to raise the value of the DM versus its
European trading partners and threaten its competitiveness. Alternatively,
the Bundesbank could maintain the rate by intervention, but only at the
cost of increasing monetary emission and, potentially, inflation. It was a difficult position, but if the EMS could function through its fixed rates to make
other currencies equally attractive in those times it would take much of the
pressure off the mark. Skeptics point to maintenance of a relatively undervalued DM and larger German balance-of-trade surpluses and growth rates
as evidence the country had not suffered from the system. Melitz (1988)
made this point, while Vona and Bigi Smaghi (1988) found that the U.S.
balance-of-payments deficits of the early 1980s provided a "safety valve"
from the implications of such trends on the stability of the system.

A second possibility suggested by Kenen (1988) was broader in concept, and more political in nature than these economic considerations. It was that the political rationale of European integration was as important as the economic aim in the founding of the EMS. By extension, the political determination of a state to move toward integration can be applied to Germany without full economic justification for EMS participation. On the integration front, however, it must also be remembered that West Germany would be reluctant to not participate in a system without which the full economic benefits of EC membership might not be achieved. Part of the incentive of Germany in the past to override its national and deep-seated reluctance to part with monetary control has been a fear of risking the customs union. It is an important lesson from the history of monetary integration in Europe that Germany has much to fear from a return to protectionism within Europe and will simply not allow that to happen.

The point of political motivation is made best when referring again to a Socialist government in France that was willing to accept those restrictive policies necessary to remain firmly in the ERM. If in those critical years France had pulled out the system would have suffered the same fate as the snake, potentially setting integration back another ten years. It is difficult to imagine a Single European Act after a collapse of the EMS. What was the difference? After all is said and done, it may be that Mitterand, the man himself, viewed himself as coming from a time and spirit of men like Jean Monnet and Robert Schuman. Of course he was French and a Socialist; but he was also a European. It is such a subtle blending of personalities, history, politics, and economics that finally makes institutions and policies.

Fiscal-Policy Convergence

Whereas a strong case can be made for there having been greater monetary policy convergence during the 1980s, the same cannot be said for fiscal policy. Federal deficits widened in the EMS period, while central government balances relative to the size of the economy did not tend toward convergence. The fear that was related to the EMS during this period was that excessive government deficits would have an impact upon monetary policy, either by inducing inflationary financing or by creating the need for tightening, in either case potentially affecting the stability of a fixed-rate system, especially one where realignments were eventually ruled out.

Asymmetry

An important hypothesis concerning the way in which the EMS worked is that it had been an asymmetric system, if not from its inception then certainly from 1983 on. This refers directly to the use of Germany, and German monetary policy, as a nominal anchor.

A "symmetrically" fixed, or fixed but adjustable, exchange-rate system would work if the central banks representing currencies threatening to diverge—because of differential monetary growth rates—were to intervene into the exchange markets by buying up the "weak" currency with the "strong." This would, within the structure of the EMS, say, be achieved by the weak country borrowing currency from the strong country (through the VSTF) and buying up its own outstanding currency. This is symmetric because the money supply of the weak currency drops while that of the strong increases, bringing economic variables (inflation, interest rates) closer into line, and solidifying the exchange-rate commitment.

To some minds, this was the way the EMS was supposed to work, but, as indicated above, the coincidental desire to disinflate according to the German model altered the system to an "asymmetric" one. In this system the weak currency country alone would intervene on the market by buying up its outstanding currency, either with previously accumulated reserves of the stronger country, reserves of another country, or borrowing reserves that are then "sterilized" for their impact on the stronger country's total money supply. This effectively would reduce the money supply of the weaker country to adapt it to the lower, constant, growth rate of the strong currency leader, or anchor, in the system.

There is good evidence that this is exactly the way the EMS developed. The original intention of the EMS was generally to have interventions in EMS currencies, and yet without any more than minimal "working balances" being kept by ERM central banks. In fact, there had been interventions in dollars at significant levels (although most of these had been by Germany to influence the overall position of the ERM versus external currencies), and interventions in DMs, previously accumulated and held for this purpose. Germany, of course, had been aware of this and had acquiesced to this use of the DM with the understanding that it would not jeopardize the net monetary growth of its currency. Likewise, for interventions that had taken place Germany had tended to sterilize, whereas the others had not, thus bringing their inflation rates down to the German norm. The ERM had become a "greater DM-area,"[26] and asymmetric in the sense that the entire burden of adjustment had fallen on the weak countries.

Empirical studies have reinforced the notion that this was the way the system developed.[27] It is not clear, however, that this had been bad, even though the term asymmetric carries a negative connotation. Since the objective of many of these countries had been to disinflate, and the system had (in the ways already outlined) abetted this desire, and since Germany had been willing to allow for something of a compromise in the use of the DM as a European reserve and intervention currency, it could be argued to have had a purpose.

There were two concerns, however. The first was that the system, by fostering a reduction in monetary growth system-wide, had also introduced a "deflationary bias" with Europe. Since the use of fiscal policy (in spite of the lack of convergence noted earlier) was hampered by a spillover into the other countries, the overall level of growth was damaged. This did not seem to be a great level of concern by the late 1980s, however, given the level of European growth rates and disappearance of worries of "Eurosclerosis." The early 1990s were a different matter.

A second problem was that although the system was perceived to have worked well in the 1980s, it had not achieved its original end. Inflation rates became quite acceptably low, this argument went, and so the system needed to become more symmetric in nature, see Folkerts-Landau and Mathieson (1989) and Russo and Tullio (1988). Some of the changes instituted in the Basle-Nyborg agreements of 1987 implied just the kind of sharing of burden that would make the system both more flexible and more symmetric. The history, of course, turned in a different direction altogether, but at the time what this would have meant was some mechanism to substitute an agreed-upon target for overall growth of ERM money for the explicit role then served by Germany. This would have taken an institutional arrangement that would have made the system much closer to an EMU.

Conclusion

The consensus view of the experience with the European Monetary System is that—at least during the 1980s—it had worked, and some would argue that it had worked well. It had worked partially because it was, or had been viewed as, a flexible system to deal with monetary problems and decisions. It was used as a structure around which to forge positive results on disinflation, even though the asymmetric approach diverged from the original design of the system. Nascent official ECUs, frequently unused financing facilities, and redundant and ignored divergence indicators were the byproducts, but in retrospect it is the rare person who views this institutional development as having been a serious problem. Instead, the system had been praised for its flexibility. Exchange-rate changes, and, increasingly, monetary policies were defined and implemented through the system, cooperatively rather than competitively, using an international institution to serve common ends. The level and spirit of cooperation—institutional cooperation—was such that not only did realignments have to be jointly agreed upon, but that countries were even seen regularly and voluntarily to accept lower than full devaluations to cover their differential inflation rates in ERM realignments.

The success seemed so complete that from 1987 countries proceeded to voluntarily sacrifice any exchange-rate changes at all. There is much more to say about this, including how such a step in moving away from the flexibility of the EMS all but insured the destruction of the very system itself, but the main point to take from the 1980s is that the discretionary use of the EMS had been viewed as a success, indeed in vanguard among EC institutions in its integrative power. Godeaux' (1989, p. 198) comment is representative: "The EMS monetary cooperation has now reached a context that largely outweighs the degree of cooperation achieved in most other areas of Community policy." This was important, for it meant that the failure following on the Werner Report of the previous decade had largely faded in memory, thus providing the base, the incentive, and the momentum toward EMU.

It is easy to lose sight of all of this in consideration of later difficulties with the EMS, but in a sense those difficulties may not loom important at all in any full appraisal of the historical value of the system. Instead, the fact remains that it was the use of the EMS that allowed these countries to come together around a common system to serve common ends, and find that, with application of the spirit of flexibility and compromise, it all worked. In fact, it worked well enough to allow for consideration of movement onto EMU. What had also become clear by the end of the decade, however, was that the EMS did not provide an adequate structure for movement toward monetary union.

FOUR

Institutional Shift
Toward Monetary Integration

Two events in 1987 dramatically altered the milieu in which the EMS had hitherto operated. Together these two events spelled an inherent inability of the system to continue to operate as it had in the past, and perhaps forced it to move onto a higher level of monetary union. These events were coincidental, and they represented broader institutional change rather than more evolutionary developments to the system. What is more important is that they both had strong implications for the way the system had functioned to that point. Although not generally linked together in the literature (probably because they resulted from different institutional incentives and came from different venues of EC decision making), when combined they implied radical changes in the nature of the EMS.

The first of these acts has been referred to earlier, and is curiously often relegated to a footnote in descriptions of the EMS. It was the Basle-Nyborg agreements of September 1987. On the surface the components do not appear extraordinary, and could even be viewed simply as institutional tinkering—at a technical financial level at that—designed to improve, or fine-tune, the operations of the ERM of the EMS. As mentioned in the last chapter, the components of the agreement were to allow for a greater level of support for central bank exchange-rate interventions through the VSTF, a slightly longer repayment period, use of the financial facilities for intramarginal intervention, more surveillance of monetary policies, and greater use of interest rates in support of exchange rates. In a Europe whose average citizens were only beginning to become conversant with the ECU, this was indeed arcane subject matter. It would, nevertheless, carry the potential to affect them much more than many if not most of the developments in the EC since the Treaty of Rome. What Basle-Nyborg did was to encourage market players to the belief that, except for movement within the narrow bands, the EMS was henceforth a fixed, and not adjustable, exchange-rate mechanism.

The second event, officially adopted in 1987 as the Single European Act (SEA), was broadly based in nature, and with implications for very nearly every aspect of Community activity. The provisions most immediately pertinent to monetary integration were those on financial integration and free capital mobility. The clearest implication of this was to remove a tool governments could use, and had used, to insulate their economies from the full effects of differential monetary growth rates.

In this way, and at the same time, EC governments were effectively stripped of two of three areas of international financial policy flexibility. The other implication of the SEA, of course, was to attempt to insure the removal of another tool of international trade policy—the types of non-tariff barriers (NTBs) that had over the years since 1958 loomed more and more decisively in constraining the free flow of goods, services, and factors of production in what was designed to be a free, common market. Either outright or veiled trade protection is, of course, a more direct way to isolate an economy than financial controls.

Hasse (1988) actually makes an even stronger case than this. He argues that there has been an artificial distinction drawn between trade and capital liberalization; and that, in essence, causation runs from capital to trade flows. That is, constraints on capital flows, such as exchange controls, alter, suboptimally, the production of goods and services, thus indirectly affecting consumption and trade. This then fosters the introduction of trade controls, such as tariffs or NTBs. This line of thought, as pointed out by Hasse himself, is quite different than that usually employed, as one can see in the institutional dichotomy in the Treaty of Rome, which deals extensively with trade liberalization, but which can be said to be lax on forms of financial integration (as noted in chapter 1). The implication is that this is part of the reason further integration movements have stalled along the way, and why NTBs had become so pervasive as to require the strong step of the SEA effectively to bring about a true internal market. One can see the wisdom then of linking financial deregulation and capital mobility with the other measures of the SEA, for unless this were done, the rest could well come to naught.

Returning to the case of Basle-Nyborg and the SEA, the joint removal of two international financial instruments brings into play an old concept in economics, that it is incompatible for a group of countries to simultaneously be able for long to maintain fixed exchange rates, free capital mobility, and differential monetary growth rates between them.[1] The tensions created by an attempt to do all three could hold implications either for the continuance of either of the first two, or for the continuance of independent state control over monetary policy. It is in this sense that 1987 may be seen as an overt institutional impetus toward EMU.

Single European Act

The Single European Act was, in a way, born with the production by a directly-elected European Parliament of a draft treaty on European Union (EUT). This called for a distinct change for more democratic Community decision making and an expansion of its areas of concern into foreign policy. With somewhat less revolutionary changes in mind, a Solemn Declaration of European Union was adopted by the European Council, which set up, in Fontainebleau in 1984, the Dooge Committee to study ways in which to further integration. The committee was perhaps established in part to avoid some of the radical changes advocated by the EUT, and yet recognizing that some positive movement was needed. The Dooge Committee recommended a number of less far-reaching but, nevertheless significant, institutional policy changes associated with creating a freer internal market. In June 1985, in Milan, an intergovernmental council was established by the European Council, in order to study the implementation of some 300 measures put forth by the EC's executive branch—the Commission—in a White Paper (proposal) designed to unify EC markets. The intent was to ensure the "four freedoms" of movement of goods, services, capital, and labor by removing a wide variety of remaining fiscal, technical, and physical restrictions, and by amending the EC Treaty to do so. Agreement on the plan, called the Single European Act, was reached by the European Council in Luxembourg in December of 1985, and was officially signed by representatives of the states in February of 1986. The final approval for amending the Treaties followed in 1987. Binding legislation was needed on all of the 300 or so measures, but the act also provided for qualified (weighted) majority rule on most areas of decision making, thus streamlining the process. The legacy of the old French desire for intergovernmentalism, or unanimity, was thus finally broken by the SEA.

The politics of the passage of the SEA are fascinating given the background of the events previously related surrounding the prior EMS negotiations. Again here it was that the French-German axis formed the basis for action. It is clear that the SEA could not have emerged unless Mitterand—in a manner similar to the French economic policy changes of the early 1980s that were designed to allow France to fully commit to the ERM—had signaled in a speech in Strasbourg his acquiescence for talks to proceed. That a socialist president of France could do this demonstrates both his level of statesmanship and his commitment to the European ideal. It also shows how important personality is to explaining institutional change.

Some have argued that Mitterand's role and commitment to integration were even stronger than this, and that the SEA was used as a means to politically force Britain's hand toward deciding upon Europe by providing the threat of a two-speed Community, with Britain "out of the game" in the second tier, unless it acquiesced.[2] The hard-line and often arrogant negotiating style of Thatcher, as well as her obvious misgivings over the potential supranational nature of a future EC, were also components. That a negative personal reaction—shared by Helmut Kohl and demonstrated in his walking out in anger over budget negotiations in Brussels in March 1984—could be influential in leading the Community toward greater integration is again one of those peculiarities that is difficult to quantify either by political scientists or economists. Further evidence of its effect, however, is provided by the raising of stakes for Britain in the 1985 SEA negotiations by establishing a 1992 deadline and the drawing up of Lord Cockfield's "White Paper" (which contained the Commission's formal policy proposals that in turn became the concrete manifestation of the SEA). When the choice of committing to the construction of "Europe" or not came, Kohl, over potentially significant internal opposition, agreed to include EMU as a goal in the preamble of the SEA. This latter was in spite of a previous Kohl-Thatcher agreement, in November 1985, but the French and Italians had, in the meantime, agreed to liberalize exchange controls as part of a process seen to eventually lead to EMU.

The British, however, could not but applaud the fact that, although the SEA specifically now included mention of, and Commission responsibility for, the EMS in the Treaty of Rome, it would nevertheless take the full amendment process of the treaty (article 236) for any new institutional adjustments to the system. Movement toward EMU, in other words, could conceivably be vetoed, and certainly stalled, by any one country, a tactic that Thatcher had demonstrated she was more than willing to employ. In spite of this tactical success, however, the parallel can be readily drawn between the development of the EMS and that of the SEA: both were integrative measures of great importance established around a French-German coalition designed in no little measure in opposition to British desires. In both cases it is certainly an open question if the integrative movement of the plans were taken further because of British opposition, and if so, it must certainly constitute a curious ironic twist in history.

Financial Deregulation

Not the least important part of the SEA provided for the elimination of cross-border restrictions on providing capital services. With the Second Banking Directive banks could do business anywhere in the EC under the regulations of their own country, and would be "largely licensed, regulated, and supervised by their home country," from Folkerts-Landau and Mathieson (1989, p. 6). A similar move toward EC-wide deregulation would apply to investment services and also insurance.

The result of this form of deregulation was expected to bring a greater degree of efficiency and lower costs of production to EC financial activities. These savings would naturally accrue as greater economies of scale were forthcoming through intra-EC mergers in this industry; although the extensive branching already then present in most countries would suggest that, at least in the retail banking area, any gain might not be significant. The level of competition would increase sufficiently, as financial services became truly an EC market, to more than outweigh any monopolistic threat that might arise from the mergers. Indeed, many saw the effects of such competition (low EC prices for banking, insurance, and securities services) as important benefits from deregulation. One report, for example, noted the highly varying prices of such services in an assessment of the benefits of "1992."

At the time it was considered that the primary economic impact of financial market integration on the EMS, of necessity coupled with the removal of capital controls, was the possibility of currency substitution on a large level. This is so because households and smaller businesses could then look upon the markets as one and begin, for the first time, to consider their monetary actions from an international perspective. In particular, they could consider using, as many large firms had for a long time, other currencies in their daily, even purely domestic, activities. The use of this type of "currency substitution" as a means to satisfy the normal uses of money with other currencies was considered a potential threat for the future stability of a system like the EMS; it could make the demand for any one country's currency less stable, thus making it harder to maintain control over monetary policy. This could be especially important in a system that used a nominal anchor, such as the DM, for it could conceivably jeopardize the ability of the Bundesbank to control the orderly growth rate of the currency that was used as the base for the other currencies in the system. Instability and even pressure to move on toward monetary union could result. At least this was considered a serious enough threat to act as one important reason for opening up the possibility of further movement toward integration on the monetary front.

One may examine a bit more closely the threat of currency substitution using the traditional functions of money as a device for analysis—that money serves as both a medium of exchange and as a store of value, while the unit in which money is denominated (e.g., the franc) allows for its use as a standard of value. The advantage of using a different currency than one's own as a medium of exchange for goods and services can be found in the potential reduction of transactions costs necessary for exchanging currencies, plus the possibility of avoiding exchange-rate risk when foreign goods or services are involved in the transactions. Currency transactions charges are not terribly large for large transactions; for example, this was not evidently the source of extensive ECU demand. For smaller transactions, especially those engaged in by smaller institutions and individuals, it would be useful to hold significant foreign-currency balances only if there were extensive intra-EU transactions or, of course, if another currency were used extensively for domestic transactions. Lacking a common parallel currency, an extensive demand for other currencies did not and does not appear to exist generally in Europe, even upon rather full EU market integration. Alternatively, lower transaction charges are likely only upon extensive economies of scale in the exchange of currencies. This could happen with the elimination of use of some Community currencies, so that the banks could make markets in fewer currencies at higher volumes, but, again, short of introducing a common currency (where exchange transaction costs would be zero), this appears unlikely. Certainly it was not the case after the removal of most exchange controls after 1990.

In terms of exchange-rate risk inducing greater substitution toward other currencies as a hedging device for protection against devaluation, much the same applies. That this can easily be an objective of the larger firms is certainly clear, and is evidenced by the existence of robust forward exchange markets and substantial use of balances in other currencies and ECUs. Whether smaller institutions and individuals would increasingly seek to cover their goods-and-services purchases and sales through such practices as the European financial markets became more integrated is less clear. Again, there is little evidence of this happening from 1990 on.

The avoidance of exchange-rate risk is also the major consideration in the use of alternative currencies as a store of value. For this reason there has undoubtedly been demand for currency substitution in Europe. The growth in the private use of ECUs, after all, had really been primarily for store of value objectives rather than to cover, or hedge, trade transactions. This development in ECU use must be considered a little more closely because it appears that the large growth rate in ECU-denominated assets at the beginning of the 1980s was due in part to a peculiarity of the EMS. ECUs could occasionally dominate domestic or other currency assets because the system provided a level of exchange-rate stability, and the ECU was nevertheless able to incorporate a weighted portion of weaker currency interest rates. In addition, it was possible to invest in ECUs without as much concern over potential or existing exchange controls. As the latter ceased to be a concern, the dominance of ECUs became less obvious, for each asset in a different currency would simply reflect any potential risk of exchange-rate changes in its interest rate.[3] There would not then appear to be an advantage of ECUs over other currencies or, more to the point, for any one currency over another. Generally, a strong currency asset could be the equal of a weak currency asset because the loss of interest on the first asset would just outweigh any risk of depreciation of the second instrument.

This leaves pure currency (rather than demand deposits or other assets upon which interest may be paid) as an asset that may influence the demand for money and yet cannot be adapted in this way. This raises the overall point that the greater level of stability in the ERM exchange markets (induced by the progressive institutionalized commitments of the 1980s, culminating in no realignments between 1987 and 1992) meant that the threat of currency substitution was also seen as minimized in a system that minimized exchange-rate fluctuations.

In looking at the standard-of-value function of money, or at least the unit of account in which money is denominated, the threat of currency substitution is minimal in a system like the EMS. In fact, it is only when a currency is inflating at such a radical rate that people begin to start discriminating against it in domestic transactions that one could say currency substitution could become a problem related to the standard of value function. This is sometimes known as "dollarization," a phenomenon usually reserved for countries with extremely high inflation rates, lack of convertibility in face of goods shortages, or both. None of this, of course, has recently applied to Western Europe.

In summary, the EMS could probably be said to have worked well enough so that any threat that currency substitution, arising from increased financial market integration, might have jeopardized the stability of money demand—and hence monetary policy—was small. The threat of such currency substitution could, nevertheless, have added to the momentum toward EMU by creating in the minds of decision makers the possibility of a form of unsustainable instability in the future. This did occur, as noted in the next chapter.

Free Capital Mobility

The elimination of capital controls may have potentially had a greater impact on the continued smooth functioning of the EMS, and in this way led to a greater openness to currency union (rather than through greater currency competition arising from financial market integration). The eventual difficulties in 1992 and 1993 show that those that held such concerns were not simply borrowing trouble.

The objective of the removal of capital controls is to achieve a better allocation of resources. To the extent that they are effective, such controls isolate the capital market in a particular country, and drive a wedge between risk-adjusted real return to investment and saving in different countries. If, for example, it is the objective of France (which it might not be) to use capital controls to keep French capital permanently at home, there could result lower real return for savers and an inadequate flow of capital to, say, Spain, where there might be relatively more efficient investment projects to be financed. The result would be an inefficient allocation and, possibly, lower overall generation of capital. Such a result would certainly seem contrary to the spirit of the SEA, not to mention a true common market—the reason attention to capital controls was explicitly incorporated into the Single European Act.

Capital controls had been extensively used by several European countries prior to the late 1980s. Whereas the United Kingdom dismantled theirs in 1979, and Germany established complete convertibility in 1981, (see Hasse, 1988), it took France and Italy somewhat longer, with major progress only coming after 1986. Most controls effectively came off by 1990, with Spain, Portugal, and Greece given more time, as noted in Gibson and Tsakalotos (1990). In the French and Italian cases, it is not clear to what extent these controls were ever intended to seriously isolate the capital markets in the long run—that is, how effective the authorities really believed them to be for this purpose—or to simply avoid "disruptive" capital flows in the periods surrounding expected exchange rate realignments. The Italians, certainly, were not consistent in their application of controls over the years. Whatever the incentive, and even if they may be somewhat effective for the long run (although there are many ways to avoid them), they seem to have promised the most usefulness for maintaining shorter run exchange market stability.[4]

One implication of the removing of capital controls on the functioning of the EMS was on the so-called "volatility transfer" from exchange-rate to interest-rate fluctuations. The rationale behind this concern was directly related to the functioning of the EMS (at least before 1987). With a fixed-but-adjustable exchange-rate system, and countries with differing inflation rates, domestic interest rates must adjust along with differential inflation rates to compensate holders for the expected devaluation they feel must be coming. This, of course, is the "uncovered interest parity" condition referred to above, and the divergence in interest rates on assets denominated in the currencies will become greater as the expectation of realignment becomes greater. In this way exchange-rate fluctuations are transferred at the middle run to interest rates.

This volatility transfer could be unfortunate because the costs of interest-rate volatility might be higher than exchange-rate variability. For instance, depending upon the degree of openness of the economy, interest-rate volatility could affect the nontradeable sector as well as tradeables, and, in addition, the facilities for hedging are greater in the foreign exchange markets than they are for interest rates. Investment is certainly socially productive, and there could be significant welfare implications if investment was to be reduced by interest-rate uncertainty. The case is made even stronger by the use of variable-rate loans, which means a company is not certain that even the financing of past projects is free from such fluctuations (especially if there is no close correlation between the variable nominal rates and true returns firms receive to finance their debt).

Since governments, themselves interest payers, find it "unwelcome," in the words of Wood (1988), to allow interest rates to move in order to induce capital to stay they "compel" it to stay by exchange controls. Several have gone on to suggest it was these capital controls that were at the heart of the very survival of the EMS, as in Giavazzi and Pagano (1988). Rogoff (1985) found substantial violation of interest parity, a clear breach of efficient markets, and questioned the relevance of an exchange rate regime based upon capital controls. Again, the difference between onshore (domestic) and offshore (Euro-) interest rates gives some measure of the effectiveness of the controls for avoiding large fluctuations in domestic interest rates prior to realignments and, indirectly, evidence on the importance of controls for the working of the system. A paper by Caesar (1988), was especially interesting in this regard, and reinforced the Giavazzi and Pagano concern at the time. Artis and Taylor (1988), using nonparametric tests, came to similar conclusions on the French and Italian case, that is, lower variability of onshore interest rates due to the presence of capital controls.

Concern over volatility transfer led to intriguing suggestions on how best to manage a fixed-but-adjustable exchange-rate system in such a way as to maintain competitiveness over time with a minimum impact on interest rates. Driffill (1988), for example, examined several methods of accommodating the EMS to the removal of exchange controls so as to limit interest-rate volatility.

In a sense, however, these studies missed an important point concerning the way the EMS had been used in the past; incentives of states within the system did not necessarily include maintaining competitiveness as a first priority.[5] Instead, the EMS had been used to help maintain overvalued, or less than competitive rates in an attempt to provide a self-imposed cost to help curtail excessive inflationary pressure. In addition, as noted, the system had increasingly moved away from any realignments at all, and toward greater fixity. Institutionally, it would then appear not to have been acceptable to design the system to adapt well to maintain competitiveness in the face of free capital movements, because it was increasingly unacceptable to have any exchange-rate changes at all.

The implication for the EMS was inescapable. Without exchange controls or a willingness, say, to frequently realign rates (as in a "crawling peg" or the kind of "soft bands" described well by Driffill (1988)), the system needed a mechanism to stem potentially destabilizing capital flows without relying upon radical changes in interest rates. Capital "flight" or, better, speculative capital flows in Europe, was large, increasing in magnitude, and also was responsive to exchange-rate (as well as political) risk, as in Gibson and Tsakalotos (1990). The implication was that private capital flows could quickly force the liquidation of an overvalued currency, thus forcing its devaluation through lack of sufficient system reserves to handle this speculative onslaught. The stability of the EMS would be in question without some mechanisms to keep capital from moving.

In other words, exchange-rate stability desired within the EC, as evidenced by institutionally revealed preferences of the Basle-Nyborg type, was threatened by another institutional preference: full capital mobility for the purpose of greater market efficiency. This point is made quite clearly in the Delors Report (1989).

System Development

It seems apparent from this discussion that there is a level of incompatibility with free capital mobility and fixed exchange rates. They are not necessarily incompatible, however, if the underlying pressure, both for potential devaluations and capital flight, is removed. This pressure is, of course, differential inflation rates caused primarily by differential money supply growth rates. The inconsistency trinity would hold implications for monetary policy coordination, then, in suggesting that the advantages of capital mobility and fixed exchange rates can be realized only as long as monetary policies are adequately aligned. Of course, if countries do not recognize the risk and continue to insist upon the application of their own differential monetary policies, they might threaten the foundation of the system. Padoa-Schioppa (1988) described the worst-case scenario as the breakup of the common market itself, a reintroduction of comprehensive exchange controls, and a general "unraveling" of Community arrangements, if sovereignty over monetary policy were not sacrificed at the state level. Although one might therefore describe it as a "high risk" strategy, like Basevi (1988), others at the time alternatively suggested that it is the very inconsistency in the "trinity" that might induce movement on the joint monetary policy front, indeed, toward EMU.

There are echoes in all of this of the old monetarist-economist debate, with the monetarist theme here being that "the liberalization of capital movements would intensify pressure on EMS countries to adopt compatible economic policies leading to convergent economic developments," as in Ungerer et al. (1986, p. 10). Likewise, the economist argument might be that "unless divergences in economic policies and performances are eliminated to begin with, freedom of capital movements will prove destabilizing," from Guitián (1988, p. 9). The difference between this and the old debate is that the removal of capital controls is an elimination of a form of control, while the original clash concerned the introduction of rules over exchange-rate movements. Indeed, in the language concerning the SEA, a distinction was made between "negative" integrative movements (removal of barriers, deregulation), and "positive" integration (introduction of common institutions and instruments). Pinder (1989, p. 107) described a process of proceeding from negative integration—giving "many economic and social problems a Community dimension, at the same time depriving the member states of some of the policy instruments with which they hitherto tried to deal with them"—to positive laws and policies to meet Community-wide objectives. The monetary case would seem to fit well into this framework, for there is evidence that the removal of flexibility over capital controls dictated by the SEA, coupled with an increasing preference for fixed exchange rates held important implications for monetary union. It was no accident that the SEA preamble recognized the connection between the SEA and monetary union, and that the European Council in 1988 decided to set up the Delors Committee to study EMU.

Regime Shift

One factor that would lead to fuller consideration of monetary union was the reduced flexibility of the EMS after 1987. Such a change was so significant that at the time it was thought to represent no less than a change in the regime itself. This sense of a major regime shift was shared by many, one characterization of which is described in Giavazzi and Spaventa (1989).

Inherent to this notion is that credibility of exchange-rate maintenance had been so well established that it had ceased to be a problem in the EMS, and that development in turn held more implications for the way the system then worked than for its long-run, or future, stability. As an example, Padoa-Schioppa (1988) might have been concerned with developing and institutionalizing adequate lines of central bank defense against destabilizing currency movements, and suggested the mobilization of reserves to fully accommodate demand for currencies (analogous to the way national central banks deal with "runs" on banks). Of course the implication of attempting to maintain the trinity as capital controls were removed, would reinforce the concern, and hence, the prescription. Such proposals could easily fall on deaf ears in such an environment. That is, if the regime-shift hypothesis were true, such institutional steps were not really necessary because such speculative market pressure was not—and would not under even fairly radical circumstances—likely be brought to bear in attack on a weak currency. The argument ran that exchange rates had been fixed (disregarding the margins of availabile flexibility), and the market was now convinced that the commitment was valid. The EMS, therefore, as noted above, had become a truly credible fixed (and no longer adjustable) exchange-rate system, a development that could have had very real implications, somewhat different but related to the concerns over monetary integration stated above.

The following scenario may be used to demonstrate how belief in a regime shift could affect reactions in what was termed the "new" EMS. Say that a country were to receive a real—nonmonetary—asymmetrical shock to a larger extent than other EMS members, for example through a large increase in investment in one country due to particularly good prospects from deregulation due to the SEA. This increase in real demand would produce an increase in the growth rate for the country, increase imports more than exports, and thus throw the current account into deficit, as well as threatening inflation. Under the "old" EMS this would have led to speculation of a devaluation, and capital flows away from the "weak" currency, thus perhaps resulting in a realignment. Instead, however, in the "new" EMS there would be no concern over the credibility of the exchange rate, and, instead capital flows in to finance the current account deficit. The joint credibility of exchange-rate fixity and the lack of threat of reintroduction of capital controls here produces a very different result.

Suppose the authorities were to become concerned over inflation, and engage in a restrictive monetary policy in order to fight it. Interest rates would, therefore, be raised, thereby inducing even more capital inflows in a market increasingly responsive to even fairly small differences in rates. This is especially true as differences in interest rates no longer reflect exchange-rate depreciation expectations. The authorities, in their restrictive policy, would be forced to sterilize the inflows, because the inflows have implications for increasing the monetary base and, hence, the money supply.

The result, again at the authority reaction level, seems worrisome, since deficits are not just financed, they are "overfinanced." The central bank is forced to use the margins to allow for some appreciation of the supposedly weak currency within the band, and countries, instead of following the German lead on monetary policy, are now actively deciding on their own policies. There is no longer any leadership provided on monetary policy, either from Germany or at the EC level. Capital flows in such large amounts can eventually call into question the stability of the system, including the preference for greater exchange-rate stability within the band.

Actual events in Spain and Italy during the late 1980s seemed to contain elements of this scenario, but suffice it to say that it would not be very long in the history of the EMS that the overriding concern would become something very different than potentially deficit countries having their exchange rates appreciate and their deficits overfinanced. Attention to this line of thought, remembering that it was not without evidence of support, is important because it provides insight into the way in which people thought of the EMS during this period, and became convinced that the ERM could go on indefinitely in empirical denial of the inconsistency trinity.[6] That is not to say that there would not eventually be the need for some greater stability within a system where monetary policies were not coordinated, but rather that people viewed the EMS as having a particularly long half-life. This element of the institutional development of the system would find later echoes in the Maastricht Treaty.

Conclusion

In review, two events in 1987 coincided dramatically to alter the functioning of the EMS. The enactment of the SEA and the agreements at Basle-Nyborg effectively meant fixed exchange rates with free capital flows. Even if these developments had not been enough to result in a regime shift toward full confidence in exchange-rate stability, they had been enough to lead to the recognition that there could be a significant threat to the system if countries insisted upon continuing to exercise complete autonomy over monetary policy. They had provided a level of economic pressure upon governments to begin to move toward greater monetary integration.

The costs of lack of coordination could be significant. In the past, for example, Germany had been reluctant to not agree to action leading toward greater monetary integration, for fear of being politically branded. Now the same pressure became strong on all of the EC states, for the fear of seriously crippling the movement toward the four freedoms and growth rates inherent in the SEA. The Delors Report would be the next step.

FIVE

The Delors Report

By 1988 the implications of the double thrust toward greater integration, provided by a much greater commitment to fixed rates, and a serious move toward financial integration were being recognized. Indeed they had already been recognized in the preamble to the Single European Act itself, which had called for movement on the monetary front. Added to this, in 1988, were increasingly real concerns over the way in which the EMS had worked, so that the status quo no longer appeared viable.

The criticisms over the functioning of the EMS were aimed directly at West Germany. Edouard Balladur, the then finance minister of France, for example, drafted a paper criticizing yet again the asymmetric way in which the EMS worked, that is by forcing weak-currency countries to adjust more than strong-currency ones. This was not so much a complaint of the old type (for France had, after all, bought into German-style monetary discipline) but rather that imbalances could be created whereby no one country would be exempted from adjusting its policy, when that policy "departs from Community-agreed goals" (Colchester and Buchan, 1990, p. 166). The paper called for a European central bank. Likewise, a paper by Giuliano Amato, Italy's finance minister, also criticized the functioning of the EMS and the German dominance of it. This was basically a restatement of the "deflationary bias" argument that suggested that an undervalued DM coupled with low growth of demand in West Germany meant, through the resultant German surpluses and the fixed rates of the EMS, that other countries were suffering from too low growth rates. Amato too, called for a European central bank to redress the situation.

The combination of basic economic sense behind the inconsistency trinity and the closely related and increasing dissatisfaction over the functioning of the EMS would lead to the Delors Report. In this document the Community states found themselves coming together, around their own interests, with the political will it would take to move forward on the establishment of a central institution that could eventually control monetary policy for them all.

Delors Committee

Notably, the first move came from Germany. Hans-Dietrich Genscher, the foreign minister, rather than taking the plausible strategy of refusing to change a system that seemed almost designed to serve German interests, instead influenced Chancellor Kohl to accept active consideration of EMU, and wrote that the "creation of a single European monetary zone, with a European central bank, constitutes the economically indispensable centrepiece of a European internal market," as quoted in Colchester and Buchan (1990, pp. 167–68).

The inexorable press of financial integration that would eventually lead to some decision of this type must have been on his mind. It is certainly not a coincidence that in June, before the Hannover Summit, the finance ministers, in the spirit of the SEA, adopted a precise timetable for lifting capital controls. As noted, France and Italy were to remove remaining (especially short-term) controls by July 1, 1990, while Spain, Ireland, Greece, and Portugal were scheduled to lift theirs by the end of 1992 (Greece and Portugal could delay this deadline if they felt it necessary). Likewise, Belgium would end its form of multiple exchange rates, which acted much like exchange controls, by 1992. Given this, it is especially noteworthy that it was Germany that put the concept of EMU on the Hannover Summit agenda for late June 1988.

The summit, with reluctant acquiescence by Thatcher, set up a committee to study the issue, and designated Jacques Delors, the dynamic president of the Commission, to be its leader. It is generally felt that Delors, a French Socialist, in searching for a way to continue the momentum following upon the SEA, felt that EMU was the proper avenue to take for a strong movement toward greater European integration. The feeling of some is that he would have preferred a different route, using a "social Europe," including significant worker participation and other social policies, but felt that this was politically unacceptable, and that the "transcendent political aim [was] building Europe," as in Cutler, et al. (1989, p. 152). Incidentally, another related view is that Delors had preferred pressing monetary union over the SEA a few years earlier, but felt the time was not right for success in the sovereignty transfer debate. His commitment, following Hannover, to EMU is indicated by his keeping the EC portfolio on monetary affairs for himself in the fall of 1988. The mission of the Delors Committee, from the written conclusions of the summit, was the "task of studying and proposing concrete stages leading towards [economic and monetary] union," from the Delors Report (1989, p. 43), and the presentation of a report by the time of the Madrid Summit in June 1989.

The makeup of the committee was impressive. It included all 12 of the EC central bank governors, three well-respected outside experts on European monetary affairs, and Frans Andriessen and Delors himself from the Commission. It has been suggested that this was a real departure from the traditional EC practice of appointing "wise men" to such a committee, people who, although respected, did not hold power, so that the results could be too easily ignored. In addition, the individuals would generally be known as Europeanists, so that the results would be foregone in any case. The risk of the strategy of appointing the central bank governors, of course, would be getting any serious supranational results out of the committee, presuming that that was considered desirable. After all, the Hannover conclusions had "confirmed the objective of progressive realization of economic and monetary union," as in the Delors Report (1989, p. 43). On the other hand, the promise held that any plan that had the commitment from such a daunting group would have a chance of success, as they were certainly in a position to make it work.

The committee met regularly from September 1988 to April 1989, when it filed its report. Agreement came with some facility, and in some ways this is quite surprising given that the committee's task was to design a system that would rob their positions of a good deal of their power, and do so in a way that would also eliminate a good deal of national sovereignty. Examination of motivation that would, of course, differ by country, is made below, but for the governors themselves there is one sentence in the Delors Report that perhaps best summarizes what must have come in on them at this time: "Once every banking institution in the Community is free to accept deposits from, and to grant loans to, any customer in the Community and in any of the national currencies, the large degree of territorial coincidence between a national central bank's area of jurisdiction, the area in which its currency is used and the area in which 'its' banking system operates will be lost" (Delors Report, 1989, p. 20). In other words, save sacrificing the single market, and all that would mean politically as well as economically, they had no choice. These remarks also reinforce the vision of this group that—although the discussion on currency substitution in the previous chapter seemed moot at that particular time in the operation of the EMS—it nevertheless was considered important to the future direction taken by the Community upon financial liberalization.

The concept that they had no choice, of course, does not apply either to the way in which EMU might be structured, or to the process leading to it. In fact, it seems that the bulk of the disagreement was over process, especially the question of Treaty revision. The French attempted, unsuccessfully, to push through a system of early pooling of foreign-exchange reserves without prior authorization through a change in the Treaty of Rome, to which the SEA had already spoken. While this was quickly rejected by the others, it is indicative of the level of French enthusiasm for the endeavor. Another area of substance to EMU that received a good deal of attention was the question of how much control over member budgets was necessary. The report is strong on this issue, but the debate would nonetheless surface again.

Delors Report

As the most important document regarding European union on the monetary front since the EMS was established, and more probably since the Werner Report, the Delors Report bears close attention.[1] Comparison with the Werner Report, examined here in chapter 1, is more than one of just degree, for there are striking similarities between the two documents. This is not entirely surprising, for when, even in the early years of the single market, the question was raised on how to proceed next, the answer was to draft a new Werner Report. At the Société Universitaire Européenne de Recherches Financières (SUERF) conference in Luxembourg in 1986, for example, J. Rey and J. Michielsen (1988, pp. 88–89) suggested the "need for a common understanding of the process through which the ultimate stage of monetary cooperation in Europe could be reached, should the political obstacles be removed. A 'Werner report revisited' might help in focusing action on the next most useful steps, be they monetary or non-monetary."

The similarities between the Werner and Delors Reports begins with structure. For each there are basically three parts: an introduction, outlining the need for EMU; a description of the final objective; and the definition of the stages necessary to achieve the objective. Much of the language, in fact, is the same, including the specific institutions and the concept of stages. There is, in addition, a shared theme that could most simply be summarized as "we have done well, but we need to do more," supplemented by "if we do not do more we may lose what we have gained, but if we do, we will benefit even more." It will be instructive to compare the two reports so as to bring out in full relief some of the most important features of the Delors Report, but it is already clear that intellectual debt is owed by the one report to the other.

The first chapter of the Delors Report deals with "past and present developments." Regarding the past it refers to the Werner Report following upon agreement for consideration of EMU at the Hague in 1969. This occurred against a background of prior successes in the Community, including an early transition to the full customs union, the CAP, and a Community budget. It mentions as well, perhaps with a little irony, the expressed "political will to establish an economic and monetary union" (p. 11) following upon the presentation of the Werner Report. Some of the history following this is briefly recounted, including the setting up of the snake and the EMCF, and that the integration process "lost momentum under the pressure of divergent policy responses to the economic shocks of the period" (p. 11). This interpretation, as evidenced in the first chapter, is open to some question, in that it is defensible that there was a lack of political will to establish other than divergent policies under any circumstances, but the point is, nonetheless, made.

In the report the EMS is viewed as a "success . . . in promoting its objectives of internal and external stability." It did this, not unconvincingly, by "laying the foundation for both a downward convergence of inflation rates and the attainment of a high degree of exchange rate stability." Again, although perhaps not empirically demonstrable, the general perception is expressed that the latter, that is reduced exchange-rate instability, had "protected intra-European trade." Finally, it had achieved this through "increasingly close cooperation among central banks" (pp. 12–13).

Immediately establishing the thesis of having come far, but not far enough, the report is quick to point out that the EMS had "not fulfilled its full potential," there not being full membership (nor all members at the narrow margins), full convergence of fiscal policies, nor movement onto the second stage as originally envisioned in 1978, that is, with the establishment of the EMF. Also the ECU, although well accepted privately, had only played a limited role officially in the EMS.

Something of the same tack is taken with the SEA, (pp. 13–14), that is seen as having imbued the EC with a "new dynamism . . . contributing to the recent acceleration of economic growth in the Community." Of course critics could point to other reasons for the pickup of growth, which reached a healthy 3 percent in 1989, such as oil-price reductions (before the Gulf War), but the investment boom that quelled concerns of "Eurosclerosis" at this time could, with reason, be attributed to SEA, so this is probably not hyperbole.

The need to do more is here established by appealing to the economic logic that since the single market increasingly links economies together there is promise for greater "economic advancement," but only if economic policy "responds adequately." In particular, the greater level of integration is seen to "reduce the room for independent policy manoeuver" (p. 14). There needs to be stronger regional and structural policies, as well as greater convergence in the budgetary field. The latter is due to the fact that the closer links forged by increasing integration would otherwise put an "undue burden" (p. 15) on monetary policy, so the broader macroeconomic policy mix needs coordination. This section, entitled incidentally "Problems and perspectives," is interesting in that it explicitly mentions the problems created for states by a "growing reluctance to change exchange rate parities" coupled with capital liberalization. It also suggests that voluntary cooperation is not enough, but that rules, the "binding rules" that are a leitmotif throughout the document, are necessary.

Finally, in this chapter, the stick is established by noting (p. 15) that the success of the internal market progress "hinges to a decisive extent" on close policy coordination; while the carrot is that, with such coordination, EMU could result in a "quantum jump [toward] . . . a significant increase in economic welfare" in the EC.

The original Werner Report contains the same basic theme. Success in the sense of advancement toward integration leads to disequilibrium, or "weakening of autonomy for national economic policies" (p. 8), and the need for policymaking at the Community level. The stick here is revealed as allowing for free movement of goods, services, labor, and capital "without thereby giving rise to structural or regional disequilibrium" while the carrot is a "lasting improvement in welfare."

The second chapter of the Delors Report, on the final outcome to be expected from the process leading to monetary integration, begins with a definition of EMU, or at least a description. The need for a change in the Rome Treaty is dealt with early on, the basis for which is the "transfer of decision-making power" from members to the EC level, covering both monetary ("one decision-making body") and other macroeconomic policies ("an agreed macroeconomic framework"). The latter again implies budgetary policy, with "binding constraints on the size and the financing of budget deficits" (p. 18).

The report is then quick to bow to the "principle of subsidiarity," a concept deemed applicable generally in all EC areas. It states that only those tasks that are necessarily best performed at a higher level should be absorbed by the EC and all others left to member states. This principle is perhaps even more than an efficiency criterion, intended to calm those with concern over excessive power flowing to Brussels. It has been criticized by these very people as sounding well but not operational in practice. This criticism is actually valid here, for there continued a good degree of debate after the Delors Report was filed over the need for binding constraints to be established over budgetary policies at the Community level.

The Werner Report contains a parallel passage on the question of Treaty change, presupposing "a modification of the Treaties of Rome," (p. 13) thereby completing a link that flows historically back through the early 1970s to a treaty in 1958 that did not speak effectively to this issue at the time—again, for understandable reasons. The subsidiarity question, on the other hand, is really more pertinent to the late 1980s debate, with the U.K. concern over "Brussels the harmonizer," but even the Werner Report warns against "excessive centralization" (p. 11).

The intellectual link between the Delors and Werner Reports is explicitly recognized at an important juncture: the definition of monetary union. The parallel is almost exact in defining three conditions: total currency convertibility, capital liberalization and financial integration, and the irrevocable locking of exchange-rate parities.[2] It seems curious that a single currency is not part of this definition, but pains are taken to distinguish monetary union from this requirement as not being "strictly necessary," although for "psychological and political reasons" it would be "a natural and desirable further development of the monetary union." This preference is based upon demonstrating the irreversibility of the union and the necessary elimination of transactions costs between currencies, and the move should, therefore, occur "as soon as possible after the locking of parities" (Delors Report, p. 19).[3]

In fact, this distinction has seemed more than a curiosity to some, but an important and unfortunate, feature of the report. This is so because it seems to remove an identifiable and appealing symbol of the necessary final goal of the process. By reducing the importance of a single currency—indeed, by explicitly eliminating it from the definition of monetary union—a tactical flaw may have been introduced that might have politically made the delicate and uncertain process of adoption that much more difficult. It turns out that in the history of Maastricht this probably was more of a tactical question than a serious strategic mistake, however, and the fine point is drawn in the Delors Report—as it was also in the Werner Report—for political reasons. Roy Jenkins (1990), former president of the Commission, for example, explains that people are reluctant to adopt new names for their currencies, referring to the complaints that arose when the United Kingdom in 1971 decimalized and dropped the units "shillings" and (old) "pence." Since, in similar thinking to the Delors Report, irrevocably pegged rates are much the same thing, it might be politically wiser to keep domestic units of account. Jenkins says "always avoid domestic opposition when you can do so without any sacrifice of principles" (p. 55). In a Europe of 1988 when the average person on the street, asked to respond to the phrase "European Monetary System," would say simply and with a feeling of finality, "ECU," these points certainly are not moot.

The report describes the features of "economic union" somewhat better than it defines the concept. To those unfamiliar with this literature, the term might seem somewhat idiosyncratic, if for no other reason than it would appear that "economic union" would seem to subsume "monetary union" under it. This interpretation would, in fact, fit better with the general usage of terminology generally applied to the integration process. Following this, a "customs union" would describe a state of free trade among its members, a "common market" would add free factor flows (capital and labor) to trade, while an "economic union" would take the process one step further and add policy integration to imply complete economic integration.[4] In this case, certainly "economic union" would constitute a sufficient rubric, without the necessity of adding "monetary." The problem is that there has been much disparity in the way the term has been used, with some authors implying that union would be essentially coincidental with total economic integration, while others require only some significant degree of policy harmonization before the condition applies. Since monetary union represents a particularly "high" level of policy integration, it perhaps justifies being distinguished.

In this light, the semantic use of "economic union" appears useful as "the characteristic of an unrestricted common market with a set of rules which are indispensable to its proper working" (Delors Report, 1989, p. 20). It includes (1) a single market, with a free flow of goods, services, capital, and labor; (2) competition policy; (3) structural and regional aid policies; and (4) macroeconomic policy coordination (presumably other than monetary policy). The single market is self-defining, the objective to which policy addresses itself, and the subject of the initiatives of the SEA. Competition policy, also part of the SEA, is mentioned so as to insure that the benefits of a single market could not be thwarted by cartelization or excessive concentration, or at least the abuse of these. Market access should be free from private as well as governmental constraint.

The perceived need for inclusion of regional and structural aid, or "development," policy at the EC level needs some explanation. A good deal of attention is paid to this in the report, as well as in several related papers that are presented along with it, including one by Delors himself called "Regional implications of economic and monetary integration." More will be said on this issue, but the proposition itself is simple. It is that the EC states differ considerably in terms of economic development, and that the Community could not yet be said to be an "optimal currency area" in the sense where factors of production actually do move—as opposed to possessing the legal ability to—easily between states. In this case differential growth, or events that affect that growth, could no longer be dealt with by individual countries with using the exchange rate as a tool, that is, if EMU were to come about. In this case some form of regional policy could substitute for the loss of the tool. This type of policy is very controversial from an economic point of view, but the report hints at a somewhat more political motivation, the necessity to "spread welfare gains [presumably from a fully efficient single market] throughout the Community," and that if this were not to happen the union would be faced with "grave . . . political risks" (p. 22). Already at this time these funds were to be doubled from 1988 until the end of 1992; and as the result of a 1988 Council decision the least developed countries (Greece, Portugal, and Ireland) were scheduled to receive in the neighborhood of four to five percent of their annual GDPs in Community aid by 1993. It is in such an area as regional funding that a full understanding of an economic institution is impossible without consideration of the political dimension. It is too facile to say that the report promises a quid pro quo, and indeed it is quick to suggest that reliance on financial aid to subsidize incomes is not appropriate,[5] but the tone is there.

Finally, macroeconomic policy, which here is really governmental budget policy, is addressed again, with another reference to binding rules on the size and financing of national budget deficits. Three reasons are given for such rules. First, differential budget policies, presumably meaning excessive budget deficits in some states, could "generate imbalances in the real and financial sectors of the Community" (Delors Report, 1989, p. 23). This means that individual states could attract excessive amounts of financing and savings from other parts of the Community by the interest rates coincidental with large budget deficits.[6] Second, excessive deficits could put pressure on for monetary expansion. Finally, the Community budget would in all likelihood remain quite small, so that any form of EC fiscal policy would need to rely upon coordinated action using state budgets, perhaps an action that would not always result from voluntary cooperation. In this way a common monetary-fiscal policy mix could be used for countercyclical use at the Community level.

The relevant passages in the Werner Report, although not quite as detailed in rationale, are quite similar. A pertinent example, here in terms of tracing the intellectual history for such a strong stand taken, after no little debate, on the budgetary issue, is "a fundamental element will be the determination of variation in the volume of budgets, the size of the balance and the methods of financing or utilizing any surpluses" (Werner Report, 1970, p. 11).

The Delors Report proposes a new monetary institution, a European System of Central Banks (ESCB), as a mechanism to control monetary policy and exchange rates. It would have full status as an autonomous Community institution, and have a structure much like that of the Federal Reserve System in the United States or the Bundesbank in Germany. The federal structure would have major decisions taken at the center, or ESCB Council,[7] while the national central banks would execute operations. It seems to be understood, again on the U.S. or German model, that although federal in structure, the bulk of real power rests at the center. It also seems that such a system was very much in the minds of the drafters of the Werner Report, where the equivalent institution is described.

The mandate of the ESCB is an area where much thought and experience is represented in the report, and in this case in contradistinction from the prior model of the Werner Committee. It strongly reflects the makeup of the committee, for the first—indeed prime—mandate, is to "price stability" (p. 25). The ESCB would support general EC economic policy, but this is put below, and is "subject to" the objective of price stability. Add to this guaranteed independence of the new institution, subject only to accountability by reports to the European Parliament and the European Council, and the meaning and parallel are clear. The ESCB is designed here to become an EC Bundesbank, to take over the role of that institution in safeguarding low inflation through a prior charter from which it would be loath to divert in principle or in practice. One would have expected no less from a committee of central bankers including among its members Karl Otto Pöhl of the Bundesbank, but also others who were convinced that the German strategy held the best hope for stable long-term growth in an unstable world. German monetary discipline lies at the very heart of the Delors Report.

Again in variance with the Werner Report, which called for a new "centre of decision-making," the Delors Report sees no need for a new institution in the non-monetary, "economic," area. Instead it feels these competencies would devolve on present institutions (Commission, Parliament, Council, Monetary Committee, Court of Justice), but leaves the specific responsibilities undefined, to be specified in the new Treaty. Finally, for the second chapter, it is likewise relatively vague regarding the external role of the EC in international monetary affairs, although it foresees a "greater say" (p. 29) for the EC in international negotiation.

Perhaps the most controversial aspect of the third and last chapter of the report lies in the introductory paragraph, which states that although progress toward EMU involves stages, the process is to be regarded as one, and "the decision to enter upon the first stage should be a decision to embark on the entire process" (p. 31). This language was not appealing especially to the United Kingdom, which among all of the then twelve states had expressed the greatest level of concern over the direction of a "hard" currency union and all that it would mean for sovereignty. The paragraph, however, makes perfect sense both historically and politically. It will be remembered that there were problems of separation of stage one of the Werner Report from the final outcome because some states viewed stage one as the desirable final outcome. The Delors Report was unlikely to repeat that mistake, if one component of a prior document wrought from a rather radical form of political compromise could be called a mistake. In addition, the experience with the Single Act indicated the need for and benefits of maintaining momentum, so the fluid movement through the stages might encourage the final outcome. There is also, however, in the statement, something of a threat, in fact, perhaps intended for the United Kingdom. Remembering the lesson learned from the EMS negotiations, Britain, even if it did not wish to fully participate in new institutions, could be counted upon to not block passage if it were threatened with non participation. The British seem to fear above all being "out of the game." With this in mind, it is interesting to see a somewhat unveiled form of threat on participation where "influence on the management of each set of arrangements would have to be related to the degree of participation by Member States" (p. 32). As Cutler, et al. (1989, p. 157) noted, the option of staying out is made as "unattractive as possible," as "the new arrangements will be run on a collective 'club' basis, and those who stay outside the club will lose any chance to influence the rules of the club."

Again, this portion of the report differs from the Werner Report in outlining the stages more completely, but it would be inaccurate to suggest that there is a lot of detail here. Also, in contradistinction with the Werner Report, and because of a view of failure of that document due to the non completion of EMU within a decade, the Delors Report studiously avoids stating a deadline, except for the beginning of the first stage as July 1990 (coinciding with capital liberalization).

A section on the ECU both suggests that the ECU would probably develop into the eventual common currency, and rejects using it in a parallel currency strategy, and gives the reasons for this. In this way, the report takes some of the ground away from a British proposal on a different approach toward eventual EMU.

Stage one is described, with the sense that it operates within the "existing institutional framework" (p. 34), and acts as preparation for the next step. During this period all EC currencies would join the ERM, and there would be what Thygesen (1989) calls a "higher profile" for the committee of central bank governors (CGCB) in coordinating state monetary policies. There would also be greater budgetary policy coordination, and greater financial market integration and completion of the single market would occur. Exchange-rate realignments would still be possible, but avoided through more effective use of adjustment mechanisms.

The second stage would be a transition phase toward final EMU. It would be a necessary phase so as to allow time for the new institutional structure to come up to speed in the use of common decision making and policy implementation. The ESCB would be set up at this time, and it is this institutional feature that would distinguish the beginning of the second stage, because treaty change would be required. The "linkage" between the two stages and treaty change was deemed appropriate within the committee because it was seen that it would be during this period that at least some beginning of transfer of decision making from the members toward the ESCB would be made. Thygesen (1989) outlines the rationale. The smaller EC states saw little problem with prior discussion and coordination of monetary policy with the CGCB, but in France and the United Kingdom monetary authority was divided between the government and the central bank in a way that would need national legislation and a treaty change to alter. In Germany there would also need to be such a consideration given its constitutional independence. The linkage would be made explicit by the convening of an intergovernmental conference (IGC) early on during the first stage to tackle the treaty question. Other characteristics of the second stage included some pooling of reserves (also, of course, requiring treaty approval), exchange-rate changes that would still be possible but "exceptional," and a further narrowing of margins.

The final stage would complete the process, and bring it to the description of the second chapter. Exchange rates would be "irrevocably linked," and there would be full transfer of powers needed for EMU, including linking rules and procedures in the budgetary field. Monetary policy, including full responsibility, would be transferred to the ESCB, where all official reserves would be pooled and henceforth managed. Finally, "the change-over to the single currency would take place during this stage" (Delors Report, 1989, p. 40).

Comparison with the Werner Report

The Delors Report, in connection with the prior Werner Report, evidences how ideas once crystallized can continue to command significant influence years after their original milieu has vanished. In grappling with the best strategy to move the Community forward, the notion was adopted to "revisit" the Werner Report, and move the EC toward EMU. What would be the accepted blueprint for EMU—the Delors Report of 1989—was in many ways strikingly similar to the prior document. Several of these similarities are important for the debates and events that followed, including of course Maastricht. Neither document is a "proper" cost-benefit analysis, each, in its way, taking the objective as desirable rather than open to analysis. The definition of monetary union is coincidental in the two reports, involving an "irrevocable fixing of parity rates" coupled with the complete liberalization of capital movements. Both lack a strong emphasis on the need for a single currency, perhaps for the reasons noted above, however, they both recognize the need for a new institution to control liquidity creation. There is the shared feeling for a need to control member state budgetary policy. There is explicit recognition that the transfer of powers with EMU is so great as to require treaty revision; the sovereignty transfer issue is dealt with head on. The process is seen in both reports as best taking place in more or less defined stages. Finally, a link is recognized between the free movement of goods, services, capital, and labor, and fixed exchange rates, a link that calls for centralized control over economic policy.

The similarities between the reports are great enough as to have prompted some to focus on the differences, whereas it is also clear that some pains have been taken to intentionally differentiate the Delors Report, so as to avoid some of the perceived intrinsic weaknesses of the Werner Report. Baer and Padoa-Schioppa (1989), for example, suggest that part of the reason that movement toward EMU was not more successful in the 1970s was due to defects in the report itself. They note several such problems, including (1) that there was not enough examination of the process moving beyond stage one toward the final objective; (2) that inadequate attention was paid to institutional matters; (3) that the report lacked safeguards against "lapses in policy consensus" (p. 57); (4) that there were institutional ambiguities on who should make decisions and "how responsibilities were to be distributed;" and (5) a lack of internal momentum by steps that would trigger market reaction. These criticisms of the Werner Report seem a little harsh given the political environment out of which it was issued. If there had in truth been the level of political will at this time to move onto EMU, then these defects may have been part of the problem,[8] but that, of course, was not the case. The criticisms are certainly more important as evidence of the way in which the two rapporteurs of the Delors Committee viewed the prior document for ways in which to improve it. There can be little doubt that the detail in the Delors Report on stages, the fuller description of institutions, the concern with prior commitment to the process, and the descriptive care taken over how market imperatives necessitate decisions all owe something to this vision. That the report is viewed as so powerful a document is partly the result.

Country Motivations

It remains to return to the question of what made the Delors Report possible in the first place. What constituted the correlation of attitudes and conditions among the member states that allowed for the political will to go forward, if only in consideration of EMU? The smaller countries, of course, in being so open, had not had a large degree of control already, and this became even more so in the 1980s when the EMS was something like an expanded DM zone. It would be better for the smaller countries to have gained some control over monetary policy through an EC institution than to leave it all to the Bundesbank, even if they shared the Bundesbank's goals.

France always plays a central role, and in the past (for example, after the Werner negotiations) it had often proved to have powerfully divergent views. By the last part of the 1980s, however, France had successfully moderated inflation close to the West German level, and had a fairly robust economy to show for it, at least by the somewhat less demanding European growth standards of the time ("Eurosclerosis"). There was really no need to question the value of an EMU committed to price stability. Moreover, EMU would allow for a way, as evidenced by the Balladur Paper that criticized the asymmetric way in which the EMS had worked, to wrest away some West German control over monetary policy by establishing joint decision making.[9] There was, as well, the political motivation of dissipating potentially increasing German independence and power, through bringing it even further under the EC umbrella. This, of course, would become even more important with unification and the potential hegemony a strong Germany could wield in the political vacuum of Eastern Europe. Casual conversations with French citizens, or indeed with other Europeans, frequently reveals a strong reflective concern over German dominance of Europe. There is more on French attitudes below, but here it is enough that the French were viewed as Euro-enthusiasts at this time, who even, as previously noted, questioned the need for treaty revision before taking some institutional steps toward EMU, such as reserve pooling.

The Italian case is very similar to that of the French, but with a twist that although the EMS had helped in stabilizing the economy, it had not been entirely successful in bringing down inflation rates or budget deficits (in the 10 percent of GDP range) to acceptable levels. The section of the Delors Report dealing with deficits seemed to be welcomed by many in Italy at this time as a form of further allowing that country to tie its own hands in this regard.

Britain, of course, was profoundly skeptical of any move toward EMU. Their position will be examined further in the next chapter, but here it is sufficient to note that the attitude in Europe had increasingly been one of 11-against-1, the position of one represented aggressively by Thatcher, and that this applied to the Delors Report as well. The position taken was to let the report go forward with the proviso that the British could present an alternative after the Madrid Summit.

The German case is in some ways the most interesting, for that country would seem to have had the most to lose by abandoning a system, the functioning EMS, that appeared to have served German interests so well. The strong case against Germany's supporting monetary union, of course, involves the loss of direct control over monetary emission by the Bundesbank, and the threat of possible inflation. Added to this were the undervalued ERM exchange rates for the DM that simultaneously allowed German control over its own money supply (and, through the ERM reduction of other states' money-supply growth rates, reduced inflation in Europe) and a stable growth rate for Germany driven by competitive exports.

As strong as this argument was, the problem was that the EMS would be unlikely to continue to operate in this fashion for long. The letters by the finance ministers of France and Italy indicate a lack of ease with continuance of the system. Growth, of course, and the "disinflationary" hypothesis, seemed to lose much of its sting as an issue with the growth spurt following the SEA, but asymmetry continued to be an issue, again more in the sense of a need for equality in decision making than in the old-style pressure to inflate that was thinly veiled by the term asymmetry. The remarks in previous chapters also indicate that Germany was no longer viewed in quite as much control of the EMS. The very success of the system in effectively reducing expectations of exchange-rate changes convinced some of an altered regime, and seemed to introduce both more control among other members and more potential instability. This may have been just a misreading of the nature of the system in a period of transition to the implications of the removal of exchange controls, but it was still unsettling.[10] As has been made clear in previous chapters, Germany, a highly industrialized country largely dependent upon intra-European trade for its health,[11] has over the years felt the need to guard not only against currency instability, but any return to protectionism that might result. Indeed the stable but persistent undervaluation of the ERM also posed this very threat of protectionism, as outlined in Pelkmans (1989).[12]

There may well have also been a political motivation for Germany. The Germans themselves, aware of current attitudes toward German hegemony in the rest of Europe, were quick to be seen as European, and willing to institutionalize this perception. Finally, however, after all of the various ways in which to narrowly rationalize Germany's attitudes toward EMU, there may be something left out. It seems difficult to explain the fact of German foreign minister Genscher's himself adding EMU to the Hannover agenda without consideration that there comes a point in European political life when one person, in a critical position, will take a stand that is not entirely explicable in terms of pure national motivation. It has been seen that Pompidou, Schmidt, Giscard d'Estaing, Mitterand, and Genscher have all done this at points in the history of the search for European EMU. It seems that it is at these important junctures that the marginal attitude toward Europe, in a personal way, divorced from narrow interests, could shift the balance toward movement forward.

Conclusion

Mirroring the events of 1969, a constellation of events, state interests, and a willingness to compromise came together in the late 1980s to move the EC to draft an exceptional report calling for EMU in Europe for the second time. The result is a document that—by setting up a central institution controlling monetary policy for the entire Community—would transfer the largest degree of sovereignty in the history of the EC. The political symbolism of a common currency alone would be enormous. One may analyze in great detail the specific political and economic motivations that had brought these states to this point, but in the broad view it was the economic reality of events—especially capital-market liberalization accompanied by exchange-rate fixity—that dictated such a movement. Any view, however, seems incomplete without considering that there was in 1988 and 1989, with the exception of the United Kingdom, the political will to acquiesce.

SIX

Movement Toward EMU

The pace of movement toward EMU in Europe accelerated in the very early 1990s, between the Delors Report and the signing of the Maastricht Treaty, and proceeded at what seemed to many to be an unprecedented rate. Indeed, the pace of the discussions seemed to echo the speed at which other historical events were occurring in Europe. The analogy is appropriate, for it can easily be argued that the events in the USSR and Eastern Europe in many ways drove the union discussions, and provided a strong external impetus toward greater Western European integration. In other words, the constellation of interests that appears to be necessary for the next step toward integration was now present to at least some extent as the Western European states understood the power of the events in the east to influence their futures, and realized their need to act together. Coupled with this was a by now well-developed institutional framework as well as an intellectual consensus over most of the main issues surrounding EMU, a structure that may have been even more important in establishing the political will necessary to move toward Maastricht.

A New Political Order

As it has so often, Germany found itself at the center of activity, with that country's unification playing the role of catalyst. Patient Germans had thought that unification might, with luck, be on the world agenda at the earliest by the middle of the following century.[1] Instead, of course, perestroika, the rapid wane of the Soviet state as a first-rank economic and political power, and the freeing of Eastern Europe from domination allowed the Germans first to voice (through amazing mass demonstrations in East Germany in the autumn of 1989), and then achieve (with a brilliant political stroke by Helmut Kohl) what had never really ceased to be a long-term desire.[2]

While these events were, in retrospect, seen as inevitable, they neverthe-less raised old fears among other Western Europeans, including the French, British, Dutch, Belgians, and Danes. It might be more accurate to say they raised old fears among older Europeans, for it seems that the concern with a perceived German national characteristic of a need to dominate, including militarily, lies more with those who remember the second world war than those born well afterward. The polls on this are persuasive. In late 1990 over 55 percent of 18–25 year olds in France were glad to see unification, while 49 percent felt closer to a German of their own age than a French person of the same age as their parents.

Nonetheless, and although (usually) expressed in quiet, unemotional ways, the fear was there. Reinforcing it was a now much larger German state which, with 78 million people, was no longer on rough parity with the United Kingdom (57 million), Italy (56 million), and France (at 57 mil-lion). Although the GDP of the new state did not increase by much upon unification, the expectation at the time was that, with the traditional Ger-man ability to create industrial miracles, it would not be long before the five new Länder (the rough equivalent of U.S. states) were on a par with their western neighbors. Finally, of course, was the circumstance of the other East-ern Europeans, poorer than ever before from the attempt to effect a transi-tion to a functioning market economy on the basis of a negligibly competitive industrial base and inadequate infrastructure. Domination from a colossus in central Europe would not be difficult to imagine.

These fears most certainly influenced French foreign policy, in the direc-tion of tying Germany into an integrated Western Europe through the struc-ture of the EC, so as effectively to moderate German influence with dilution among the twelve, and, eventually, even more members. A direct economic advantage with such a policy is that it would also ensure an easy, open, and free access to the potentially lucrative markets that Eastern Europe would eventually provide, for even if Germany were not seriously to threaten, po-litically and even militarily, to dominate the broader region, it could do so economically, and in a protectionistic way. Barzini (1984, p. 150) provides the colorful metaphor of "an embrace so close that it would control and par-alyze Germany like a straitjacket."

Less colorfully perhaps, but no less to the point, Huhne (1989, pp. 19–20) feels that the "only strategy which can protect Western European in-terests is a continued and accelerated process of economic integration, whether motivated by old-fashioned fear of German revanchism or by a fresher desire to provide a powerful western pole of attraction for the liber-alizing Eastern Europeans. Only the integration can ensure that conflicts are resolved within the Community by the rule of law, rather than between na-tion states by the rule of the powerful."[3] The irony here is that it was also

German policy to allow itself to be tied to Western Europe in exactly this way. Sommer (1991, p. 41) states it in a charming way: "We don't mind at all being tied in, tied down, or tied up, but would gladly be contained in every sense of the term—within the larger encasement of a uniting Europe."

This had, moreover, been German policy for many years, and the country as noted in earlier chapters had not even been reluctant to use the fears of others to help forge instruments of greater integration. In a case noted earlier, for example, the Germans emphasized at the Hague Summit that those who feared growing German economic strength ought to have embraced British entry. In this case, a similar form of subtle blackmail was current, including a hint that the Germans might change their minds on Europe, so it was important to take advantage of the window of opportunity. A similar threat had it that if the Social Democrats were to return to power there would be less enthusiasm for political unification. Specifically on monetary union, the notion was that Germany, if given time for greater consideration, might withdraw from the loss of sovereignty over the DM, and the more uncertain fate for price stability, that merger within an EMU would entail.[4]

The fact that this initiative worked is no clearer than the way in which Helmut Kohl was able to insist that discussion on EMU would not proceed unless there was also progress, through the establishment of a simultaneous IGC, on political union.[5] In this fashion he was able to force debate on a federal Europe, a Europe with greater democratic control through increased powers for the European Parliament.

The importance here of these subtle threats, and the expansion of the political dimension of the Community, is not so much in either the veracity of the threats, or the final outcome on political union, but rather in the way events in the Soviet Union and Eastern Europe hastened the discussion on monetary union. Although it was initially questioned whether these events might detract from the incentive toward furthering western integration, both of the single market and EMU, the opposite turned out to be true, at least at the time. One part of the original idea, of course, was that Germany would be too preoccupied with German unification to be able to pay attention to European unification. The results belied this scenario due to the will with which the Germans wanted to reassure the rest of Europe—and the world—that they were "good Europeans." In fact, if it took threats to forge adequate institutions to prove that point, all the better.

Another event at this time—although in retrospect probably not as important as the above—contributed to the pace at which Europe would consider EMU. This was the resignation of Margaret Thatcher as prime minister of the United Kingdom. This action removed a source of great contention within Community decision making from the scene, and promised increased consensus on EC policies in the future. The diplomatic goodwill that accompanied John Major's introduction into European Council discussions was in sharp contrast with prior meetings, leaving behind the specter of Thatcher as one against the other eleven. Compromise was in the air, which, by bringing the United Kingdom along, could not help but achieve greater cohesion on difficult issues.

Actually reinforcing this point is the proposition that it was Thatcher's view on Europe, encapsulated in a famous speech in Bruges, that led to her being replaced as the head of the Conservative Party in Britain. It was the core support group for the party, especially the financial interests associated with the City of London, that decided it would be antithetical to the future of British financial services, including insurance, to not be a part of the common currency area that was being fashioned. It was not lost on this powerful interest group that the United Kingdom had always entered late and at somewhat disadvantageous terms, if only to have been excluded from the design of the new institutions that comprised the European Community. This had been true of the Coal and Steel Community, the original EEC, and the EMS. The shift in attitude of the City at the time, although that was certainly not all, made it impossible for Thatcher to continue to stand in the way of further unification efforts (even though, as events subsequently demonstrated, anti-Europe factions were still strong within the Tories). The possibility of being left behind was too great.

Another current of thought had it that Thatcher, by being so acrimonious—indeed hostile—in her attitudes and the way she expressed those attitudes to her peers in Europe, had actually fostered greater unification. In other words, the other Europeans would take steps and approve policies that were at the margins of their acceptance levels because Thatcher was so negative, forging a cohesive group to push back against her. In this case, her resignation would actually lower the pressure upon others to acquiesce to plans that, upon careful, close, and empirical examination, were not necessarily to their liking.

Finally, another view is that Thatcher was actually speaking for other minority interests in Europe, countries which were only too glad to let her do the talking, and provide the roadblock, so as to save them from having to take on the task, with potential loss of political capital. Now, all that would happen is that these other groups (including the Spanish) would have to come forward.

In many ways the intent to further integrate was great enough in the rest of the EC, and along the famous Bonn-Paris axis, that it probably did not make much difference what the United Kingdom felt, except to the United Kingdom. In other words, the changing political order on the continent was seen as very important to furthering EMU, important and strong enough to effectively encourage the British first to join the EMS, and then even to be an active party at the IGC on monetary union.

Without in any way depreciating these events as catalysts toward the faster and more serious progress toward EMU that occurred in the early 1990s, it is posited here that such a movement would have been impossible without the strong institutional and intellectual framework that was already well in place by 1990. Without this framework it would be hard to imagine, as the history in this work suggests, any serious coming together over a common plan. With the framework in place, however, the next steps seemed not only possible, but plausible. EMU could certainly be sidetracked by external events, but, likewise, momentous historical changes could just as likely allow people to argue for taking those next steps necessary for EMU based upon a structure that was already well advanced.

The institutional framework is, of course, well documented here, as are the changes in, and perceived success of the EMS in establishing a zone of monetary stability in Europe, not to mention a successful move toward a single market incorporating the freer movement of capital. Wayne Sandholtz (1991) presents an interesting hypothesis that puts this institutional development into the neofunctionalist school of thought regarding integration. This allows for the theory of a "spillover" from one institution to the establishment of another, that is propelling integration, due to pressures from one form of integration (fixed exchange rates and free movement of capital) toward another (a single currency).[6] This theory is hardly new, but Sandholtz also allows for the impact of domestic interest groups on international bodies, or better, collective decision making among states. The argument is that domestic groups found, in these years, their own interests (low inflation and avoidance of recessions) being well served by the price stability and monetary discipline that was represented by low monetary growth rates and fixed exchange rates. EMU would not only encourage maintenance of these policies for these groups at the EC level, but also solidify the gains from market integration that were the single market.

The intellectual framework was also present by this time, allowing for a form of consensus over the desired shape of EMU. Without the guide of the Treaty of Rome, the shape of EMU had to be forged over time. The similarities between the Delors Report and the Werner Report explored before provide abundant evidence that by 1990 there were enough common ideas in circulation that an adequate basis existed for an agreement on institutions. It was in this way that the Delors Report set the agenda for EMU, and EMU no longer seemed remote for Europe.

In fact, the structure of what follows in this chapter is based explicitly on the similarities between the two reports. This is appropriate, more so than, say, using a chronology of events, because it is now clear that it was around these items of similarity that controversy could occur. In other words, the similarities had been already accepted by most as the proper direction for movement, the details being left to debate. The details were hardly inconsequential, as will be seen; but in the minds of most Europeans, the structure was now in place, and acceptable as such.

Incidentally, then, the chronology was as follows.[7] After the Delors Report was accepted in April 1989, the Commission began to work on some of the more controversial aspects of the report, with an eye to developing proposals that would lead to a draft treaty. The result in March 1990 was the "Working Document," otherwise known as "Economic and Monetary Union: the Economic Rationale and Design of the System" (EC Commission, 1990b). This was an important document, both in terms of developing acceptable language and in addressing some of the objections to the Delors Report, with an eye on compromise (especially in the budgetary area).

On July 1, 1990 the first stage of EMU began. In August the EC Commission spelled out what it called its "Final Proposal" to elaborate upon several points, again including member state budgets (1990a). The United Kingdom entered the ERM early in October (at the wider band) and just a bit later the European Council met in Rome, where eleven of the twelve heads of state essentially accepted the ideas contained in the two prior papers. They decided to begin phase two of EMU on January 1, 1994 (instead of 1993 as originally proposed by the Commission), and agreed to limits on Eurofed (the term circulating at the time for the new monetary institution). The movement to the second stage, incidentally, was conditional on progress regarding policy convergence.[8] The Rome meeting allowed for the opening of the two IGCs, EMU and political, in mid-December in Rome. In the meantime, the Commission[9] published "One market, one money," which, by being a cost-benefit analysis, simultaneously attempted to answer some critics who suggested that EMU was being implemented without an adequate basis of evaluation of its economic effects, while also hoping to reap something similar to the public relations impact the Cecchini Report had had on the success of the single market. After extensive discussions of proposals dealing with the subjects below and made by the Commission, central banks, and governments, there would be an acceptable draft treaty by the end of 1991 in order to allow for ratification by the states, ideally by the end of 1992.

EMU Definition

It will be recalled that monetary union in the Delors Report is defined as consisting of (1) currency convertibility; (2) capital liberalization and financial integration; and (3) the irrevocable locking of exchange rates. A single currency was not necessary, but would constitute a desirable further development. Economic union would entail: (1) the single market; (2) competition policy; (3) structural and regional development policies; and (4) macroeconomic policy coordination.

Subsequent developments on the economic union front concerning primarily the appropriate level of coordination of state budgetary policies had been substantial. However, the definition or, better, description of "economic union" had not effectively changed.

In the monetary sphere, however, there had been a significant change in what "union" means and indeed, in how it is defined. As early as the Working Document "a single currency, the ECU," was now considered an "essential feature" of EMU, in order "to exploit to the full the potential benefits of the single market and monetary union." This was followed by the Final Proposal, which was even more emphatic on this point, reusing the "essential feature" language, and adding that it should be clearly written into the treaty. The text of "One market, one money," Directorate-General for Economic and Financial Affairs (1990), in a similar vein, actually includes a somewhat idiosyncratic reading of the Delors Report, saying that the report "identifies the definitive monetary regime as consisting either of a fixed exchange rate system or a single currency system" (p. 17). It prefers the latter on economic grounds, although a fixed-rate regime is also examined in the volume. The point here is that, rather than a "natural and desirable further development" of the system, a subtle but significant change occurred during 1990 that made a single currency the centerpiece of EMU and the definition of monetary union.

This change was probably driven by two factors. First, there seems to have been recognition that a single currency simply was superior on economic grounds (again, to be examined below). The second, although there is no direct evidence to support this, is that the time was ripe for the political and psychological move that would symbolize greater unity.

On the point of free capital mobility and fixed exchange rates, an early date (July 1, 1990) was chosen so as to encourage states to begin to adhere to these characteristics of monetary union, with some success. As noted, the United Kingdom entered the ERM around this date, albeit at the wider band of 6 percent,[10] leaving only Greece and Portugal out of direct participation. Also, France and Italy had dismantled virtually all of their exchange controls by the July date.

The debate that surrounded British entry into the ERM has been described. In spite of what was undoubtedly an overvalued exchange rate upon entry, the initial experience with official maintenance of sterling in the system proved to be generally favorable within the first year. As expected, but what is no less an objective of the mechanism, exchange rates became more stable (see Brittan, 1991). In addition, interest rates had dropped, due to both moderated inflation, and the phenomenon observed by other ERM members, of a level of confidence in the long-run stability of the currency that also allowed for interest-rate cuts.[11] Reinforcing the confidence, or stability, argument was evidence that wage settlements were being moderated, and that productivity was increasing, along with continued high levels of investment in spite of a recession in progress. The seemingly splendid statistic of a lower U.K. inflation rate than that of Germany, however, lost some of its glamour upon recognition that this was due more to an increase of the latter (with increased demand and taxes resulting from unification) than a decrease in the former.

Single Currency

It seemed clear in these days that the ECU would serve as the single currency, which was now the prime objective of EMU. Christopher Johnson, Chief Economic Advisor to Lloyds Bank, was not only speaking to the financial interests represented in the City of London when he offered the opinion that irrevocably fixed exchange rates were a "poor substitute" for a single currency, because, "to a politician, nothing is ever irrevocable,"[12] and that the single currency "[would] have to be the ECU...." (1990, p. 78). He saw advantages in not having a parallel currency, in order to avoid the risk of excess monetary creation, as well as seeing no need for a currency broader than the DM for the role.

Current at this time, even into the negotiations of the IGC, was the "hard ECU" proposal of the U.K. Treasury, which at its heart was an entirely different approach to achieving EMU than the institutional route specified in the Delors Report. It was intended to provide a market-based incentive by which a strong ECU, issued by a European Monetary Fund separately from the basket ECU and with proper attention to a low monetary growth rate, could find a following in the private sector as a currency with salutary characteristics for stability. As such this would find Europeans substituting toward the new currency, which would in turn induce member states to pay similar attention to their currencies (since their central banks would be forced to buy their weaker currencies back with hard ECUs). In this way, movement toward greater monetary convergence would naturally evolve toward eventual union. The advantage seen in the parallel currency plan was, again, that it would provide a more natural, market-driven approach than establishing an overweight, centralized bureaucracy.

The arguments against the proposal on the continent included the fact that the proposal tended, if anything, to pull away from the then perceived success of the EMS by reducing the direct structure established for exchange-rate stability that was the ERM. Moreover, the conservative Germans were concerned that a system that split monetary control between the proposed European Monetary Fund and the central banks, thus making money harder to control rather than easier, would raise the apparition of uncertainty and inflation.

These concerns do not seem entirely fair to the proposal, which, if fully embraced and efficiently implemented might well have added a level of stability rather than instability to European monetary affairs. But, in the end, the arguments were probably moot for, and with some justification, the plan was always viewed as a mechanism to detrack the progress on EMU in the Werner-Delors mold, since the United Kingdom was never terribly enthusiastic about the end result in the first place. It is interesting that, given the opposition (except for occasional bouts of interest shown by Spain), the proposal remained in place as long as it did. It finally died quietly in the interest of demonstrating an altered, more positive view of the United Kingdom toward the EMU debate, if for no other reason than to avoid being left behind in a two-speed Europe.[13]

A New Monetary Institution

It was also during this time that a new monetary institution, built along Bundesbank or Federal Reserve lines, became accepted as the model for control over monetary policy and ECU creation. In structure, its ruling body would be a federal council—composed of the central bank governors—and a board charged with the day-to-day implementation of the common monetary policy. The council would be independent of member states and other EC institutions. Debate centered around the level of reporting to the European Parliament and the finance ministers (Ecofin) by the president, but in no way was independence ever seriously questioned, as this was a minimum condition for German participation. This would mean, of course, that each member state central bank would need to be independent as well, giving pause to both France and Britain.

It was broadly accepted at this time as well that the central bank's prime objective, as had been spelled out in the Delors Report, would be price stability. In this way the bank would insure continuance of the successful German model to which now almost all adhered. Without this objective in the treaty, again the Germans, as well as the Dutch, would not agree to any change from the status quo. The German fear of inflation runs deep.[14]

It is at this point that reunification began to give pause to some Germans, who began to look at EMU somewhat more skeptically. It was true that the forces that would lead to quicker movement on the integration front (reunification) were in place, as described at the beginning of this chapter, but that in a way was the point. Would Germany sacrifice its hard-won and long-defended price stability and strong DM on the alter of European unity? Again, it is true that independence and price stability were at the front of the EMU agenda, but would these be given away to, say, French pressure to politicize the new central bank, thereby allowing it to escape taking the hard choices necessary for monetary stability? The facts around German unity itself were not comforting, for it was Kohl's political decision to establish German monetary union very early, against the wishes, and even without full prior notification, of the Bundesbank. Moreover, the exchange rate for German monetary unification was politically chosen; it overvalued the East German mark and practically insured extensive extra unemployment in that part of the new Germany. This was against what had been the prior thinking and advice of the Bundesbank on the subject.

Although these kinds of concerns had helped to lead the controversial and colorful Pöhl to resign his position in 1991, it is also now clear that they had steeled his colleagues at the Bundesbank and led to an accepted draft treaty that did not diverge from the dual planks of independence and price stability for the new central bank.

State Budget Controls

Even though both the Delors and Werner Reports agreed on control over state budgets, there would be few issues leading to EMU that would foster greater disagreement and debate. It will be remembered that the Delors Report had been particularly strong on the point, calling for a system of "binding rules" on the size and financing of budget deficits. Given the degree of sovereignty transfer already inherent in monetary union, member states were not exactly enthusiastic about the proposals. In order not to allow EMU to go off track, the Commission considerably softened the language in the Working Document by offering "binding procedures" rather than "rules." As such it effectively shifted the mechanism from general control to encouraging individual countries not to run excessive deficits. It specifically recommended two rules that, if respected, would allow for quick negative political and market reactions to a particularly high budget deficit. They were: (1) that there would be neither financing of public debt through increases in the money supply nor special access to international capital; and (2) there would be no "bailing out" of states in financial straits, either by the EC or other states. In addition, during the first two stages member states would design and effect economic strategies to reduce potential or existing deficits that would eventually be implemented into law. Surveillance by the

Community was to take place, and, if countries did not adhere to their plans regional funding could be withheld.

In the Final Proposal that followed the point was reinforced that excessive budget deficits should be avoided by suggesting this should be part of the treaty. If the multilateral surveillance were to prove inadequate, and a member's budget deficit excessive, peer pressure could be exerted in private first, in public next. Then, in the words of Hyde, "if the country is still unable to reduce its fiscal deficit the stick of withheld regional funds is replaced with the carrot of the promise of a new special financial support scheme in the form of grants or loans to help members in economic difficulty" (1991, p. 10). In addition, here there was the first attempt to give some specific guidelines regarding acceptable levels of deficit, including deficit and debt to GDP ratios. They relied on a generally accepted rule in the economics literature, that is that a deficit should not exceed public investment expenditure. As the Final Proposal puts it, this "appears the most satisfactory from an analytical point of view and is the only one widely applied in existing federations."

Acceptance of these general principles in Rome in 1990 did not keep the debate from heating up again in the IGC in 1991, where Britain and Greece opposed the public investment rule, while the southern EC members generally would hear nothing of the sanction of removing regional aid for excessive deficits. By this time the Commission had pulled back even further from binding rules and sanctions, in curious agreement with the British, who felt that market pressure would be adequate (the Commission seemed simply to be looking for compromise). Those with the strongest stand on rules and sanctions, the Germans, were also in a mood to compromise given the high cost of unification and the rapid loss in their current account surplus, so the final accepted draft treaty was relatively mild on this point. Surveillance and possible public debate were deemed adequate to the task.[15]

Treaty Revision

It had been generally accepted, except for a period of time by the French, that a new treaty would be needed to move on to EMU. The British were particularly insistent upon this point, perhaps feeling that they could veto it if necessary. As it turned out the treaty process allowed Germany to insist that a political IGC meet in tandem with that on EMU in order to bring some level of parliamentary decision making into the process, as well as to expand the venue of "Europe," a certainly undesirable result from the British point of view. In addition, the treaty that emerged had allowed a majority of at least eight countries to decide when to enter upon stage three, allowing for a two-speed Europe of some countries going ahead before others (see the following). This was also not a British objective, but one they could hardly deny to the others if they clearly desired it.

Stages

The topic of stages also led to debate following the Delors Report but, again, by this time no one except the British seriously questioned the proposition that there should be stages, there should be three of them, more or less what the stages meant, and that they should be fairly well defined going in. This was the legacy of the thought that went into the Werner Report, followed upon by the strengthening of the same ideas, and avoidance of "mistakes," by the Delors Committee.

This is not to say there was complete agreement on the details, however. From the stages described in the Delors Report (see chapter 5), by the Final Proposal of August 1990 the Commission recommended the beginning of stage two on a specific date, January 1, 1993, coincidental with the single-market deadline. The second stage was seen as being "brief," but with enough time for the establishment of the single, politically independent system of central banks and for "intensive preparations" for a common monetary policy and a single currency. Stage three would introduce the single currency (now an essential feature of EMU), and its timing would depend on the political agreement of EC leaders.

By October at the Rome Council meeting it was decided to postpone the beginning of the second stage to January 1, 1994, upon fulfillment of the conditions outlined earlier. It was also decided that within three years from the start of stage two the Commission and the nascent central bank would report to Ecofin and the General Affairs Council on the functioning of stage two, in order to help decide on moving on to stage three.

During the IGC there was disagreement over stage two. The French wanted the central bank established at the beginning of 1994, while the Germans felt it should wait until just before the final phase. The French argument was that the existence of the bank in place would focus the attention of member governments, and encourage them to get their economies in order. The Germans, however, were concerned about rivalry with the Bundesbank from the new institution—again a split in authority that might hamper strict monetary policy—and insistent on convergence of economies (deficits, debt, inflation, and interest rates) first. Since they had already agreed on some form of institution at stage two, they proposed at the beginning there be a "council" of the central bank presidents, only in order to improve cooperation and without any real authority.

The compromise was accepted to set up the bank at the earliest in 1996, but this was coupled with language that ensured there would be enough economic convergence, and objective criteria satisfied, for the positive decision on the single currency. The interesting thing about this debate was how closely it seemed to echo prior confrontations on the nature of stages. The French, in pure "monetarist" fashion, were arguing for the establishment of institutions that would encourage the members to insure the conditions upon which the institutions could effectively function; while the Germans, true to their "economist" heritage, argued for adequate convergence before any serious move toward the setting up of institutions. It seems that old disagreements can have lives of their own, often as strong and lasting as long as ideas leading to economic integration.

Centralized Control over Economic Policy

The German insistence on economic convergence raises another point of similarity between the Werner and Delors Reports, that of some form of control over economic policy that is broader than simply control over deficits; but here again there was hardly what one could call a quick and easy consensus. Surveillance was generally accepted as advantageous, and, in practice this began under stage one, as did attempts to define "adjustment" programs for some higher inflation states. The strength of the German stance on this was such that they did not favor participation by those members unwilling to converge, or what the press began to call "economic weaklings," and thus the insistence upon strict criteria. Of course, this is not the same thing as centralized control, but it does imply strong direction on outcome, a point about which the British were again not enthusiastic.

The problem with the German position from the view of Delors and others was that it implied a two-speed Europe, or at least acceptance of such an idea. From a long-run view of the Community becoming a cohesive, centralized unit, it is easy to see the concern if the EC were to consist of states that would be in some Community institutions but not others. Nevertheless, the British views played strongly into this conclusion, in effect by forcing the others to say "if you refuse to go along, we will leave without you." There is not finally that much difference between allowing a reluctant traveler out and keeping out one without the right ticket.

It was symbolic of how much EMU meant to Delors that he offered a critical compromise in mid-1991 on the British issue. The compromise was that if the British signed the draft treaty they would be allowed to defer to a later British parliament the final decision whether to participate in the eventual union. Ironically, this reasonable concession was seen in Britain as exactly what it was, a tacit endorsement of a two-speed Europe, but they could hardly both not accept the concession and then hold up the others, perhaps especially as Thatcher was now gone, and many in the country had decided that they were indeed part of "Europe."

Regional Finance

Another point of similarity between the Delors and Werner Reports is the longer vision of the need for regional aid to the lesser developed countries of the EC. The Delors Report, and Delors in particular, had been insistent on this. Nevertheless, when it came to the IGC on EMU, the Commission softened its tune considerably, and tried to divert discussion away from the topic altogether.

The reasons are not surprising. The Spanish were vocal about the need for a link in the discussions between further movement on EMU and aid, even to the point of insisting there be a revision of the then current five-year budget in favor of the poorer countries. They hinted broadly about lack of enthusiasm for signing a treaty, and they seemed to get support from Greece, Portugal, and Ireland.

Again, however, the Commission wanted an outcome, and they feared that if the budget were brought up coincidentally with the negotiations it could fatally affect the talks. Moreover, they were aware of the strong German reticence on the issue. Germany's concern seemed not only to be the lack of convergence of economic policies separating those states ready for EMU from those not, but also, less clearly articulated, the difference in income levels. Pöhl, in his usual candor, however, did articulate to the European Parliament that there would be a problem with a Community that had monetary union without economic "harmony," requiring "vast capital requirements, a transfer of welfare benefits and a highly critical exacerbation of the production and employment situation" (Gillies, 1991). It was perfectly natural that the Germans, beginning to pay dearly for the reunification and the attempt to bring some harmony between East and West Germany, would extrapolate their situation to that of a more closely integrated Community. This view was not lost on other, northern, EC states, so that the debate over a two-speed Europe was as much about this disparity as anything to do with convergence. The Commission took the tact of emphasizing to the southern states the doubling of aid in the then present program (to 60 billion ECU) ending in 1993, as well as suggesting a series of planned reforms on disparities, and found reward in defusing the issue in the final draft treaty.

External Relations

Finally, external relations were dealt with to the extent of considering which body had the right of proposal in what would become common external exchange-rate decisions. Although the Commission was keen on reserving the right for itself, it was given to the Monetary Committee (made up of central-bank and finance-ministry officials).

Conclusion

The process leading from the Delors Report up to the signing of a draft treaty at the end of 1991 was fraught with controversy. Examples include the strong debates on budget deficits, the date of establishment of the new central bank, and economic convergence and a two-speed Europe. The negotiations within the IGC were often heated, and the compromises difficult to come by. Nevertheless, come they did, and to a successful conclusion.

What was the reason for this success? Political will is one answer. Prior negotiations had broken up many years earlier, largely because of the lack of this joint will. In this instance a good case can be made that the political conditions of the time—the tremendous upheaval in Europe traceable to the collapse of the Soviet system and the liberation of Eastern Europe—contributed significantly to a Western Europe seeking greater unity. Without denying this geopolitical influence, it can also be said that it is hard to feature meaningful movement on the monetary union front without what was by then a long, and slowly developed, institutional and intellectual framework. In spite of points of disagreement between them, the areas of agreement in the Werner and Delors Reports provided the broad basis for consensus and allowed for further development. The existence of a then well-functioning EMS, operating within an increasingly single market, was, perhaps, no less important to this result.

SEVEN

Maastricht Treaty

The IGCs had opened in Rome in December of 1990 and continued on in Brussels during 1991, with the final meetings at the highest level in December of that year under the Dutch presidency in Maastricht. The resultant treaty would become known as the Maastricht Treaty (1992, with pertinent excerpts included here as Appendix 3). Given the close proximity of many other European states to this city in the southern part of the Netherlands, Maastricht was a logical site for the negotiations.

The difficulties of the negotiations had been great, and there still needed to be final decisions taken at the head-of-government level at Maastricht in order to resolve some of the remaining thornier issues. The final treaty that emerged was based on the Delors report, but with significant differences due to the final compromises effected.[1]

The final document would call for the creation of a common currency by 1999 at the latest, at least for a subset of the member states. In spelling a transfer of authority over money creation to a common central bank the treaty would carry implications for moving Europe much closer than ever before to the form of economic as well as political integration implied by the phrase "United States of Europe."

Institutions

The final treaty would establish, by the third stage, a European Central Bank (ECB), within a European System of Central Banks (ESCB), the latter composed of the ECB and all member-state central banks. The ESCB would be governed by the decision making bodies of the ECB, the Governing Council and the Executive Board. In turn, the Governing Council would be composed of the members of the Executive Board of the ECB and the governors of the national central banks. The Executive Board would be composed of a president, a vice president and four other members, appointed by the member state governments on recommendation from the Council, in consultation with the European Parliament and the Governing Council of the ECB. The board members would serve for eight years in nonrenewable terms.

The new institutions would all be independent through article 107 of the Maastricht Treaty (1992), stating that they would not "seek or take instructions from Community institutions or bodies, from any government of a Member State or from any other body." They were, in addition, in article 105, committed to the goal of price stability, as "the primary objective." The ESCB would support the "general economic policies" of the Community, but "without prejudice to the objective of price stability." It is easy to see the hand here of the Bundesbank, with this language intended to save the new central bank the fights it had had over the years in maintaining price stability without as clearly worded a mission for itself, as noted in Henning (1994). They wanted, in addition, a legal basis for the objective because they feared that political pressures would be greater for a European central bank than they had been for a German bank, which at least could count on a broad national consensus for such a goal.

The treaty also specified that the bank would have full control over all monetary instruments. As an important part of protecting this control, it was written in that the bank would not fund government deficits. Again, foreseeing potential pressures from governments in this area, there were the supplemental transition "convergence criteria," especially budget constraints, that would continue after the establishment of the ESCB. This not generally well-known provision was intended to provide safeguards against states running excessive deficits, using the methods of surveillance, recommendations, and eventually even fines. This, too, was a prior requirement of the Bundesbank that was dutifully funneled through the German representatives into the Maastricht Treaty, as noted by Henning (1994).

The general operating role of the Governing Council of the ECB, was to "formulate the monetary policy of the Community including, as appropriate, decisions relating to intermediate monetary objectives, key interest rates and the supply of reserves in the ESCB, and . . . establish the necessary guidelines for their implementation," see Maastricht Treaty (1992, p. 154). Decisions were generally to be taken by majority rule, with one vote per participant.[2] Operations would include standard central bank tasks, such as carrying on open market operations, requiring minimum reserves of banks and other credit organizations, insuring efficient check clearing and payment mechanisms, buying and selling foreign exchange, and issuing banknotes. Again, the treaty is quite explicit in terms of prohibiting the central bank from covering overdrafts of, especially, national governments or of purchasing debt instruments directly from them.

On the external side, that is in monetary relations of the EU with the outside world, the final compromise was that the Council would retain control over both external exchange-rate setting and participation in any external exchange-rate regime-setting. This could be considered to be a potential loss of control over monetary instruments and, indeed, the Germans were not finally happy to have made such a compromise. However, the final wording has it that any decisions in this area not be such as to jeopardize the price stability objective.[3]

Stages

Recognizing that the first stage had already begun, the treaty dealt with the need for member governments to continue the process of eliminating residual capital controls as well as any other impediments to factor flows. Common rules on competition, taxation, and any other governmental interference with the internal market were addressed, as was the need to begin to coordinate economic policies, to avoid excessive deficits as a precursor to being able to satisfy the convergence criteria, and to start the process of establishing the independence of national central banks.

The treaty specified that the second stage would begin on January 1, 1994, and established the European Monetary Institute (EMI) as the transition institution that would lead in the final stage to the European Central Bank. It was not, in bow to German wishes, to be seen as the ECB, and did not carry any appropriate powers to such an institution, so as not to create confusion about who actually continued to run monetary policies at the state level. Instead it was designed simply to facilitate the transfer process that would later occur. Its role would be to take over the functions of the EMCF of the EMS, to monitor the EMS, to help strengthen coordination between the national central banks and their monetary policies, to prepare for the carrying out of a single monetary policy in stage three, and to consider appropriate rules of operation for the national central banks in the ESCB. The EMI would be composed of the governors of the national central banks, with a president from outside approved by the governments.[4]

As can be seen from this structure, there was a good deal of compromise inherent in the structure of the EMI. The Commission and the French, in particular, had wanted a full-fledged ECB at the second stage. The Germans, as indicated, wanted none of this as they were fearful of giving up any control over monetary policy without full authority having been transferred. There was also the notion that the new bank might lose some prestige if it did not have full control during this period, but certainly it must have been foremost in the minds of the Germans that a similar attempt at EMU two decades earlier had failed, and they wanted to reserve all power to themselves over the DM until the structure was entirely in place. The Germans generally prevailed here, but it is true that there was acquiesce to the French desire for an outside president as well as the possibility of the central banks being able voluntarily to transfer reserves to the EMI.

The third stage would take place when the ECU, then thought to be the name for the eventual currency, would be irrevocably fixed. The dates of the beginning of this stage were an issue of no little discussion and compromise as well. As it exists in article 109, the Council would receive reports from the EMI and the Commission on, especially, "sustainable convergence," associated with the several criteria stipulated. The Council, based on these reports, would then decide which countries met the criteria and, no later than December 31, 1996, whether a majority fulfilled the necessary conditions. If so, it would set a date for the beginning of the third stage. Later agreement, given the conditions present in the Community, saw to it that this would not happen as early as this time, but the treaty then specified that if there was no setting of a final date, the third stage would start on January 1, 1999. Before halfway into 1998 the Council, constituted as the heads of state, would decide, based upon the same convergence criteria, which states would be included in the clear beginning of monetary union.

The question of setting a specific date as the supposedly incontrovertible beginning of the final stage represents one of the few areas of great significance where the wishes of the Bundesbank were not respected in the treaty. The French wanted a final deadline; the Bundesbank did not. The French view on this issue was very monetarist in flavor in that a deadline would focus the states on the inevitability of the final outcome, and encourage them to prepare for it. The Germans perhaps remembered the Werner Report and its final date for EMU, and that the drafters of the Delors Report considered this to have been a mistake. Probably more to the point, however, was that a final deadline that came without the full convergence of member states could bring significant pressure to go forward with the final stage anyway, thus substituting a political for an important, in Bundesbank eyes, economic decision. This, of course, was the economist position, with the addition of the need to insure that the new institution, in coming into being, be equal to or stronger than even the Bundesbank in its structure and resolve, supplementing the basic economic conditions of the member states, to insure price stability.

This would be one of the few areas in which the German government would diverge from Bundesbank wishes during the establishment of the final conditions of the treaty, and the only one in which Kohl would be seriously criticized in the process. It is clear that Kohl decided to take the European step—some would call it a leap of faith—at this time, in order to encourage the others about the seriousness of the Germans to the project, as well as to encourage their adoption of restrictive measures in anticipation of a real event in the offing, as in Henning (1994). But, given the stakes, it is nonetheless an extraordinary move, and one of those moments referred to occasionally in this work that must finally rely upon the decision of one person at one moment in time to take a stand in spite of the risky consequences. Kohl at this stage, no less than Mitterand had in 1983, and it could be argued with less pressure, decided for Europe.[5]

Convergence Criteria

From the very beginning the Bundesbank took a stand on the need for strong convergence criteria—a stand agreed to by the German government. Even into the final negotiations, this was also agreed to in principle by all of the states. The states with reputations for economic restraint concurred, of course, but so did the other states who were attempting to prove that they too could follow the road of the Germans.

The final criteria, as represented in the famous Article 109j, were as follows. First, there should be price stability of a member state, as represented by an inflation rate that was close to the three "best performing" member states. "Close" here meant within 1.5 percent, for a period of one year prior to the examination, and as measured by an appropriate consumer price index. Second, long-term interest rates should similarly converge, within two percentage points of the three best performing states, over the period of one year. The measure of interest rates was to be long term government bonds or comparable securities. Third, the member state should have respected the "normal" fluctuation margins in the ERM of the EMS for at least two years before the examination, and, "in particular the Member State shall not have devalued its currency's bilateral central rate against any other Member State's currency on its own initiative for the same period." Finally, the government budgetary position should not have been deemed "excessive," here defined as greater than 3 percent government deficit to GDP ratio, and greater than 60 percent government debt to GDP ratio.[6] This last criterion was only one part of what would be ongoing consideration and avoidance of excessive deficits under article 104c of the treaty.

The need for such convergence criteria, and the specific criteria themselves, have provided grist for much discussion over the years. The inflation criterion probably raised the fewest objections given the seemingly agreed need for all who wished to move on to monetary union that they had to bring their inflation rates down and into line with the others. This was to be able to prove their willingness to adhere to the price stability objective of the new regime before it would come into force. If there has been criticism it has been that actual inflation rates at any one point in time do not necessarily identify underlying tendencies, or long-term proclivities towards greater inflation rates than those aspired to or achieved by the group of states with which one wishes to be associated. The second problem raised was more technical, in that the consumer price index would not necessarily measure inflation well. Such indices, even if they could be constructed equivalently between countries, would not measure many of the goods and services actually produced and absorbed in an economy. Furthermore, they would not provide a good level of comparison between countries because of the fact that nontradeable goods prices can diverge significantly between states with little or no impact on the levels of competitiveness that could cause difficulties. To reinforce this point, Crockett (1994) added consideration of the need to compare absolute price levels, rather than or in addition to inflation rates, as being important, this presumably for any final setting of exchange rates upon entry into monetary union.

Giovannini (1994) focused on the first of these issues. He felt that some measure for propensity toward inflation was more important than actual measures, at least partially for the reason that the actual measured inflation could diverge significantly between countries through variability in nontradeable goods prices. Long-term interest rates were a superior measure of propensity toward inflation according to this argument, because they are composed only of real rates and inflationary expectations.

Presuming real rates were more or less equal motivated the second Maastricht criterion for interest rate convergence, at a low level, for member states. The problem, in turn, seen with such an argument was that too much could be read into such rates, not the least of which is that the rates themselves could be influenced by the exchange-rate regime in which the country participates. Take, for example, a country participating in a fixed-but-adjustable exchange-rate system that "borrows" credibility from a nominal anchor country. Such a state may find that it is able to enjoy low nominal interest rates over fairly long periods of time, so goes the argument, without the market punishing it for not paying attention to underlying monetary and fiscal fundamentals. The curious result would be that what was being measured was not discipline, but rather participation in an institution.

This raises the next criterion specified by the treaty, that is maintaining participation in the ERM of the EMS at the narrow (although the treaty significantly refers to "normal") margins for at least two years. There is no clearer evidence of how the EMS had become viewed at the time of Maastricht than this criterion; it had become considered a fixed-rate system. Moreover, this was deemed a sign of success of the system, evidence of the convergence of policies and desired outcomes. The EMS, in other words, could serve as the basis upon which countries could simply enter intact into EMU.

The inclusion of this criterion into the treaty has been controversial. It has been considered risky at best, especially in light of the exchange rate crises that subsequently occurred in 1992 and 1993. In other words, with a long transition period—such as that included in the final treaty—any lack of full convergence would lead, in a fixed-rate system, to inconsistencies in exchange rates and underlying inflation that would possibly be unstable. The possibility of one-way bets by speculators in a world with a good deal of capital mobility would add weight to such an outcome. In addition, however, the same level of divergence would almost certainly imply the need for some realignment of currencies soon before entering the third stage, thus further questioning a criterion that called for central rates up to EMU.[7]

The final, budgetary, criteria were included in the treaty for a number of reasons, several of which are outlined in Crockett (1994), and they certainly were considered important given the lack of emphasis in this area of the Delors Report. First, even though independent, there could be strains placed on the ECB by governments wishing to reduce their debt burdens by monetary financing through the central bank, thus jeopardizing the price stability objective. Second, the risk of default by a member state, measured in some way by the specific criteria employed, could carry with it significant implications for partner states, again placing undue pressure on the bank to diverge from its objective. Third, a large public debt could pre-empt savings, through higher interest rates, from other countries, savings that could possibly be more efficiently allocated elsewhere. Fourth, large swings in budget positions could affect other countries as well. The last two reasons do not necessarily imply any constraint on the ability of the ECB to do its job as much as they suggest some perceived negative results of government financing on other states. The connection implies that a much greater integrated financial market due to monetary union makes such spillovers greater.

Finally, there could be added the specific concern that Europe lacked the kind of safeguards of other federal states to reduce the risk of such events coming to play. The United States, for instance, is composed of states that generally have strict, even constitutional, limits on running deficits. Also, there is a greater level of leverage there, through the federal budget.

A lot of attention was paid to this particular convergence area. First, it was asked whether or not the budget should be viewed, in association with GDP, independently of the business cycle. Would not the structural deficit, calculated without consideration of the loss of revenues that occurs with recession, be a better and more representative measure?

Second, should government investment expenditures be treated any differently than other expenditures in determining deficits, the basic notion being that investment, whether it comes from the government or private sector, adds to capacity and the ability of an economy to produce, and is not to be considered the same as expenditures on consumption. It was even carefully thought about early on in the negotiations to include as the criterion that deficits not exceed public investment, and such a consideration did survive as an additional standard under the deliberation of excessive deficits, under article 104c(3). This was, in fact, the "golden rule" of public finance (see Sandholtz, 1993), and was certainly well appreciated by the Germans, but in practice such a rule can be difficult to apply. For example, assuming education adds to human capital, how does one seriously distinguish impact on the final "investment" of expenditures on school buildings versus teacher salaries?

A third problem seen was that the figures in the treaty, assuming no adjustment for cyclical augmentation to a structural deficit, were too low for what would constitute actual conditions. Remembering especially that the treaty provisions here were ongoing in terms of excessive deficits, and that the recessions of the 1990s resulted in actual, measured, deficits well in excess of 3 percent even for what might be called responsible states, the point was made.

A fourth, and perhaps more fundamental, criticism was that the excessive budget criteria were simply unnecessary. This was because private markets would impose sufficient discipline on deficit states by charging higher interest rates, compelling states to balance their budgets over time.[8] Indeed, such a constraint on governments might even be considered undesirable, because the loss of monetary policy associated with EMU would limit the tools available to deal with those asymmetric shocks that might affect some but not other member states. In this case the rules would unnecessarily tie the hands of governments, preventing them from doing what they needed to deal with such situations.

Without necessarily dealing at great length with these arguments concerning the convergence criteria of the treaty, it makes sense to reiterate their core rationale. Valéry Giscard d'Estaing articulated that the criteria were simply "designed to show whether it [would] be possible [for a state] to remain within the system and whether the state of various participating economies [would] be such as to allow them to content themselves with the traditional adjustment mechanisms without recourse to the monetary mechanism" (1994, p. 169). This summary would hardly apply to the opinions of the Bundesbank, which wanted a very strict interpretation of the criteria, but may finally have applied to those of the German government. This is because, in the negotiations, the very question was raised about how closely to apply the criteria in practice, when a final decision would be taken on who would enter and who would not. In the end the German government acquiesced to some level of what might be called "interpretation" of the data by the Council in its decisions. There is, most clearly to this point, the ability to decide that a state does not necessarily exactly meet the excess deficit and debt criteria, but that it might go forward if "either the [deficit to GDP] ratio has declined substantially and continuously and reached a level that comes close to the reference value; or, alternatively, the excess over the reference value is only exceptional and temporary and the ratio remains close to the reference value," and likewise, the debt to GDP ratio can diverge from 60 percent if "the ratio is sufficiently diminishing and approaching the reference value at a satisfactory pace" (Maastricht Treaty, 1992, p. 27). The final decision, in other words, is flexible, open to discussion, presumably on what the data suggest to be the overall case to be made on convergence of the country, rather than the specific criteria being satisfied. Whether or not such a determination can be unduly influenced by political considerations is an important question. But the consideration here is that, at least in the minds of many, many of the questions regarding the exact criteria chosen are beside the point, which is the ability of the criteria to evidence commitment to the final stage of EMU and what that entails in terms of foregoing monetary policy as a macroeconomic tool.

It would be unfair to suggest that such a view is not without risks, because it chances obscuring what might be key questions on the value of the convergence criteria themselves. First, how critical was the notion of a fixed EMS as leading toward EMU, that is as given institutional substance by being included in the language of the treaty, in the subsequent breakup of the EMS itself? Second, would a strict interpretation of the budgetary criteria threaten the later creation of EMU itself, and, even if not, would it unnecessarily subsequently tie the hands of governments looking for tools to deal with asymmetric shocks? Finally, what implications would the criteria hold for a two-level Community, and what would be the implications of such "variable geometry"?

Variable Geometry

John Major, in spite of the warm reception he had gotten early on as prime minister, and the willingness to work with him demonstrated by the other Europeans, came to Maastricht not wishing to commit Britain in any way to EMU. As mentioned, this worked in well with the German insistence on, and general acquiescence by the others to, convergence criteria, so as to imply that not everyone would go forward at the same time. Indeed Delors himself had raised the possibility of a "two-tier" EMU as early as late 1990, and the Bundesbank at about that time was simultaneously suggesting it would accept nothing else.[9] In other words, countries might not go on because they either did not wish to or they could not satisfy the requirements. The treaty itself is not, by design and compromise, terribly clear on the nature or structure of a two-speed Europe. Nevertheless, cursory conditions are specified for those not satisfying the convergence criteria, and, of course the criteria themselves and the decision on who will enter and who will not, imply such a result. Of course the opt-outs for the United Kingdom and later Denmark are clear; the British opt-out was written as a decision open to being taken later, while the subsequent Danish one was to opt out of the system altogether.

The actual language of the treaty had it that any countries left behind, as it were, had a "derogation" from going forward, and that they were not to be included in the decision making process of the ESCB, their votes not counting in the Governing Council. They were not, however, to be left out of the decisions on who would go forward, and this too was a compromise in favor of solidarity of the union.

A two-speed Europe was a great concern. It was certainly of concern to those who would be left out, but it also had implications for the EU, raising the possibility of Europe à la carte, and threatening the political visions of economic leading to eventual full political union. This concern was reinforced by the United Kingdom's also opting out of the social charter of EPU as part of the Maastricht agreement. In any case, there appeared to be no alternative, and certainly the Germans would have it no other way, but it was recognized as a potentially significant problem.[10]

Conclusion

At the end of 1991 and the beginning of 1992, with the official signing of the Maastricht Treaty, the Community seemed to be at a high point in its history of progress toward union. In spite of the acrimony during the protracted negotiation process that left many of the most difficult issues to be resolved at the last, most of the participants felt they had received something from the compromises and could claim a form of victory for their positions. Moreover, the cause of Europe had been enhanced with a political treaty— EPU—that, although still very intergovernmental in nature, at least broached the areas of foreign and defense policy, justice and home affairs, and a variety of other joint concerns. Mainly, however, it was in the monetary area that a treaty that promised a common currency by 1999 at the latest was achieved, at least for a subset of the member states.

The treaty meant that sovereignty over monetary creation, arguably on a par with national defense in those terms, would be given over by the states to a Community institution. This institution, a European central bank, independent and committed to price stability, would also have some powers over fiscal as well as monetary policy in the economic sphere. This would all come about with a full legal framework and, as such, held the possibility of taking Europe much closer to becoming a United States of Europe in the following millennium.

As in the past, there was a confluence of interests that would bring the states together in such a way as to move toward a greater level of integration. In this case a common interest would be an underlying concern over the implications of exchange-rate flexibility, but there was also more. A successful single market and a shared view of the best form of macroeconomic policy seemed to almost demand a common currency. In addition, the EMS as a well-functioning monetary institution appeared effectively to set the stage for the next act. It turns out this act would prove close to a tragedy for those in favor of a smooth transition to EMU.

EIGHT

After Maastricht

The signing of the Maastricht Treaty on February 7, 1992 was a high point in European integration, promising movement toward economic and monetary union by 1999 at the latest. Furthermore, there had been movement toward greater political unification in several areas, and, in spite of the difficulties in the process of negotiation, things were looking very robust for greater integration in Europe. Following soon after the signing of the treaty, however, there were two immediate crises. Although related in time and cause, they were conceptually distinct. The first was a crisis in ratification, while the second was a rolling crisis in the European Monetary System leading to a result adequate of the description "breakup." In spite of what was clearly a strong threat to the EMU objective, the will to move forward held. The comparison with the failed attempt to achieve EMU two decades earlier was striking, but so was this very important difference. Why did the states not falter in this historical instance? Certainly the fact that there was a signed treaty in place contributed, but finally one must consider that the constellation of interests that had brought the states together in the first place had not disappeared.

Following Maastricht

After formal signing, the process was to have the treaty go to the member states for their political ratifications, understanding that in the case of Ireland and Denmark there would need to be referenda of the people, as dictated by their respective constitutions. In all other states the elected representatives would suffice, except when some form of legal opinion of constitutionality was also needed by a supreme court.

In the meantime, Portugal entered the ERM of the EMS in April of 1992, with a vision and commitment to entering monetary union "on time." In May 1992 the Danish government dutifully ratified the treaty, and scheduled a referendum of the people on June 2 of that year. Although Denmark was well known for its ambivalence toward the EU in general, there was initially little concern over Maastricht. When crucial popular votes had been taken in the past, those that would determine the fate of the country with regard to its continued participation in the Community, the vote had always been positive (in spite of spirited and divisive discussions prior to the polls). This had happened in 1972 upon entry—in contradistinction to the Norwegians who decided not to join the EC at the time—and again in 1986, when ratification was sought for the single market under the SEA. Therefore, the government, and indeed everyone else in the Community, was a bit complacent in advance of the vote. The Danes, of course, voted no, and the world learned a Danish word: *"nej."*

The reasons for the negative vote were varied almost down to the individual. Losing control over the Danish krone, although of course that was a concern, was not often actually at the center of the discussions. This was perhaps because such a small state as Denmark, in close proximity with and engaging in a good deal of trade with such a large state as Germany, did not have a good deal of independent control over its currency anyway. This was reinforced by a strong Danish commitment to German economic policy, as evidenced by that country having generally played by the rules of the monetary link through the ERM. This all did not mean, however, that the high interest rates that were the result of such a link were not an issue. Maintaining these rates had been hard on Denmark, and a good deal of the high Danish unemployment rate, albeit perhaps extensively structural in nature, was blamed on Germany.

Another issue was the loss of national identity, an important point for a small nation that has a largely homogeneous population and a proud past, and can feel threatened by decisions taken by the large countries that surround it. This identity would also be considered to be threatened by the emergence of strong, and potentially even arrogant, European institutions that would have little respect for the concerns of a small state. Many Danes, specifically, felt they might have needed to sacrifice their interests in fisheries, the maintenance of social welfare and environmental standards, and the avoidance of an overly assertive defense posture at the European level.

Wrapped up in all of this was that if the identities of individual countries were to become blurred in a more integrated Europe, coupled with a now much larger and potentially more powerful Germany, Denmark might lose in its fight to remain culturally and politically distinct from that "resurgent" country. The latter was not necessarily publicly discussed in the same way, say, as the threat to environmental policy, but it was certainly in the minds of many Danes at the time of ratification.[1]

Finally, in Denmark there was a good deal of public resentment directed against politicians and government in general.[2] In this, Danish opinion reflected European opinion, a point then not fully recognized, at least by the political establishment at the time. This, the first complete public statement that there was a severe problem of confidence by the people in their political leadership, was to be important even after the middle-term ratification crisis was eventually resolved, important to the residual difficulties in what was intended as the transition process toward monetary union.

The immediate crisis raised by the Danish *"nej"* was real. As Maastricht was a treaty it had to pass by unanimity, and by all rights the question of ratification should have stopped right there as one of the member states had, by public referendum no less, voted against it. But, Denmark was not Germany or France, and it was hard to see how a country with only five million people could keep the rest of the Community from going forward. Nevertheless, those were the rules.[3]

Two weeks following the Danish referendum came that of Ireland. The Irish vote had seemed secure, but in the atmosphere of the time nothing any longer was certain. Much more attention was paid Ireland, and the politicking was intense, with the potential loss of regional aid surfacing as a major point of the proponents, while many of the same concerns voiced in Denmark were posed by the opponents.[4] In the result the electorate voted yes by a strong majority.

After the Danish rejection Mitterand, as president with significant powers, decided to hold a referendum in France on September 20. France, as noted, did not need to do so, and the treaty would have passed easily through the two French houses, but the decision to go to the people was political. It was designed, by all accounts, to reaffirm French support, at the level of the public, and hence put EMU back on track. It was also designed, within the swirling vagaries that are French politics, to split conservative political opposition (that is to the Socialists) at home, which was not necessarily of one mind regarding Europe. Mitterand's decision to hold a referendum in France at this time, with a solid majority in his pocket, and in light of what must be viewed as mixed motives, was a very risky move. There resulted an active public debate, albeit begun somewhat late by the proponents, that raised many of the same type of views represented in the Danish vote, especially regarding loss of national identity and EU control from Brussels.

As it turned out the vote was positive for the treaty, but very close, at 51 percent in favor versus 49 percent opposed.[5] Such a close vote, a *"petit oui,"* did anything but reinforce strong public support of the project by the people of one of the states that had been most committed to it, both in theory and in practice. Although the positive vote barely avoided a quick and complete rejection of the treaty, it had not left Europe any more certain about the future than it had felt after the Danish results.

In the meantime, that is between the Danish and French votes, there was mounted in the financial markets a concerted and powerful assault on the supposedly fixed exchange-rate system of the EMS. The events were hardly unrelated, although there will be more to say later on the causes of the exchange-rate crisis. First to come under attack was the Finnish markka, not an ERM, EMS, or even EU member at that time, but nevertheless one that had announced voluntary pegging to the ERM, and it collapsed under speculative selling of the currency. This was soon followed by a similar strong push against the Swedish krona, against which the government was able to maintain its peg, but only with at one juncture 500 percent interest rates (on an annualized basis).[6] Again Sweden was not then officially part of the system, but the next country to come under pressure, Italy, certainly was.

These events led to a somewhat infamous meeting of the Community's finance ministers at Bath, England on September 4 and 5, where Germany was pressed, particularly by the United Kingdom, to lower interest rates in reaction to what some then and later viewed as excessive zeal by the Bundesbank in fighting inflation in the face of reunification demand buildup. The Germans, and the Bundesbank in particular, responded that what was needed was a realignment of rates within the ERM. This was not accepted at the time, remembering how the system had become fixed in people's minds and the political credibility that any currency would lose upon devaluation.[7] In the interim, massive support was needed by the Bundesbank to help the Bank of Italy shore up its currency.[8] Finally, it could go on no longer, and the Bundesbank president, Helmut Schlesinger, appealed to a little remembered agreement upon the establishment of the EMS that could have the German central bank, lacking a necessary agreement to realign, refuse to intervene in the support of other currencies. The German government, and Kohl in particular, saw the bank's position and carried the day with the other governments. There was an agreed devaluation of the lira on September 13, accompanied by a reduction in German rates. The realignment of the lira, however, was only 7 percent, well below what most thought had been the intervening differential inflation over several years and subsequent misalignment of the currency. When Schlesinger was quoted in the press (from a comment that he considered would not be for public consumption) that the bank had wanted both a larger devaluation of the lira, and a broader one to boot, including sterling and the Spanish peseta, both considered overvalued, the markets saw blood.

On September 16, "Black Wednesday," these three currencies came under heavy speculative attack, especially sterling and the lira, and despite unprecedented intervention,[9] the Banks of England and Italy could not hold out. The United Kingdom and Italy dropped out of the system, it is significant that they did not try to maintain a connection through devaluations of their central rates, and proceeded to float their currencies.[10] Spain stayed in, but only with a 5-percent devaluation and a reintroduction of capital controls several days later. Attention next turned to the French franc, and either devaluation or forced removal from the ERM was averted, again with massive support from the Bundesbank, that let it be known that it was quite serious in maintaining this currency link with the DM.[11]

Turbulence continued on through the rest of 1992 and into 1993. Under further pressure the franc still did not budge, although others did. Spain and Portugal, the latter very reluctantly, devalued by 6 percent on November 23, 1992, while Ireland, needing to follow the British down as they are major trading partners, devalued 10 percent on January 30, 1993. The Irish as well, and not exactly in the full spirit either of the SEA or Maastricht, reimposed capital controls, but it would be difficult to criticize a country that at one juncture had needed to institute interest rates of 300 percent (see Andrews, 1995).

It will be remembered that while these events were creating crisis in the EMS, the ratification crisis was still unresolved. Soon after the Danish rejection the heads of state met in Lisbon in late June and decided, essentially, to go on with the process of ratification as though Denmark had not happened, or, at least to give the Danes time to make some concrete suggestions on what to do about the impasse. In the meantime, however, the question of public dissatisfaction at least with the potential for abusive and excessive power at the Community level was addressed with a greater emphasis on subsidiarity, which, after all, carried an important place in the Maastricht Treaty (article 3b).

The Edinburgh summit in December 1992 reinforced the emphasis on subsidiarity, and dealt with the Danish question by offering the Danes the chance to vote again. This time there would be opt-outs for the country, similar to those for the United Kingdom, here read as nonparticipation in EMU[12] and the common security and defense components of EPU.[13] Offering here a different treaty for a second vote was an interesting development, as was the further implication of the proposal for Europe à la carte, but the chance was embraced by the Danes. The campaign was taken most seriously this time, and, in May 1993, the vote was yes. This, as extraordinary as the process was, saved the day and allowed the rest of the states to move on.

The United Kingdom, having postponed its vote in Parliament until after the second Danish decision, entered into what many considered at the time an interminable debate, giving exercise to many of the aspects of British politics and political traditions that make for incomprehension on the Continent. The result was approval in the House of Commons on July 21, 1993, and, with the legal question settled, the United Kingdom had agreed. The last hurdle was also legal in nature, that decision taken by the German constitutional court on the acceptability of the treaty to the German Basic Law. This too passed, in October, but only in association with the ruling that it would be unconstitutional, again by German law, to dismiss the convergence criteria of the treaty (see Henning, 1994). Moreover, and not well known, the Bundestag was given the right to hold a second vote, prior to entry to the last stage, to decide whether in their opinion the other member states had satisfied the criteria. In any case, with all members having ratified, the treaty entered into law on November 1, 1993. The ratification crisis was over, but hardly the questions regarding the future of the Maastricht Treaty.

With the final ratification by November, stage two could, and did, begin as scheduled on January 1, 1994. There were then several decisions made that had an impact on the second stage and the transition to the third stage. First, it was decided to set up the EMI, as well as the future ECB, in Frankfurt, which would ideally carry with the very location some of the reputation of the Bundesbank, also located in that city.[14] A second decision was taken to name the putative common currency the "euro," rather than the ECU. This was done over the objections of the French, who, as mentioned, had attraction to the former name as that of an old French coin, and also in some ways ignoring the treaty language on the issue.[15] The argument prevailed, however, that the new currency should not carry with it any association with a prior system that included as part of it any less than excellent performance. Third, it was decided that 1999 would, in actuality, be the earliest one could expect movement toward EMU, the treaty language again aside. Finally, an IGC was set up to begin in March 1996, with the hope that it would deal with many of the residual problems swirling around EMU. As it turns out the problems were intractable enough so as to allow for early agreement for their being largely ignored for the meetings, that agenda taken instead by another Community problem of how to deal with voting and other issues in a potentially much larger Community.

Things seemed to have settled down in the foreign exchange markets by the middle of 1993. With two major currencies out of the ERM and several others having devalued there was a feeling that the markets had sorted out the major problems of misalignment and were more or less content with the result. This was not to be the case, however, as yet another massive assault of selling of French francs against the DM began in July. The fundamentals of the French economy behind the franc, including inflation rates and external position, were not considered by most as out of line, although there was the question of how long the government would continue to take the high rates of unemployment implied by its continued linkage with German policy, called the "franc fort" policy. The Bundesbank intervention in this instance was again huge,[16] but this time it could not hold and the system cracked. It was decided on August 1, 1993 to widen the bands of the ERM from 2.25 percent on either side of par (or 6 percent for the old "soft" margins), to fully 15 percent, or 30 percent potential divergence between currencies.[17] It is significant that the governments, again given the pressure, did not abandon the system altogether, but then it could also be argued that such broad bands were no longer any system at all. Nevertheless, there may have been advantages to the way the final decision was taken. The event, however, does call for the description "breakup" of the ERM, because that is virtually what happened under the onslaught of overwhelming pressure from those who were to gain from forcing governments away from their commitments in the exchange markets. The causes for such a momentous result, with obvious damaging implications for movement toward monetary union, require examination.

EMS Crises

The reasons for the EMS crises of 1992 and 1993 have been extensively explored with recognition that there were overlapping explanations. The first potential reason is an early fixing of the exchange-rate mechanism in the EMS. The ERM began to be viewed as a fixed system from the 1987 Basle-Nyborg agreements, in an understandable attempt to provide some real stability to the area covered—the zone of monetary stability that was the objective of the system—and also to demonstrate solidity with the core notion of all the states involved achieving price stability around the German model. Again, the system would work purposefully in an asymmetric fashion to forge the result, focusing the attention of states on the need to demonstrate macroeconomic restraint through not allowing for matching realignments with underlying differential inflation. The success of the system bred a form of prestige associated with not realigning, and in a subtle fashion, as soon as talk of EMU was current, it became viewed as the fixed system that would move smoothly, as on a "glide path," to the common currency. It was subsequently embodied in the treaty with that view.

What was, of course, forgotten was the inconsistency trinity. It is curious that it was forgotten, because in many ways it was this idea that served well as an understandable economic motivation to move from EMS to EMU. In fact, if the ERM could be viewed as permanently fixed, successfully permanently fixed, why even bother with the effort to move on? The answer, of course, is that the capital mobility required by the single act, and reinforced by increasingly integrated capital markets, coupled with fixed exchange rates simply could not, in the long run, coexist with independent monetary policies.[18] An argument could be made that as long as monetary policies were consistent among themselves around the German model of low money supply growth then there was no "inconsistency," but that was not the case. Countries' inflation rates were different, and the tensions would only build up over time, as in a pressure cooker, so that eventually the top would need to blow off (as in fact, it happened), or the fire could be turned down through the now-dreaded realignment.

A second reason for the crises was the institutional reinforcement of the exchange-rate fixing of the EMS through one of the convergence criteria of the treaty, where countries were to maintain their exchange rates within the "normal"—this was intended to mean narrow—margins of the ERM for two years prior to the start of the final stage of EMU. Again the rationale of such a stipulation was entirely understandable. Participation in the system, successfully so by avoiding parity changes, evidenced, even market-recognized, commitment to the price stability and economic convergence which would be necessary preconditions for governments to satisfy others of their intentions to abide by the implications of a system where they would seriously sacrifice the use of the monetary tool. Nevertheless, the point is that the markets would also recognize that the institutional reinforcement only further added rigidity to a system that simply could not continue to exist as a fixed but not adjustable rate system. Speculators were even more certain, in other words, that there would not be easy access to realignment, and that something had to give.[19]

A third point related to this but distinctive enough to warrant separate consideration was the institutional fixing of a date, a final date, and again in the treaty, when EMU would take place. This understanding of a final date by the markets could exacerbate a crisis because participants could fairly accurately gauge the inconsistency of the date with the increasing divergence of the fundamentals behind the exchange rates, most especially the divergence from purchasing power parity (PPP). The participants would recognize the need for a final realignment, at a certain date, and as that date approached more profits could potentially be made on a one-way bet against certain currencies.[20] The "one-way bet," of course, refers to the very high probability that the change could only go one way if it happened, and the only cost of the bet would be if the change did not come off.[21]

A fourth cause was German economic policy at the time of reunification, which could be characterized as a relatively easy fiscal policy (with taxes insufficient to cover the extra expenditures involved) coupled with a very restrictive monetary policy. The Bundesbank, naturally, insisted upon the latter in order to constrain the inflationary implications of the higher level of spending on the eastern part of the country. This was an asymmetric shock if there ever was one in the history of Europe, and, through the ERM, the resulting high interest rates were transferred to the rest of the members of the exchange rate system (as in Filc, 1994). The resultant recession and high levels of unemployment were felt by market participants to be so strong as to be unsustainable. This would be true even for those countries not in any way otherwise misaligned in terms of economic fundamentals, and so could provide pressure against even relatively strong currencies. In other words, there could be states that had low inflation rates and balance-of-payments deficits that could, under this reason, come under scrutiny by the exchange markets for the maintenance of their currency in the ERM, under the expectation that their patience would politically wear thin and they would begin to inflate to deal with the most severe recession since the second world war.[22]

Finally, there was the question of the Danish and French referenda results having provided at best tepid support for EMU. This raised questions about the political viability of the project, perhaps negatively reinforced by the strains of recession, and its potential abandonment due to lack of political will (as had happened during an earlier run at EMU). It will be remembered that the first EMS crisis occurred coincidentally with the ratification crisis, and so it would not seem inappropriate to search for reasons there. This explanation can be read the other way from one which suggests it was the premature fixing of the exchange-rate system that was the problem, because it says that it was only the referendum results that called the glide path of (otherwise successful) exchange-rate rigidity leading smoothly into EMU into question. Of course there is no necessary inconsistency if one simply submits that it takes a particular event, such as the votes, to draw the attention of the markets to an otherwise untenable situation.

Each one of these explanations contains a level of plausibility. The first explanation, which might be called premature fixing, seems to be able to bear a great deal of the burden of the facts surrounding the crises. The inconsistency trinity applies when country fundamentals are increasingly out of line, and that was certainly true at this time. Both Thygesen (1994a) and Artus and Bourguinat (1994) had suggested that the Italian exchange rate was some 15 percent out of line, due to intervening inflation rates higher than others, while Henning (1994) referred to Italy's budget deficit being out of control. Boyer (1994) similarly found Spain's exchange rate 17 percent misaligned in comparison with its EU members, between 1985 and 1992, while Artus and Bourguinat (1994) had it at 25 percent. The United Kingdom, although perhaps not in quite the same position, nevertheless was operating at below average interest rates, and by general agreement had entered the ERM in 1990 at too high an exchange rate.[23] In the case of all three of these countries, those that received the most speculative attention at the beginning of the extended period of crisis, annual inflation rates were at least two percentage points above German rates.

It is a powerful argument that if these countries had devalued in a timely manner the potential profit from further speculation would have been dissipated, and the markets would have been well satisfied with their subsequent positions in a stable EMS. The alternative argument that realignment would simply have rewarded speculators and actually threatened the stability of the system seems less convincing than the position that the market never saw the need for the system to be fixed in the first place, and it was only when it became so misaligned that there was the first heavy assault upon it. Again, orderly realignments would seem to have been more consistent with a road to monetary union that was built upon the need to adjust exchange rates in the face of independent monetary policies.[24]

Given the above, at least for the initial phase of the crisis that involved seemingly misaligned currencies, it is not clear how much additional blame can be placed on the inclusion of fixity into the treaty. Again the purpose was to demonstrate the credibility and commitment of the governments involved, but it is significant that the language of the treaty is that the margins be maintained only for two years prior, leaving enough time for appropriate realignments. As noted earlier, there was a general expectation of a final realignment anyway, which would have been more easily handled politically for a country that had kept to its central rate for a few years. In this instance, unless one believes that it was the inclusion in the treaty that caused the EMS to become viewed as fixed, somewhat turning the facts upon their head, then one needs to ask how much harm was caused by putting into writing what everyone had already determined to be the case anyway.

As to the inclusion of a specific date for the beginning of the third stage, it is again understandable why a final date was considered valuable, even though it had been purposefully avoided in the Delors Report. The French, in particular, felt that it could help force convergence. The remarks above on any separate blame to be borne, in this case by the setting of the date, apply in some force here as well. The traders on the markets seemed to be reacting to the premature rigidity of exchange rates and subsequent excess overvaluation of currencies, and not to a fixed date for EMU. Together with the inclusion of language on fixity, these thoughts lead to the conclusion of little extra blame to be allocated to institutional problems associated with the treaty for the eventual EMS crises.

The same cannot necessarily be said for German economic policy at the time of reunification. People have argued for a different policy mix, and that the actual policy chosen emphasized German concern only for domestic issues, at the expense of European objectives, perhaps most especially movement toward EMU. This was evidenced in a failure to increase taxes adequately at home to finance reunification, allowing for more latitude to lower interest rates. Such a policy mix would have, again through the ERM, shifted much less burden to the rest of Europe.[25]

The point here, however, is that asymmetric shocks, whether or not exacerbated by macroeconomic policy errors, are perhaps best dealt with using the exchange-rate instrument. A revaluation of the DM would have seemed appropriate. The fact that the crises continued into 1993, even though the bulk of misalignment appeared to have been resolved, culminating in the breakup of the EMS through the large widening of margins, reinforces the independent importance of German policy and its impact on the rest of Europe. Thygesen (1994a and 1994b) makes this point with some strength, and draws a distinction between the two episodes of crisis, with 1992 representing misalignment and 1993 representing reunification pressures, with the latter affecting even otherwise strong countries. The point remains, however, that the independent level of blame, that is separate from premature rigidity of the EMS, must be considered small. If the exchange rates were viewed as adjustable, in other words, either to account for misalignments or for asymmetric shocks reinforced by the policy reactions of one state, then the inexorable pressure on the system might have been avoided.

Finally, there is the question of the Danish and French votes. As indicated it appears as though these events, in being coincidental with the first September 1992 round of crisis, triggered the attack on overvalued currencies. The "new" EMS also came unraveled at this time, suggesting that there was something in the events that, although not fundamental to the problem of misalignments, nevertheless precipitated extensive market reaction to them. The new EMS, of course, included countries that even though they had rates of inflation higher than their partners, were able to borrow credibility by their ERM-EMS participation, and convince the markets for some period of time of the strength of the exchange-rate linkage. The inflation rates could be ignored, and the current account deficits in some cases overfinanced with inflows of capital, drawn by higher interest rates. Instances of such "excess credibility" had occurred before, of course, and there was evidence that foreign exchange–based stabilizations generally become inconsistent with the persistent inflation differentials, and the exchange rate peg collapses (Giovannini, 1994). Artus and Bourguinat (1994, p. 156) pointed in such a situation to the requirement of a "small shock," specifically they mentioned the "Danish 'no' and the French limited 'yes'," as adequate to "lead to the explosion of the crisis." The later speculative attacks, moreover, not justified in terms of the underlying economic conditions, may also have owed something to market perceptions of political will to withstand the implications of staying with the system in the face of reunification-oriented German economic policies. To this extent, as well, the votes could have introduced uncertainty in the minds of market players on the commitment by European citizens, and, eventually by extension, their representatives.[26]

In summarizing the exchange crises then, this analysis is fairly gentle on institutional mistakes, at least in terms of treaty language and German policy errors upon reunification. It is less forgiving, however, of what might be considered a premature rigidity of the EMS in leading to EMU. By implication these results give little weight to a significant malevolent role for speculation itself; the markets probably in the long run simply react to underlying problems rather than create problems of their own, as easy as it is to criticize them at the time of crises. It is finally history in the conditional to try to decide whether or not the EMS could have weathered the storm if it had been allowed in the first stage of the crises to adjust to currency misalignments (1992), and then, in the second, to adjust to German reunification implications (1993). And even so, it could be that the lack of political will itself, as reflected in the Danish and French votes, might have been enough to call the EMS into question and undermine the system. As it was, however, the breakup of the EMS that appears to have resulted from premature fixing served to worsen the political milieu in which any progress toward EMU had to operate.

Finally, there was the result that EMS was not entirely abandoned in 1993. Irony could suggest that the "bands" of the ERM had turned into "boulevards,"[27] but it was nevertheless true that the system was still on the books. In fact, given that reality, there were several positive results to be seen to follow. First, after the widening of bands the speculative pressures generally abated, and a good deal of stability returned to the markets (Andrews, 1995). No doubt the greater width of potential exchange rate movements introduced more uncertainty into the speculative process, thus eliminating the one-way bets that could yield huge gains (Artus and Bourguinat, 1994). Second, they provided a continuation of official participation in the EMS, so as not to violate at least the written institutional basis of Maastricht. Third, they provided a mechanism by which, in voluntarily keeping well within the broader bands, countries could continue to demonstrate the credibility of their commitment. In fact, many of the participants strove to continue to maintain the old narrow margins after August of 1993. Next, the bands also provided a mechanism by which to define what is meant by "normal" in the treaty, thus allowing for potentially even easier transition into the last stage. Putting these last three notions together, the wider bands would not only allow for countries to establish their disinflationary credibility and maintain the institutional basis for entry into EMU, but they would also effectively allow for a last realignment within quite large margins before the event, something most see as an important option for further healthy operation of the system once it is in place.[28]

Continuing Transition Issues

There was eventually an end both to the ratification crisis and the EMS crises. Involved in both were questions of political will, not so much stemming from political representatives as from the citizens of EU states; these questions would not end during the 1990s.[29] There were several possible reasons for such malaise about the future and promise of European integration. For example, there appeared at this time a resurgence of nationalistic feelings in Europe, associated with a good deal of uncertainty in general about the pace and direction of change in the world. The breakup of the former Soviet Union, the reunification of Germany, the attempted rapid shift of Russia and the former Soviet-dominated states toward capitalistic democracies, and the war in Bosnia were all events of momentous import occurring during a short span of time in the European theater alone. Associated with this, there was a renewed level of emotional identification with the state and, as one particular manifestation of that, concern over the loss of one's currency, especially with uncertain benefits to follow. In addition, there was an even accelerated distrust of politics and politicians at all levels. The seemingly never ending succession of politicians found involved in corruption only reinforced a feeling that true leaders were only of the past.

There was also an increased degree of economic uncertainty, in a way that would have a direct influence on the ordinary person. Unemployment, at least in Europe, was high and seemingly not capable of being influenced by old-style macroeconomic policies, in other words largely structural—as opposed to cyclical—in nature. Furthermore, the era provided uncertainty even to those who had jobs in the face of world wide "restructuring," where there appeared to be little concern for, and much less loyalty to, employees by corporations driven only to serve shareholder interests.

For these general, and undoubtedly many more specific, reasons there was indeed a stepping back by European citizens from the process of EMU, a distinct reduction in enthusiasm for the task and the result. This showed up in Germany as much as anywhere, perhaps especially because the Germans felt that they had the most to lose in a strong DM and an underlying structure that fit their needs well.

One example of German hesitation was a manifesto signed in 1992 by sixty German Economists (1994) that was very critical of Maastricht. Briefly, the manifesto had it that there was no economically convincing argument for monetary union in a Europe not ready for it, politically, economically, or socially; the convergence criteria were too lax and in danger of being "watered down" for political reasons; the ECB could not ensure price stability, which was not necessarily a seriously shared objective throughout Europe; there were no sanctions for countries not adhering to the stability criteria; and substantial transfer payments were implicit in the process. Many of these concerns were responded to by another group of economists (see Gros and Steinherr, 1994), but the point is how strongly the opinions were expressed and, obviously, held.

Another example of German concern over the implications of moving forward was a renewed resolve, and at all levels of government, not to apply anything less than strict interpretation to the convergence criteria of Maastricht. This included no consideration for the fact that countries' budget deficits, and hence the deficit to GDP ratio, could be influenced negatively by recession. In fact, application of the criteria was considered so important that there were considered proposals to continue and substantially strengthen them after monetary union. Measures that included potential sanctions were approved in Dublin in 1996 to encourage such strict budget discipline.[30]

Of course one possible outcome of such a flagging of enthusiasm was that the EMU project would not go forward. Another almost certain outcome, especially with application of very strict and even potentially stronger convergence criteria, was that there would most likely be a two-speed Europe, thus leaving some states out, and possibly for a good deal of time (if not in some cases permanently). At the midpoint of the 1990s there began to be serious thought applied to the implications of a core of countries going forward, not necessarily quickly followed by others, some of whom, of course, could choose not to participate. In addition to the questions raised about the political nature of a union that had some participating in some aspects but not in others, there were the technical questions of how to deal with those left out, issues not fully addressed in the treaty.[31]

The other side of the coin was the way in which the ratification crisis and especially the EMS crises did not seem to finally deter governments from continued commitment to the goal. It could have been, as occurred in the 1970s, that there would be wholesale dropouts, all focusing on domestic policy decisions independent of the larger picture. It is significant that this did not happen, and most of the participants took the EMS debacle in stride, and settled back into attempting to satisfy the convergence criteria. This was true even in spite of what appeared to have been an easy ride for the United Kingdom and Italy after dropping from the system, and the competitive edge they thereby secured by an extensive drop in their respective exchange rates.[32] Instead, these other states, France and the "hard core" kept well within the now much larger bands, and left this room for maneuver unexploited. A series of competitive devaluations could easily have been the result if they had not.[33] In fact, the message was even received by the southern states, including Spain and Italy, who sensed the seriousness of the project and strove to prepare for as early an entry as possible.

Reactions from the participant states following the Werner Report and the Maastricht Treaty, facing similar pressures of political will, asymmetric shocks, and exchange market turbulence, could not have been more different. The difference was certainly in part due to the institutional and legal structure in place in the period following the Maastricht Treaty. It could also be attributed, however, to a level of economic and political self interest that these states saw in continuing the course, interests that were neither as clear nor as well developed in the earlier period following the Werner Report.[34]

Conclusion

During the 1990s history seemed to have come full circle. After an agreed document outlining a plan to achieve economic and monetary union by the end of the decade, the smooth transition to such an end was abruptly challenged by a large external economic shock and coincidental lack of political will to go on. The same thing had happened two decades earlier, ending in a formal agreement to abandon the project. In this instance, however, most of the parties reacted with a quiet resolve to go forward. These states, especially the hard core—who had always been identified with Germany in monetary and macroeconomic sympathy—but also now significantly joined by France, seemingly ignored the damage done to the European Monetary System by the exchange crises directly following Maastricht. They voluntarily kept to the old exchange-rate margins of the now broken exchange-rate mechanism and refused to resort to the competitive devaluations that have always been a risk in a Europe closely tied together through trade. They kept to the economic processes necessary to allow them to satisfy the convergence criteria of the treaty, including the difficult budgetary requirements that now Germany in particular insisted would be inviolable. The other states, the Italys and Spains of Europe, planned for as early an entry as possible. The potential new member states of Eastern Europe specifically understood in their enthusiasm for eventually joining that one of the requirements and, indeed, benefits of membership in the union, would ultimately be being included in the monetary union. Again, none of this seemed easy, and the questioning and perceived lack of support from many citizens still threatened to throw the process off track, in sympathy with the lack of will shown after the Werner Report, but here percolating up from the grass roots. Nevertheless, the will seemed to hold at the governmental level.

What had been the difference? Certainly institutions do finally matter, and the fact was that a treaty had been signed. The treaty might have been difficult for many to understand—vague in places and clearly the result of many compromises. But it had finally been fully ratified, and was going forward. The other was that the constellation of interests that brought the states together to draft Maastricht had not gone away, or were not in this instance so fragile as to dissipate easily. They included the fact that Europe was now very different from what it had been two decades earlier. It was now much closer to a common market, thanks both to the growth of intra-European trade and—not unrelated—the institutional results of the Single European Act. Added to this was an international economy that, although hardly one, was interconnected enough through capital and goods markets to make it difficult to continue to run autarkic macroeconomic policies. Also, there still seemed to be the residual lesson that few talked about any longer (but was a good deal of the basis of the original EEC), that is, a political objective to bring Europe together for its own good, in order to avoid the negative results of nationalism. Few still considered the chance of another world war beginning on European soil as the result of old antagonisms. Nevertheless nationalism, resurgent as it appeared to be, seemed anachronistic in a time when the world looked to one voice from Europe on the many problems that continued to plague a post–Cold War environment.

Finally, there seemed to be a lingering feeling that monetary union made sense, both economically and politically. That is not to say that there were not radically different views on these issues, but, at least among many Europeans, this seemed to be the case. It is those economic and political issues that need to be examined next.

NINE

Economics of Monetary Union

In what has become a traditional approach, the economics of monetary union in Europe is now commonly analyzed in terms of costs and benefits. This approach has the advantage of using a format that is generally understood by economists and others alike to emphasize the general fact that everything has a cost, and proper consideration of a proposed project needs to assess the costs as well as the benefits. In addition, such an approach holds the promise that a rational decision can be forthcoming if the costs and benefits are correctly identified and measured.

Having said that, this approach, although generally used, has suffered when applied to the question of monetary union in Europe. It has not seemed to have meaningfully informed the decision making process on EMU, and, in fact, many of the results have simply been ignored by policymakers. This is unfortunate, because economists should be able in an instance of this type, which is at heart an economic question, to be important players in the policy process. The powerful tools of economic theory should by all rights be brought to bear on this question, with no less powerful results.

Instead it seems as if what has happened is that economists have generally used an extant body of thought—optimum currency area theory—in addressing the question in terms of costs versus benefits, and found monetary union in Europe wanting. Indeed, the best many have done is to find that monetary union might be desirable on political grounds, but only if states are willing to pay what might be considered a net cost on the economic side.[1] Again, and almost in spite of these conclusions by professional economists, there is a wide body of opinion in Europe that a single currency could be beneficial, economically. Moreover, to make the lack of effective communication worse, many of the views expressed by those in Europe supporting monetary union mention economic reasons and concerns that simply do not enter into either the analysis or results of economic examinations.

This is not to say one side is right and the other wrong; instead it almost appears as though the two sides are close to talking about different things.

One hypothesis of the difficulty here is that the approach itself may be creating an analytical structure that (again, although hardly wrong) asks the questions in such a way that the analysis incorrectly addresses what is most important to those who are affected. The use of the structure of cost-benefit analysis—especially in a case like this where existing measures of both costs and benefits are severely lacking and open to a good deal of dispute themselves—in other words emphasizes features of monetary union that are of somewhat less concern to many Europeans while ignoring those features of greater concern. Specifically, a cost-benefit approach (just in terms of structuring the questions), when supplemented with some of the interesting and important results of optimum currency area theory, results in close examination of such issues as labor mobility as an antidote to asymmetric shocks, loss of the exchange-rate instrument, and the impact of transactions charges on currency exchanges. On the other hand, when one listens to policymakers and members of the public talk of currency union one more often hears of such concerns as competitive devaluations, imported inflation, reintroduction of exchange controls, and potential loss of the common market.

This chapter will take a somewhat different approach to the examination of the economics of monetary union, and will focus on broad and generally accepted economic goals. It will be seen that most of the same considerations and concerns will enter as in the traditional cost-benefit analysis. On the other hand, an approach using economic goals as the basis, while being no less objective, will nevertheless allow for inclusion and adequate consideration of many of the concerns of policymakers and the public.[2]

It will be seen to follow that a two-speed Europe is a distinct possibility, based on trade dependence and similarity of industrial structure leading to a strong preference for avoiding exchange rate fluctuations. Also, concern over growth seems to favor EMU through an appeal to long-run stability issues, including avoiding competitive devaluations and a return to capital controls as threats to the single market. Finally, the modern loss of much of the effectiveness of standard macroeconomic tools makes a common central bank seem a less costly option in Europe.

Growth

The first general economic goal that might be affected by the adoption of EMU in Europe is economic growth, especially that arising from a more efficient, and ongoing, allocation of resources. One aspect of such growth is associated with the traditional gains from international trade, here of course related to the impact of foreign-exchange risk on the decision to engage in trade. The optimum structure of an economy, according to this argument, could be negatively affected by such risk, so that relatively more resources would be devoted to nontradeable production, and growth of such, and less to tradeable goods. A larger allocation of resources to the tradeable goods sector, in other words, would otherwise promise to utilize existing resources more effectively, even in a dynamic fashion. This can be seen most clearly through specialization in exports in the areas of comparative advantage, leading to gains from trade arising from exchange for relatively low-cost imports, produced by others with a comparative advantage in those goods. There is also, however, the possibility that firms might eschew the potentially profitable production of importable goods, because their prices, as well as those of exportables, are influenced by the "risky" foreign sector.

One pertinent aspect of monetary union is the avoidance of short-term volatility of exchange rates. A frequent answer to this problem, and one referred to in an earlier chapter, is that hedging such risk is possible, and, indeed a good number of firms do so. Financial institutions offer forward contracts for most currencies, at least for those in which trade is invoiced, so this should not be a problem even for smaller firms that cannot manage their own corporate portfolio in such a way as to mitigate foreign-exchange risk. A problem with this response is that many firms do not in reality hedge their risk, concerned that such hedging is too expensive, whether or not it is in practice.

This has often led governments to assume some of this risk from private traders by attempting to peg their currency in various ways with other countries, of which the EMS is only one example.[3] It will be remembered that the EMS was established as a "zone of monetary stability," one important component of which was to dampen exchange rate fluctuations, and that result was viewed as part of what was then deemed a successful system for years. Here is one area that Europeans, in other words, pay attention to as being important, and it is arguable that such a concern is related to the openness of their existing markets to international trade. With the advent of generalized floating, as was noted earlier, it was the Europeans who were much more concerned than, say, the Americans about the prospects of such a "system" for their own structure of trade.

Related to the concern over short-term volatility is the question of transactions charges in foreign exchange markets, because these influence both the transfer of foreign money for domestic money in the trade for goods (in the spot market), and the possibility of hedging (through the forward market). The charges here are in terms of bid-ask spreads required by traders for both spot and forward exchanges, and besides some minimal level of remuneration required for maintaining inventories and the facilities to provide the service, these charges vary with foreign-exchange risk.[4] Transaction charges are generally agreed to be relatively small in magnitude, however, with the Directorate-General for Economic and Financial Affairs (1990) estimating them in the range of one half of one percent of EU GDP. Nevertheless, these charges do constitute a cost, and represent resources that could be effectively used elsewhere.[5]

More important than either short-run volatility or transactions charges, however, would seem to be longer term misalignments of exchange rates affecting longer term decisions to, or not to, enter trade. The argument is the same as above regarding resource allocation, but here the problem is that such longer term misalignments—exchange rates that do not match underlying inflation—are not easily hedged,[6] or only at some real cost, and even then generally only for the larger firms through their own portfolio management (including issuing long-term debt). Fixed exchange rates, of course, are no protection against this type of risk, as it is the real exchange rate one is concerned with, and, moreover, fixed rates are hardly fixed forever and will not necessarily serve even in the long run to fully counter underlying inflation. Flexible rates—somewhat against what was their original promise when looked to in the 1970s after the breakup of Bretton Woods—do not seem to guarantee against this longer term real exchange rate risk either. It was thought that in allowing exchange rates to be more flexible there would be a greater chance, especially in the longer run, of their better reflecting purchasing power parity in currencies (even in spite of temporary over or undershooting as exchange rates adjust to news more quickly than the underlying price structures), but this does not seem to be the case.[7]

The result is that traders can be expected to look upon the existence of exchange rates in general as risky. It is only recently that empirical studies have begun to identify negative effects of floating on trade; it was previously difficult to draw any conclusion from the significant body of work devoted to this issue.[8] But here it is important to note that the empirical results on exchange regime compare fixed rates with floating, whereas perhaps the better basis for comparison under potential movement to EMU is no nominal exchange rate changes at all. In other words, although it is clearly possible to have different "exchange rates" in real terms in a monetary union (as prices may differ by state or region within such a union) this is not the same as systems where nominal rates can change, and should be viewed differently from an empirical vantage point.[9]

This is one particular point where the concern of the person on the street or, better, the average businessperson, is not frequently given direct consideration in the academic literature. Surveys of those in business, for example, identify "reduction in monetary fluctuations" as first among the reasons to adopt monetary union in Europe (see Directorate-General for Economic and Financial Affairs, 1990). One difference here, again, is that the academic literature most often responds to the question of exchange-rate risk, even long-term risk, with the lack of strong empirical demonstration of the impact of exchange-rate risk on trade, based often upon the strong growth in trade upon floating. A problem here is that measures that fail to show that floating seems to have affected trade are conflating the alternative systems of exchange rates with no exchange rates at all. In this sense the measures speak more to a comparison between floating and an EMS, rather than an EMU. Again, although it is reasonable to identify real exchange-rate fluctuations within monetary unions, based upon price level differences, there is nevertheless a large difference between this and instances in which actual exchange rates might move. Within a monetary union the only changes that can occur (save the introduction or reintroduction of currencies) are price-level changes between regions, which are generally more slowly made and are due primarily to real factors that can influence one region differentially. The potential of actual exchange-rate changes, however, whether in "fixed" systems or not, adds a level of risk on top of variations in price levels, changes that can both occur more quickly and reflect monetary as well as real disturbances. This is not even to mention misalignments created by the fact that exchange rates are properly viewed as asset prices subject to change, reflecting the views of market participants at any one point in time. To this extent, monetary union must be less risky than virtually any modern type of exchange-rate regime.[10]

Whether or not this may make a large impact on decisions to allocate resources within a country in order to take advantage of trade is, of course, a different question, but it is probably the better question to ask. The advantage frequently expressed, for example, of EMU making the price system within the EU "more responsive" speaks to this concern. In the case it would make for more of an EU-wide price system, rather than several country-specific systems that are not entirely coincidental, and make comparisons between prices in different centers easier. This should in turn make consumer welfare greater as it makes it more difficult (save other barriers) to price a car, say, much higher in Germany than in Italy. The point here, however, is that it should also make resource allocation based upon Community trade more efficient.[11]

In this fashion, then, one might view one money as advancing one market. It is not necessary for a single market, perhaps, to have a common currency, but it seems a natural analog as it enhances the very efficiency sought in moving toward a true common market in the first place.[12]

Perhaps the most important point to be made in this connection is this: At least until the breakup of the EMS, there might have been considered to be a fallback of fixed rates through a quasi-monetary union that could provide a level of exchange-rate stability adequate to the purpose of trade. But the events of 1992 and 1993 only reinforced what many thought even well before, that such systems cannot be expected to be stable in the long run. This point applies to the single market as well, and in two ways. The first is a point made earlier, that the single market itself provides a kind of environment in which maintenance of a fixed rate system is very difficult, if not impossible. The other follows upon this fact: the only default left to the EU is floating or much more flexible exchange rates which by their very nature threaten a single market through the risk of competitive devaluations.

Competitive devaluations have always been considered a real risk in the minds of Europeans, not the least due to the radical reduction in trade that occurred as the result of such devaluations between the two world wars. That it is a real risk depends at least partially on the degree of openness of most European nations, but also on the way in which trade linkages exist between them and what can happen to the competitiveness of one if another devalues. There can result something of a chain reaction of devaluation following upon devaluation (as in Welfens, 1994). It can be appreciated that this would be a significant risk in the minds of traders and the governments that represent them alike. The real risk, as it were, then follows, as certainly everyone cannot devalue against everyone else; it is a return to trade protectionism. Again, such a result is often in the minds of those who have understood and seen the benefits of movement toward a single market. The final risk, in other words, is that of losing the common market and the gains associated with it over the decades, including those most recently stemming from the SEA.[13]

In this sense, then, it may be necessary to move from one market to one money. Again, this is not exactly the kind of consideration that would naturally enter into economic modeling or inclusion in the optimum currency area approach, although it could do so in terms of game theory. But it clearly is a concern, and one that can drive actual political decisions in the direction of EMU, even with full understanding and appreciation of the other costs involved.[14]

The comments above address the question of growth as related to the efficient allocation of resources domestically, especially concerning those resources best devoted to trade. The same concerns generally apply to investments that might be made abroad, seeking greater return there either in terms of portfolio or direct investment. The question of efficient allocation that applies here, however, is how investment might be affected within the EU itself (with the question of certain regional areas being discriminated against in the growth process dealt with later).

Much investment, most especially of course that which is direct, is long term in nature, and the remarks on the difficulty of hedging to avoid exchange risk are pertinent here. Risk of loss of value upon repatriation of earnings or the investments themselves must weigh on the minds of those who invest abroad. It can be, in addition, that the reduction of exchange risk through monetary union can potentially also affect purely domestic investment. The linkage can be seen best through reference to such a system as the EMS, where states had chosen to keep their currencies associated with a nominal anchor such as the DM, and had to suffer higher than normal interest rates as the result. Such interest rates could be identified as providing a damper to domestic investment, hence reducing domestic income and growth.[15] The higher interest rates would, in general, not be the result of a strong asymmetric shock such as German reunification, as outlined earlier, although that certainly was of major macroeconomic concern in the 1990s. Rather they would be ongoing in nature, and associated with a risk premium that markets would insist be represented in a country's interest rate in order to reward anyone who wished to hold that currency against even a rare probability of devaluation against the anchor currency.[16] To the extent that domestic investment is thus harmed, elimination of such risk premia would be welcomed through EMU.[17]

In summary, it is fair to say that there has not been the kind of empirical work that would necessarily speak strongly to large benefits being reaped from reducing exchange-rate variability to zero. Nevertheless, by focusing the question on growth what emerges most clearly are two areas of significance. The first is the possibility of greater growth by encouraging resource allocation based upon comparative advantage, stemming from freeing economic agents of the need to worry about any nominal exchange rate changes at all. This, coupled with a reduction in risk premium on interest rates adding to investment, although also not well measured, suggests EMU being considered a natural complement to the single market. What is perhaps most striking here, however, is how the fear of competitive devaluations and the prospect of a return to protectionism enters the argument. In this case it becomes clear how proponents of EMU can conceive of monetary union as being important, even necessary, to maintain the gains of the common market already in place, and how avoidance of competitive devaluations can resonate to those with a sense of political and historical reality.

Stability

The second area that can be expected to be influenced by movement to a common currency is economic stability, including inflation and unemployment. The impact in this area includes a loss of countercyclical policy, including most obviously monetary policy. Monetary policy, of course, is not lost to the union, but to the individual states that sacrifice their currencies and hence money creation to the common central bank. Moreover, if the

ECB is true to its charter, the Maastricht Treaty, it would in addition find itself constrained in its ability, even at the Community level, to do much in a countercyclical way. This is because a large amount of monetary growth, even under some recession, might find itself reflected in later inflation.

The constraint on policy is not limited to monetary policy; it is extended to fiscal policy as well. Again, if the spirit and letter of the treaty are to be respected, there are rather strict limits on the degree to which governments can use fiscal policy in an expansionary fashion. Also as mentioned, the German government argued for even greater restrictions than those in the treaty, which would even further limit the possibility of running deficits at the state level to deal with recession and unemployment. In this instance there is no serious fallback at the EU level, as the budget itself is so small as to preclude serious possibilities for countercyclical use. Finally, there is the limiting factor on fiscal policy of debt sustainability. The argument is that if governments attempt to run deficits, say, to fight unemployment there will need to be an increase in the interest rate as part of the issuance of extra government debt. If this increase in the interest rate exceeds the growth rate of the economy there is set into motion a dynamic that can quickly lead to unsustainable levels of government debt, the only cure being long and protracted budget surpluses to bring the debt to GDP level back into line (as in Demopoulos and Prodromidis, 1994). If this were not enough there is yet one more constraint. Governments are limited in their ability to tax in common markets, thus constraining the potential for eventually running the surpluses that would be needed to offset any deficits temporarily run for countercyclical reasons (as noted by Bayoumi and Eichengreen, 1993). The message is clear. Fiscal policy in all likelihood cannot be relied upon to deal with unemployment in nearly the way it could by the states independently. As a result, it cannot be relied upon to act in lieu of lost monetary policy.

This might not be considered a problem in general, however, if one accepts what has been a general conclusion of modern macroeconomics, that there is no long-run tradeoff between inflation and unemployment. If, in other words, a country's rate of unemployment will always return to a long run "natural" level based upon structural factors, then countercyclical policy, either monetary or fiscal, is simply ineffectual in the long run. What is being sacrificed is something that finally is not useful, and indeed can be harmful. With a vertical long run Phillips curve, states that are tempted to inflate find themselves both frustrated by not finally being able to lower unemployment while facing accelerating rates of inflation. In this case most now accept the proposition that lower rates of inflation are better than higher, again because there is no positive gain, and zero inflation is best.[18]

The loss of perhaps both traditional forms of macroeconomic policy is supplemented in currency union with the loss of exchange-rate policy, and it is here that one strand of optimum currency area theory is pertinent. If there are asymmetric shocks that can affect one economy more than others then the ability to use the exchange rate to adjust for such a differential impact is lost.

Shocks might be different for different states due to differing industrial structures (as in Kenen, 1969). In such a case, if prices and wages are inflexible, then unemployment could result in that sector of the economy potentially affecting the entire economy (as in Mundell, 1961). If, however, labor is able to move easily from one area to another area not so affected, that can effectively redress the problem; thus labor mobility is one (of several) criteria that can be used to identify optimum currency areas. Alternatively, if capital can move sufficiently, it too could serve to solve the unemployment in the disadvantaged sector.[19] Lacking factor mobility the exchange rate can be changed, according to the theory, in order to quickly realign relative prices and eliminate the unemployment.

Although hardly the only component of what Tower and Willett (1976) prefer to call the optimum currency area "approach," due to the multiplicity of criteria, it is this core vision placing an emphasis on factor (especially labor) mobility that has most often been brought to bear upon the European situation. The question is: How does Europe satisfy the criteria of an optimum currency area in order to best deal with potential asymmetric shocks that could, lacking sufficient labor mobility and an exchange rate to change, leave a country defenseless to respond and having to suffer continuing excessive unemployment?

In the first instance there is the question of how diversified the European states are in terms of their industrial sectors. The very high levels of intra-industry trade that exist between the EU countries speaks to a diversified industrial base that would find any one country less exposed to asymmetric shocks. More direct studies of industrial structure reinforce this conclusion.[20] There is, however, the possibility that the further development of the single market might work in the opposite direction, and yield greater levels of specialization based around specific regions. Reinforcing organizing production around comparative advantage within the broader common market, there is the regional concentration of certain types of industrial activities that could emerge and continue on based upon economies of scale (as in Krugman, 1991). Although hardly a given that the EU will develop in this way, together these outcomes could spell a Community where sector specific shocks could more easily become country specific, in the future yielding the very problem outlined here.

That raises the question of labor mobility, which is generally agreed to be quite low in Europe, and can be expected to remain low based on continuing cultural and linguistic differences.[21] In addition, and as addressed below, although capital mobility is rising and could be even more mobile under EMU, it is not clear that capital will move in such a way as to come to the aid of areas with high unemployment.

In these circumstances then, it is important to ask whether prices and wages are or could be free to move sufficiently to counteract the impact of asymmetric shocks, and thereby avoid the need to have factors move in the first place. There is evidence that such flexibility may be adequate to at least mitigate some of the negative effects of shocks that have an impact at the entire EC level. On the other hand, nominal wage adjustment in response to regional asymmetric shocks that negatively affect employment appears small now (as in Abraham, 1993, and Abraham and Van Rompuy, 1992). Coupled with price stickiness this could indeed indicate a problem, but again the issue is as much dependent upon what the future holds as on present conditions. Could the development of the labor market under conditions of a single market coupled with a single currency influence regional wage flexibility? Bofinger (1994) already notes the willingness of German workers to demonstrate wage restraint and "to accept considerable nominal wage reductions if this is required to secure employment." The argument is that as it becomes clear to labor that there is no longer the exchange rate tool available to be used, then it is clearly up to them to decide whether or not they wish to push for maintaining or increasing nominal wages, or will instead accept the wage levels necessary to yield fuller employment.[22] Again, theoretical models find the need to maintain exchange rates as a tool to deal with sticky prices and wages, but the wage and price reactions themselves may be influenced by the exchange regime in which they are made.[23]

Some evidence, although not perfect, that this may be the case lies in the way Austria has reacted to the establishment of a credible exchange-rate commitment, linking the schilling closely with the DM. Once the commitment was made and seen to be serious, as well as accepted by the major players, according to Hochreitner and Winckler (1995), it forced the unions into adjusting their wage demands around their implications for employment. The proposition here is that Austria in the 1980s actually became an optimum currency area with Germany, although factors were not mobile and asymmetric shocks did occur. The level of nominal and real wage flexibility needed to maintain employment was altered by the regime chosen, in this case a "hard" currency option. Application to an EMU where, once established, the choice of regime will have been virtually permanently made, speaks to the possibility of the same forces operating at the Community level.

At least two factors, however, act to question the applicability of the Austrian case to the EU after EMU.[24] First, Austria possesses a particularly strong system of "social partnership" between industry, labor, and the government, one that favors cooperative solutions. Second, labor is very well represented by the unions, which can act as representatives in this process as well as understand that decisions which are made can be expected to have a larger than localized impact. In this latter way it could be suggested that the structure of the labor market might make a large difference on how wage flexibility could be expected to emerge after monetary union. If labor is well represented by large unions the case could be similar to that in Austria, taking the broader vision. Alternatively, if labor is not well represented, and is more atomistic, then competition will ensure pretty much the same result, maximizing employment opportunities through wage flexibility. It is the intermediate case where unions bargain with strength enough to increase or maintain wages in the face of unemployment, yet do not reflect on the way in which their individual actions affect the entire labor market, that is more problematic. De Grauwe (1992) presents results (due to Calmfors and Driffill) that identify EU countries by their level of centralization in the wage bargaining process, suggesting (p. 25) that countries in the intermediate level "may find it costly to form a monetary union. With each supply shock, wages, and prices in these countries may be affected differently, making it difficult to correct for these differences when the exchange rate is irrevocably fixed." It is interesting, however, and somewhat reassuring to those who believe in the possibilities of a regime shift influencing wage flexibility, that Germany is included in the intermediate range but, as noted above, seems (even in advance of monetary union) to be experiencing some success with wage moderation.[25]

Even if nominal wages are not adjustable enough to insure continued high employment, it is a question of whether or not the exchange rate is an instrument capable of inducing a positive outcome for employment. The theory, of course, is that by devaluing the exchange rate the relative price of tradeables will be increased, thus reducing the demand for imports and increasing the foreign demand for exports. This should be enough, even without any redistribution of factors in the longer run, to put unemployed labor back to work. The devaluation can substitute at the policy level for wage and price flexibility and save the long time that might be required for such flexibility eventually to occur, thus saving a long period of unemployment and less than full output.

There is a question, however, whether such a tool can actually be expected to work in practice in Europe in reaction to asymmetric shocks. First, if the shock hits one or a few goods only then the exchange-rate change would be affecting the entire price structure rather than the ones that specifically need to be changed (as in Bofinger, 1994). Second, exchange-rate changes might not necessarily be an effective tool for achieving relative price adjustment at all. If prices of tradeable goods increase in the country this both increases costs of production and reduces the real income of workers. If there is a response to this with an increase in wages, which further serves to increase prices, then eventually the entire beneficial change in relative prices of the devaluation will be dissipated through price inflation, leaving the country in no better position than when it began. The benefits will "wither away" as it were, and De Grauwe (1992, p. 39) suggests that "there is a lot of empirical evidence . . . that for most of the European countries this withering away of the initially favourable effect of a devaluation will be strong." Indeed, when one examines real wage rates in Europe, that is nominal wages following underlying price levels, one finds they are stable, suggesting a relatively quick responsiveness of wages to prices. This is perhaps especially true of the smaller, more open economies, a point further explored below, and one that would reinforce the choice of a country like Austria to adopt a hard currency option. But the lack of real wage flexibility seems to apply to more than simply the smaller countries (as in Abraham and Van Rompuy, 1992).

Several points are worth making here. First, if it is true that much of the impact of devaluation is lost, then the loss of the exchange-rate instrument is, of course, less important. Second, flexible exchange rates are no option here either, as they are no less than decided devaluations, susceptible to continuing devaluation-inflation spirals. Combined, these two reasons are part of the rationale countries have in the past chosen the hard currency option, in some cases actually revaluing in the face of balance-of-payments problems. As attention is focused on the fixed exchange rate commitment, as above, actors ideally adjust their behavior and make the commitment credible to all, including the outside world in the form of foreign-exchange market participants. Third, even if devaluation can be expected to work in the normal textbook way, the textbooks are also quick to emphasize that absorption has to be cut in an economy in tandem with devaluation. Exchange-rate changes, in other words, are not substitutes but rather complements to restrictive policies, which in turn implies that no matter how it happens, asymmetric shocks of a negative supply type will have to be borne by the economy through a lower standard of living. This does not mean that devaluations, again where effective, cannot serve a useful purpose in switching prices and putting an economy on the path toward stability and the proper resource allocation—especially when that has become skewed—but rather that absorption cuts are probably in the offing anyway.

The final point to be raised is the actual prevalence of asymmetric shocks. Real shocks, it can be argued, such as oil crises or German reunifications, are rare (as in Bean, 1992).[26] Alternatively, differential monetary shocks would disappear completely with monetary union. Obviously there would only be one money supply, so that the kind of shock created in different states in this way would disappear. Moreover, there is evidence that the demand for money is more stable at the EU level than in the individual countries. This holds implications for avoiding demand-oriented shocks that could easily be disruptive, as well as holding promise for the ECB being able to introduce more monetary stability through the EU monetary policy.[27]

Related to the effectiveness of exchange-rate policy above is another area in which a somewhat different strand of optimum currency area theory can be applied to the question of a common currency in Europe related to economic stability—specifically, the area of price stability. As proposed by McKinnon (1963) the more open an economy to trade the more it loses the effectiveness of exchange-rate changes on its balance of trade. Here the more open economy finds that tradeable goods prices represent a large share of total prices. Much of a devaluation is simply and immediately lost to domestic inflation, without an adequate amount of change in relative prices to produce the desired result. This, too, might be an extension of the notion of one market implying one money, in that a single market would involve a more integrated structure through trade and more open economies. A result would be loss of control of exchange rates as effective policy elements. Countries that are more open to one another in trade, in other words, should consider adopting a common currency; openness becomes another criterion for an optimum currency area (De Grauwe, 1992).

An important point raised in this regard is that exchange-rate changes between countries that are open to one another would threaten price level stability. In fact, this was a large part of the argument that money in such a setting could even begin to lose some of its effectiveness if threatened by inflation emanating from—even unnecessary, because they would be ineffective—devaluations (McKinnon, 1963). In a Europe increasingly interested in maintaining price-level stability around the German model this becomes a substantial issue. I have, for example, developed a model in which countries find that their domestic inflation rates are influenced more upon exchange-rate changes the more open are their economies (Overturf, 1994b). Other influential variables include relative price and income elasticities and how critical it is to a country to avoid inflation—where it can be demonstrated that the price and income elasticities are also related to openness (Tower and Willett, 1976). Expansion of the model allows for the conclusion that exchange-rate alterations should be limited, again in order to limit inflation, especially in regard to those countries with which one shares a good deal of trade. Empirical application of the model to the EU suggests again a core group of countries that are good candidates for currency union given this criterion alone, and they include especially the northern European states most usually associated with Germany, but also France. A critical issue has always been what Germany gains from monetary union. While it is certainly open by large-country standards, it is still small enough to reduce the imperative of entirely sacrificing its currency and exchange-rate instrument. Germany nevertheless appears open enough—again it must be emphasized with the "core" group of countries—to consider currency union, especially when its aversion to inflation is explicitly and empirically recognized.

Exchange-rate devaluation, as discussed above, can also threaten to import inflation as the large open (tradeable) sector prices its goods on an international standard and adjusts domestic prices for any exchange-rate changes. However, even with the loss of the exchange-rate instrument due to its ineffectiveness, inflation in close trading partners can easily be validated domestically, again in order to keep tradeable goods prices the same in the different centers that are linked so closely through trade.[28] In this way inflation abroad will be "imported" into the country.

Although not given a great deal of attention in academic literature this is an important point, especially for the Germans, and perhaps even more so for the Bundesbank. That institution had always been loath to sacrifice the possibility of realignments, particularly DM revaluations, in the EMS for the salutary effect they could bring to German domestic inflation under pressure of prices coming from abroad. They would find such revaluations effective and advisable even with the implications for domestic producers of tradeable goods (Kaufmann and Overturf, 1991).

Monetary union could be a two-edged sword for those countries that worry about inflation in general, and imported inflation in particular. This refers directly to the nature of money creation under monetary union and how effectively the ECB might in the long run carry out its mandate under the treaty for price stability. If the ECB is as or more effective in this capacity than, say the Bundesbank, then there should be no concern. Moreover, it could assure even greater price stability as it would avoid the problem of imported inflation.

Central bank credibility has been receiving a considerable amount of attention, with much of it centering on the notion of time inconsistency. The idea itself is simple and persuasive.[29] Given no long-run tradeoff between inflation and unemployment, the optimal level of inflation is zero for an economy. A government might commit itself publicly to such a target (or, alternatively, to a very low rate of inflation). Microeconomic distortions with implications for unemployment, or short-run political motivations, however, might tempt the present or future authorities to inflate somewhat so as to take advantage of a short-run inflation-unemployment tradeoff.[30] In other words, the commitment in the long run is not credible (it is time inconsistent) because the private sector is aware of this temptation and will expect the government to eventually bow to it. Economic agents, therefore, will bid up prices and wages in expectation of what the government might do, and will actually do so to such a degree as to force the authorities out of the temptation altogether, because inflation would already be high enough to counteract the inducement. In such a setting inflation is built into the structure, although obviously it is not optimal because no one desires the existing, or even any, level of inflation.

The only way out of this conundrum is for a country to demonstrate its commitment. A monetary authority without a long-standing reputation for low inflation might do this, for example, by setting its money supply growth rate to fix the exchange rate of its own currency against that of a low-inflation country. Here again, however, exchange rates can change, and there must be something about the exchange-rate commitment that makes it more credible than simply an announcement to not inflate. Another possibility for a high inflation country would be to give up its monetary policy entirely to a central bank with greater credibility on this front—one issuing a common currency. This would work, presumably, but a low inflation country, such as Germany, would need to be more concerned about giving its money creation up to such an organization.

What is the expectation for the ECB in this regard? The structure of the ECB includes the central bank governors of all of the participating states on the governing council, which in turn includes several countries with less reputation than the Bundesbank. On the other hand, they are central bankers from independent central banks. That by itself implies a reputation for a commitment to price stability. In addition, the ECB—besides being forced by its charter to adhere to price stability—is independent, and several studies have demonstrated the relationship between independence and lower inflation rates. Whether or not that would continue to be the case is another question, as is, perhaps more importantly, whether the ECB would find itself able to operate free from political influence at the Community level.[31] Ideally, it should be less influenced than present central banks simply because it would represent the entire area rather than the separate states. National politicians carry less weight here, as do electoral cycles (see Bofinger, 1994). There should be less pressure as well to deal with regional problems, because the monetary instrument is less applicable here (see Beck, 1992). Moreover, there should be less confusion about the nature of shocks affecting individual economies, due to money demand evidently being more stable at the EU level and the reduction in number of potential monetary shocks emanating from different central banks (Wihlborg and Willett, 1991), again lowering political pressure on the ECB. Alternatively, EU-wide pressure to inflate could become an issue, especially in the face of large amounts of unemployment, which could be translated through the European Council in a way that might be difficult to ignore. Put against this must be a broadly felt understanding of the long-run costs of inflation and the lack of power of monetary policy to do anything other than lower unemployment in the short run.

In conclusion to this section on economic stability, there is reason to find a small group of countries, a "core" of northern European states most attracted to EMU. The greater degree of interdependent industrial structure (implying less concern over asymmetric shocks) and the greater amount of openness (implying less value for the exchange rate as a policy instrument) among these states, the more sense it makes to have a two-speed Europe.

In the broader question of whether EMU makes economic sense, the considerations here find all of the difficulties associated with the traditional optimum currency area approach—at least in its asymmetric shock emphasis—in application to Europe. Nevertheless, it appears that further development of the single market may speak to an increased value for one money flowing naturally from one market. In other words, independent exchange-rate policies may not be effective in a growing single market (even if market structure does not become more consistent among European states and labor remains immobile). Moreover wages and prices might develop the degree of responsiveness that would make independent exchange-rate policies redundant in one market—even if asymmetric shocks would be more than rare events.

A somewhat different strain of optimum currency area theory—that devoted to price stability related to openness—can also explain why countries would be attracted by EMU. As Europe comes closer together in trade, and maintains its aversion to inflation, such considerations as the limitation of value of the exchange rate as economic policy because of inflation come more into play. In addition, imported inflation in a more open environment also becomes more critical, and elicits a closer look at creating a monetary institution at the EU level that can be designed in such a way as to adhere to a stated objective of price stability.

Justice

Movement toward monetary union raises the objective of distributional justice on at least two levels, one at the EU level with regional disparity, and the other at the state level dealing with social welfare programs. Regional disparity in the short and medium runs could be expected to be influenced by asymmetric shocks, and, lacking either an adequate measure of price and wage flexibility or factor mobility, there would certainly be call to ease some of the regional pain involved. There is not the type of fiscal transfer system at the EU level that is present in more federal states, nor is there expected to be for a good period of time. Bayoumi and Masson (1994), for example, note how much the existence of a federal government—to which tax payments may drop and from which transfer payments may increase—can ease the impact of recession and unemployment. They estimate such stabilization effects to be on the order of 30 cents on the dollar in the United States and 17 cents in Canada. As much of this role has been taken by individual European state governments in the past—and their budgets will be constrained under monetary union—it is unclear how much this will lead to pressure to establish a larger part to be played in the future at the EU level. There is great controversy, of course, on the appropriate role the Community should take. One opinion is that real shocks will eventually need to be reflected in the standards of living of those in the affected area, and such transfers can only delay this result, with possible negative impact on encouraging factor mobility.

Longer run regional disparities may also be created through differential Community regional growth rates encouraged by a single market. Briefly the argument is that economies of scale, economies of agglomeration and a dynamic allocation of resources based upon comparative advantage could find some areas growing much faster than others. Backwaters, according to this theory, could occur, that might require transfers from the richer areas in order to reflect questions of equity and to insure political cohesion in the Community (as in Costa, 1990). There is a good deal of controversy here as well, including that of whether one can expect the single market to develop in this way at all.[32] This is an area that has nonetheless been accepted as being implied by movement toward EMU, at least at the EU institutional level. As indicated earlier, German opinion has become less pleased with the prospects of large scale redistribution within the Community, perhaps providing yet another argument for a two-speed Europe where union is implemented first among the core states.

The second area regarding economic justice is how social welfare preferences differ within the Community on redistribution of income at the state level. It will be recalled that the Danes, living in a country that values such redistribution highly and supports it heavily with one of the highest tax-transfer systems in the world, considered this one of the problems in voting for Maastricht in 1992. Their concern would seem to be legitimate, for even though one might suggest it is possible for individual states to maintain these systems, the single market and implied harmonization of taxes across the EU point in the other direction.

Freedom

The separate objective of economic freedom could include the freedom to trade across state boundaries, and as such it could add to the section above on free trade and growth. Here it is enough to pay attention to freedom of capital movements and state seigniorage, especially as these have been expressed areas of concern in association with EMU.

Freedom from exchange controls, or other restrictions on the free movement of capital, is only recently part of the history of the European Union, and there is always a risk that they might be reintroduced by governments alarmed over capital outflows. This again is an area of some concern expressed by Europeans that has not found full representation in economic discussions. The ability to make efficient decisions on the location of capital argues for a system in which the risk of losing the ability to repatriate earnings is low (as in Costa, 1990). This would be especially true in a single market, and was part of the thinking in including freedom from restriction of capital as part of the SEA, not to mention the Rome Treaty. EMU would add to the permanency of capital freedom through making exchange controls obsolete and other forms of limiting capital movements more difficult.

Seigniorage is the ability that governments have to issue money to purchase government debt, the loss of which would also accompany EMU. At one time this was considered an important issue, as several southern European countries had a significant portion of their budgets financed in this way, relying upon it in lieu of a more efficient tax system. That is now much less so, as seigniorage is much lower in these states (see Bean, 1992, and De Grauwe, 1992), and so does not seem to enter more than marginally into the debate on currency union.[33] The fact that it is an unfair tax through inflation, hence its inclusion in this section, and would need to be eliminated anyway in a single market without capital controls only adds to the insignificance of the issue.[34]

Conclusion

Several conclusions may be drawn from an approach to the economics of monetary union based upon emphasizing economic objectives. First, and perhaps most clearly, a two-speed Europe, at least in a monetary dimension, emerges very frequently in the examination. A core of northern states would seem to benefit from currency union, based on the degree to which they are, and can be expected to be, dependent upon one another through industrial structure and trade. This leads to the importance of eliminating exchange risk, perhaps especially in a longer term sense, and eliminating the exchange-rate changes that can create price instability. The potentially heavy political pressure that could arise from non-core states for regional transfers reinforces the possibility of several states going on ahead at, say, an earlier stage of the process.

Second, and more generally, a concern over growth would reduce the traditional emphasis placed in such examinations on short-run volatility of exchange rates on trade and investments, and focus instead more closely on the allocation decisions made in the long run and how they are influenced by exchange-rate misalignments. Perhaps most interesting, however, is highlighting the risk of competitive devaluations and the risk of return to protectionism, and how currency union might be considered a major advantage in this regard. One market, one money, in other words, may make sense as a reasonable rationale in this regard, and not simply a slogan.

Third, by suggesting decreasing usefulness for the standard macroeconomic tools in their efficacy in achieving economic stability, again in an increasingly integrated Europe, there is the possibility of little cost in their sacrifice to a common central bank. Moreover, gains in avoiding inflation enhanced through avoidance of imported inflation enter the conversation. The question of the credibility of the new central bank, however, especially under political pressure at the EU level, needs to be left unsettled.

Fourth, and also adding to the uncertainty, is the potential need for fiscal transfers as evidence of economic justice. The very value of these transfer payments is of no little controversy itself, both from political and economic vantage points.

Fifth, regarding economic freedom, the avoidance of reintroduction of exchange and other controls on the free flow of capital speaks again more forcefully for some movement toward EMU in a Europe that seeks to maintain and enhance a single market.

Finally, it might be reiterated that the discussion framed in this way has the advantage of speaking directly to the concerns frequently expressed by Europeans when they debate monetary union. These include avoiding competitive devaluations, establishing a zone of monetary stability, mitigating imported inflation, and avoiding (perhaps forever) protectionism, controls and the loss of the common market.

TEN

Political Theory and EMU

In the realm of international relations, integration theory comprises a fairly well-developed body of thought devoted to the process of integration and the interaction of states dealing with economic issues. These "grand theories" are examined here in reference to monetary union; much of the purely descriptive analysis dealt with in many political works is contained in the preceding chapters that deal with historical development.

These grand theories include neofunctionalism and realism, theories that have been the basis for controversy and disagreement among scholars over the years. Besides being considered in many ways alternative explanations of the same events and outcomes, there is not even full agreement that the theories themselves possess the kind of explanatory power that would allow them to be accepted as reasonable paradigms in approaching the interactions of nation-states in this area. In addition, there is the feeling that empirical work in support is only at the initial stages, and is, at this point, inconclusive (Eichengreen and Frieden, 1995).

Nevertheless, and in spite of often withering fire, the theories have survived and proved resilient enough to continue to serve as the basis for much of the theoretical work related to the EU and well beyond in the field of international relations.[1] The resiliency of the theories is undoubtedly due to the insights that follow from their application; insights that would not necessarily follow from other explanations. In this chapter I will adopt these approaches in order to identify relationships and results from the monetary integration process in Europe that would not clearly follow from focusing on a more detailed historical analysis or from consulting economic theory and measurement. Political theory, in other words, provides a view that can be useful in supplementing history and economics in describing the movement toward EMU, as well as the potential for changed conditions that might alter the calculus that brought together the agreement at Maastricht. Caporaso and Keeler (1995, p. 47), again in full recognition of the drawbacks, find that "grand theory, in this sense, provides an encompassing structure to help us make sense of 'findings' and identifies gaps and inconsistencies in the collective research enterprise."

That is its purpose here, as well. It is not to provide another article to add to the score in what seems to have become a question of dueling theories. Rather it is to fill out, to complete, an examination of monetary union in such a way as to make as understandable as possible a complex area that entails the intersection of historical, economic, and political variables. To this end, then, both theories will be looked to for evidence on how they can inform the process of monetary integration in Europe, even if one does not feel the need to accept the entirety of assumptions and implications of neofunctionalism and realist thought.

In addition to reinforcing some of the conclusions that follow from an economic analysis, as presented in the previous chapter, the political view adds several critical notions that illuminate a difficult process leading to monetary integration. First, both broad forms of political theory stress the importance of external influences. Second, spillovers remain an important component of the integration process. And finally, monetary integration seems to make sense in the somewhat narrowly defined calculus of political power presented by the realists, even, in the most difficult case, for Germany.

Neofunctionalism

A proper definition of neofunctionalism, even for the limited purposes required of it here, demands a good sense of its predecessor, functionalism. Functionalist thought developed after the second world war in the concern of Mitrany (1966) and others for avoiding further wars of the kind that had devastated Europe. Accordingly, this approach contains the strong normative flavor associated with the elimination of war, and as part of this the associated system of nation-states and the political ideologies that drove them. Functionalists felt that peace could come by increasingly marginalizing the state through non-political actors responding to technical and economic forces. The conditions of the postwar world, according to the theory, supported such a result. There was, for example, a waning of the older intrastate ideological conflict between labor and capital in favor of greater overall productivity, or, alternatively stated, there was a greater emphasis on productivity over distribution. Likewise, there was an increasing degree of technological interdependence in the world, one that called out for solutions at the international level. Economics, then, was considered one of the prime areas of concern for the functionalists, because economies of scale would imply increasingly larger markets to reap the significant benefits of such large-scale production.

Indeed, it was these technical and economic factors that provided the driving force in pure functionalism. The theory was "functional" in the sense that it suggested the importance of responding to felt needs, responses that promised to improve the people's standard of living, and that could only be enacted beyond the territorial constraints provided by states and polities. These latter needed to be overcome, as it were, and when they were there would be the integration that would eventually make them unnecessary.

The integration resulting from this process was quite special. It was more administrative than political in nature, with tasks being performed by groups better described as coordinating agencies than political governments. It would correspond best to a smooth running, rational technocracy, with experts coming together to solve international problems of coordination in specific task areas for the benefit of all. Moreover, in simply responding to the economic needs and opportunities provided, the shifting away from the political sphere would not be controversial or threatening. Instead, the venue would be international and non-territorial, cutting across boundaries in a very quiet, unobtrusive fashion. Ideally, the resulting coordination, coalition, and integration would not even be regional.[2]

The progression of this salutary change was to occur as people saw that the new institutions were successful, and support for them was developed as they demonstrated their ability to solve broad functional problems. Again all of this was to happen in response to technological and economic imperatives, and to felt needs. "Spillovers" from one area to another would propel the process forward, and these spillovers could either be between sectors or within them. A pertinent example of the former would be if a customs union seemed to demand coordination of monetary policies, while one of the latter would be if monetary coordination between states was not adequate to the job and required direction by a central organization.[3]

The transfer of authority to the broader organizations was to be painless. Nations were seen to obstruct the most efficient administration, and so, as it was learned that international institutions could do a better job, there would be an increasing delegation of authority. The states, however, were not the prime actors in this process; it was the technical elites who in their quiet and efficient way would gradually wrest control away from the national states. The loyalties of the people would follow in this transfer, and they would support the process.

It is evident even from this brief description that there was room for more development of the theory itself, as well as some sense that the normative basis of the theory, laudable as it was, might conflict with the continuing power of political forces. Indeed it was in these very areas that the neofunctionalists—a group early on associated with such names as Haas,

Lindberg, Nye, Puchala and Schmitter—developed their generally sympathetic elaboration of functionalist thought.

The neofunctionalists, for example, found that there was a need to define the "dependent variable" of the analysis, and concluded that it was integration itself, specifically regional integration. This implied a distinct end product for the process, although it was generally agreed that the process of integration would form the best basis of examination, and one that was not the same as that of the functionalists. In fact, some criticism has been aimed at the neofunctionalists because, by focusing upon states forming larger groupings—in some ways bigger states—they were seemingly reinforcing the state system rather than suggesting a reduction in its power.[4]

The neofunctionalists also found it more realistic to not ignore the political side. In fact they considered all things political, even if there was a possible distinction between economic and social concerns ("low" politics) and more traditional political and legal issues ("high" politics). In particular, as the functionalists had put the greatest weight of their attention on nonpolitical actors, the neofunctionalists addressed the importance of those political actors residing, as it were, in international organizations that could help act as catalysts to change and lead states toward greater integration.

There were, of course, concepts the neofunctionalists closely shared with the functionalists. These included the attention to more global social and economic concerns than state-centered interests. The basis of impetus toward integration was still functional in nature, still "rational," in considering efficient international responses to technological and economic structural changes. Spillovers were an important—indeed, very important—part of the process. Likewise, cooperation at the supranational level was seen to eventually transform those in society, both political elites and the general populace, into altering their incentives and allegiances to the higher level.

Upon this base the neofunctionalists attempted to establish a unified model of dynamic change, again leading to the integration of states. They constructed a theory of politics, establishing exactly how economic and technical details become translated into political integrative outcomes. Specifically, integration comes through the interaction of political forces, in the form of interest groups that create solutions to problems with the help of those in the supranational organizations themselves. When these solutions are successful, there is a shifting of loyalties, expectations, and political activities to a new center.[5] Actors then move beyond the state as a basic framework of action through elite interaction, the interaction of those who can gain by supranational organization with those in the international institutions themselves, who act to help engineer changes and outcomes. The latter, in fact, are especially important, and they actually can be counted upon to "go out and look for business."[6]

Spillovers, again, are key, as they provide the dynamic for change. They can either be functional or political in nature. Functional spillovers occur from the discontinuities implied by prior integration moves, creating pressures for further acts of integration to resolve the inherent problems. Lindberg (1994, p. 107) says that "in its most general formulation, 'spillover' refers to a situation in which a given action, related to a specific goal, creates a situation in which the original goal can be assured only by taking further actions, which in turn create a further condition and a need for more action, and so forth."

As simple as it sounds this concept is actually sophisticated because it requires that the assigned tasks be "inherently expansive," needed so as to overcome a "built-in autonomy of functional contexts."[7] Helping in the task expansion are a convergence of state goals and expectations, an understanding of the gains to be had by delegating difficult problems to the higher level, and again, the players in the central institutions themselves creating situations where integration makes sense. Connected to these last thoughts is the concept of political spillover, whereby loyalties are transferred to the new organizations, encouraging even further movement of decision making to the supranational level.[8]

In these ways then, the neofunctionalists saw integration as proceeding in a manner that recognized the political side. Opportunities for action brought forth by those that could gain by them were used in a supranational setting, and abetted by those who were in the organizations themselves, to imply more and more transfer of authority to Community institutions. The public was not really a part of the movement or analysis, except to the extent that they would follow the results with their allegiances. The purely national states and actors were thus subverted, and although the process was hardly smooth and spillovers hardly unidirectional and inevitable, the power was there to integrate.

During the 1960s and 1970s there was a significant and general slowdown, and even reversal, of the integration process in Europe, due as much as anything to the reestablishment of intergovernmentalism associated with de Gaulle, and reinforced by divisive reactions to the oil crises. This was accepted at the time as a major blow to the neofunctionalist theory, because it suggested that integration in Europe, much the source and evidence behind the theory, was not inexorable. It is true that the neofunctionalists had emphasized that the process, including the concept of spillover, could not be deemed automatic, that it was contingent upon conditions, and even that state actors could be important impediments. But there was nevertheless inherent in the theory the notion that the description of the integration process was adequate enough to be applied to Europe. In the instance it appeared as though there was not a sufficient power in spillovers, that loyalties of elites were not being transferred to the community level, and that Community institutions were, if anything, almost powerless.[9] Indeed, some of the caveats introduced into the theory appeared more predictive than the theory itself, including the possibility that spillovers were mainly autonomous. The result was a rather mixed system, where the states would remain strong and supranational organizations weak, the latter devoted only to fulfilling certain specific tasks. Low politics, in one particularly famous and difficult reappraisal of the value of the theory by Haas himself, would remain low and inadequate to the task of moving on to eventual political integration.[10] Political forces were too strong to be overcome.

In spite of the fact that the theory was almost abandoned, several events that occurred during the 1980s led to its rediscovery and reapplication as theory. The events were first, the actions leading to a more genuine single market associated with the SEA, and then EMU. Not only were spillovers again to be viewed as important to integration in these cases, but the impetus behind them was still the low politics of "civil society, socioeconomic interests, and technology," or the "transformative potential of civil society."[11] Economics, in other words, was again driving political integration.

Much of the original functional and neofunctional thought could now be applied to the single internal market. First, external, economic, and technical forces argued for an integrated response at the European level. A first condition, however, was the greater openness to international trade in Europe (associated with the worldwide growth of trade), as reflected and enhanced by the gradual multilateral removal of many trade barriers during the postwar years, but increasingly represented in European intra-industry trade that could take advantage of economies of scale. This, in turn, is related to the greater competitiveness and growth of the U.S. and Japanese economies, a development not ignored in Europe, and again seen to be associated with the ability to utilize economies of scale in a large market. The turnaround of both of these economies from the disastrous effects of the years of oil crisis argued that here was a model for emulation, a model that needed European cooperation in order to follow. Finally, there was the revolutionary growth in capital mobility. Technical advances in particular made transferring monies across borders easy, even often in spite of capital controls, and insured the interdependence of economies and their polities in the ways described in previous chapters.

The underlying conditions for a more liberal policy, enhancing the flow of goods, services, labor, and capital among the European economies, were ripe. Labor was not strong, this being important because at least organized labor often finds itself in opposition to free trade. In addition, macroeconomic policies were converging, at least attitudinally, in terms of the accepted model of states around the German prototype.

In such a setting, there was what has been described as the "surprise" of the SEA, which can be explained using a neofunctionalist interpretation.

First, and reiterating, the conditions were right, and provided the kind of external stimulus of a technical and economic type needed to create an integrative movement. European firms, as very interested elites, had a distinctive stake in creating the conditions for extension of their market well beyond that implied by the national borders of the individual states. In the liberal setting, again accompanied by relatively low pressure in the labor markets, such an expansion of production to serve the greater area could be viewed as complementary to, and even an example of, general deregulation and reduction of government control and direction to industry.[12] More typical state-led methods of enhancing growth had been judged to fail during the early 1980s, and it was seen as the right time to do something about it.

Second, the way in which the SEA was brought off can also be argued to fit the neofunctionalist mold. As the objective was to bring the states closer together so as to allow for more secure production and trade at the EC level, the community seemed a natural basis for the desired outcome of freer markets. Here Sandholtz and Zysman (1994) find that the single market was the result of elite level bargaining between European industry and EC institutions, leading to freer trade and factor flows. Governments acquiesced because of the positive implications promised for growth of their economies. Although the governments were there and did the negotiating, in the purest neofunctionalist fashion it was the EC and non-political elites that forged the result. Again, Sandholtz and Zysman (1994, p. 205) suggest that "the significance of the role of business, and of its collaboration with the Commission, must not be underestimated. European business and the Commission may be said to have together bypassed national government processes and shaped an agenda that compelled attention and action."

Third, spillovers were present, in spite of the surprise registered by many. Of course, within the bargaining around the single market was the need to move from unanimity to majority voting, for without this it would have been impossible to move forward. It was unlikely that agreement in all of these areas could have taken place in a purely intergovernmental setting among the original six; in an expanded EC it seemed impossible. The many individual components of the SEA needed the same movement on the political front, majority voting, that had in fact caused the celebrated retreat from integration associated with the years of de Gaulle. It will be remembered that the voting only applied to the components of the SEA itself, and not even all of those, but it was still a remarkable step.[13]

Another evidence of spillover here is the prior existence, since 1979, and perceived smooth functioning of another collaborative EC institution, the EMS. The establishment and success of this institutional forerunner, even during the dark days of Eurosclerosis and pessimism, allowed the players to think in terms of the EC as a proper venue for institutionalizing the single market. In fact, it is most difficult to imagine a move on to the single market without the prior, at least perceived, success of the EMS.[14]

The next institutional move as represented by Maastricht also can be said to fit parts of the theory well. This includes an external component, the technological advances that allow for massive flows of capital from one center to another virtually instantaneously. This fact, coupled with the objective of the single market, which includes capital mobility as an important component, carries implications for independent monetary polices among the states of the EC. The result is that, again due partly to external forces, it would be difficult in the long run to come to an intergovernmental result that would be as satisfactory. It would not take long for the exchange markets to reinforce the notion of the inconsistency trinity that a quasi-union, as represented by the narrow-band EMS, would not be stable in these conditions. And so bargaining occurred that would promise to take Europe on to a higher level of at least economic integration, with a considerable transfer of authority to be made to a European central bank.

There are several cases to be made for spillovers, as well. First is the classic spillover that the single market requires EMU to function well. There is no need to reiterate the arguments, both pro and con, of this proposition, but there is the notion that without EMU the single market could be lost through competitive devaluations and a return to protectionism.[15]

Second, a more political, or at least power-oriented, spillover has been specified in the literature. This suggests that the single market and the prior stability of exchange rates has led to interest groups concerned with maintaining conditions for the maintenance of open markets and exchange-rate stability. These broadly include those engaged in open trade, of course, but also financial interests that represent foreign investments. Stability is important to these groups, and increasing central bank independence has only strengthened their interest and, indeed, power.[16] In such a setting a natural spillover would be the need to "lock in" monetary stability, which could be more insured by an independent ECB devoted by charter to price stability than it could by state central banks, always at the risk of political pressure.[17] International institutions are difficult to create, but, once created they produce "more consistent, routinized and enduring international behavior."[18]

A third spillover, of course, moves the argument on to the next level. That is, if the ECB is to be able to follow its mandate of price stability of a single currency among a group of states that have independent budgetary authority, the success of the institution could in some circumstances be threatened by fiscal excess. This is the German position, and one that, irrespective of its veracity, already finds articulation in the treaty. Moving sovereignty over money creation to the EC level can also be seen to imply the need for greater coordination and control at that level over state budgetary policy.

In some ways, however, the neofunctionalist approach does not seem as fully applicable to the SEA and EMU cases as the points above suggest. First, it is not clear how much the EC leadership itself was instrumental in bringing about the final results. The same might be said for European industry and financial interest pressure. It could be that, as Moravcsik (1994) posits for the SEA but could just as easily apply to Maastricht, the results stem simply from intergovernmental bargaining in the realist mode, albeit with states representing positions formed from domestic interest groups. The governments did the actual bargaining in both cases, and it could be said that the results coalesced around the lowest common denominator of state interests, with as little power as possible flowing to the Community.

It is also not clear how much the extension of authority that has occurred or is expected to occur is not limited to a particular sector. The limit of majority voting to single act provisions, for example, was quite specific, while the EMU seems finally to be limited to monetary affairs. The development of the EU in general, according to this view, is overwhelmingly economic and barely political; an economic adult accompanying a political child. The question remains, then, how far and how fast can the Community extend, raising many of the questions applied to broadly functionalist theory during a time when there appeared many fewer applications than the late 1980s and early 1990s.[19]

Somewhat more positively in summary to this section, it might be agreed that neofunctionalist political theory as applied to EMU adds value to the analysis in terms of the importance of external economic forces needing to find recognition in some form of Community institution building, this reinforced by the concept of spillovers. Moreover, the actual transfer of authority that was agreed on at Maastricht does not seem entirely consistent with a result of the lowest common denominator; nor does it seem compatible with an entirely strict limit on the future transfer of sovereignty. As pointed out before, there are few stronger signs of the sovereignty of a state than the creation of its own money. Even the limited movement toward EPU underscores this fact. Finally, the presence of the institutions themselves and their representatives in providing a forum for the negotiations, as well as the burgeoning interest in international lobbies at the EC level, indicate the need for caution in rejecting the value of international actors in the process of integration.[20]

Realism

Some of the criticisms noted over the application of neofunctionalism to European integration mirror a larger debate among political scientists on the value of neofunctionalism in general. The problem is the reduced emphasis placed on state bargaining as a critical part of the process in analyzing European integration, and the lack of attention to state priorities in the more general theory. Again, in the European case, there is felt by some to be too much emphasis on international actors, almost to the exclusion of those who actually do the bargaining and forge the outcomes, that is, those who speak and act for the states. Governments, in this alternative view, matter a good deal. To degrade their influence, say, by placing greater emphasis on the low politics of economic interest group motivations, misses much of the important consideration of the establishment, the use and interaction of state power. What is missing, in other words, is the state, and the calculations of states when they come together with others to decide outcomes that will imply their sharing of power, or even sacrificing it to a larger grouping. By paying less attention to the gains and sacrifices of the power of states in such negotiations, neofunctionalists, according to this view, are missing the most consequential parts of the analysis.

An alternative is to focus much more closely on the power, interest, and conflict resolution that are at the center of realist thought.[21] For realism, power is the most important variable, often associated with security interests, as represented by the international distribution of power. Nation-states here are the dominant players, representing the final nucleus of power in a world that is anarchistic at the global level. As states finally have nowhere else to look than their own resources for their maintenance, they must be continuously concerned about keeping and increasing their power; they are power maximizers in the language of social science. The state, therefore, is at the center in deciding its own interests and objectives, which it does in a rational way, and it can be expected to represent those interests at the international level in its (even violent) interaction with other states.[22]

In this vision then, the states are dominant, and all other actors in the system are subordinate. In pure realist thought, adding in no little measure to the simplicity and elegance of the theory, there is, consequently, little concern with underlying influences. Party politics, pressure groups, and the like are of small importance here. The theory is not what might be termed "bottom up," as it is the role of the authorities to only represent their own natural, or state interests in an uncertain and even dangerous world. More specifically, there is little serious influence that can be brought to bear by international organizations or the people that represent them. They really do not enter effectively into the state calculation of interests, except to the extent that they might be used to further state power. They certainly do not represent any higher level of authority than that of the nation-state; and giving up power to them makes little sense in a setting in which states are clearly loath to sacrifice their sovereignty. Likewise, realism has until recently had something of a difficult time in handling economic interests because the economy has traditionally been viewed as being shaped by the states to best serve their own interests. Politics drives economics.

Similar to the case of neofunctionalism, there has been something of a resurgence of realism in application to the integration movements of the Community. Part of this is due to the criticism leveled at neofunctionalism regarding its depreciation of inherent state interests. Another part is surely due to the openness of modern analysts who work in the realist model to changes in the international scene that are more than simply structural alterations in the distribution of power, changes that in turn can make an important difference to states as they are concerned with their power. Allowance for these external influences—what some call "process level" variables that can include the type of economic and technical considerations important to the neofunctionalists—adds a richness to the analysis that does only little damage to its purity. Mansfield, for example, quotes Nye saying that "at the systemic level, in addition to the distribution of power, states experience constraints and opportunities because of changes in the levels of world economic activity, technological innovations, shifts in patterns of transnational interactions, and alterations in international norms and institutions" (Mansfield, 1994, p. 8).[23]

Realist theory has, in a similar vein, been adapted to allow for recognition of domestic actors and politics. Without necessarily sacrificing attention on the role of states and their concern with their own power, this expansion of the theoretical base informs the way states identify their own interests. National interests, in other words, are often now seen to be constructed at one level from the underlying confluence of domestic interests, which are then taken by those acting for the state and translated into positions to be taken in interaction with other states.[24]

The realist approach can be used to provide further insight into the subject of monetary union in Europe. One important question that the structure of its theory can address is exactly why states would be willing to sacrifice their own sovereignty in this way. In fact, it is somewhat puzzling why Europeans would have even seriously considered EMU in the first place, and why the pressure for EMU has continued, in spite of some variance in enthusiasm, since the breakup of the Bretton Woods system. This way of phrasing the questions goes beyond economic and historical examination, and beyond neofunctionalist contributions, to the very heart of the matter. The power of the state needs to be at the center of any analysis that attempts to explain a sacrifice of sovereignty.

The answers to these questions are perhaps easier for the EU states other than Germany than they are for Germany itself. The small, open, economies of the Community, being heavily influenced by the larger states in trade and capital flows, have had little to lose and at least something to gain in terms of some minimal influence over Community monetary policy that would arise from the establishment of a European central bank. To some extent this rationale applies equally to France. In being forced by greater international interdependence as well as induced by the logic of the model to commit to policy austerity as the best means to foster growth, France has found itself tied to German policy not of its own making. Losing effective policy control in the EMS after adopting the goals of low inflation and fixed exchange rates was probably the clearest manifestation of this. By embracing EMU France would be able to at least have a seat at the table, even if that seat is in the very restrictive environment of the constitutional ECB.[25]

The most difficult question, however, is that of Germany itself. Why would Germany be willing to sacrifice the DM, what some consider the best currency in the world, for a euro over which it would of necessity have less control? Moreover, and as outlined in the work above, Germany has been frequently at the forefront of integration efforts in the monetary realm, including the Werner Report, the EMS, and Maastricht. The fact that it emphasized the importance of convergence as a necessary precursor to EMU does not diminish this seeming enthusiasm for the endeavor.

The typical answer that EMU is an economic manifestation of a political commitment to Europe in a sense begs the question, especially from a realist perspective, that would still find the need to identify why Germany would wish to sacrifice its sovereignty in any fashion to a broader Europe.[26] There remains, in other words, the issue of whether or not it is possible to see a benefit for Germany to join a common currency, in spite of the lack of apparent economic rationale.[27] Again, it must be remembered that at Maastricht the national executives did the actual bargaining, and approved the outcomes (as in Smith and Sandholtz, 1995), so it remains material to identify their motives, as no one, including perhaps especially the Germans, was in the position of blithely sacrificing sovereignty.

Once more, it is in structuring the question in this way that calls most clearly for a realist response. Much of the material presented to this point can be brought to bear on this question, but it is only by explicitly using the model that makes it the most difficult to justify German incentives that one can fully appreciate the result. Neofunctionalism, specifically, justifies the move to EMU in some ways too easily, by identifying spillovers and not fully considering the forfeiture of power that the move entails. In this case realism, by explicitly recognizing state actors and the importance of power, promises not only to help explain EMU but to determine if there may be implications for the future of the EU as an institution that might not follow from other approaches, specifically in reaction to altered world conditions.

As international power lies at the heart of the objective of the state in this approach, one needs to define the basis of that power. Critics of realism have found this to be something of a defect in the analysis, as the theory does not always allow for a clearly defined and potentially measurable objective function for states, as opposed to individuals in a more economic computation, to attempt to maximize in a system of constrained optimization. Attempts to define a state utility function in a realist model have not always been persuasive. The "national capabilities" variables do not always convey the full sense of actual political power, for example, and are often difficult to see as being additive in any actual calculation.[28]

For Germany this difficulty in defining power has not been so large a problem during the postwar years, as it could be much less concerned with the military side of its objective function. This does not mean that there was no need for the state to be concerned with security, but constraints on rearmament, both external and internal (the latter including an inherently pacifist attitude engendered by memories of the past), reduced its importance. Germany, in other words, could simply focus on economic growth as virtually the sole component of its objective function. Economic growth needed to be tempered with low inflation if for no other reason than for avoiding the social instability Germany has traditionally identified with inflation, but this was hardly a problem in a country whose message to the world has been that inflation actually hampers growth. This notion fits well in the realist model because it associates German views on its own power clearly in a structural way, the reorganization of power that resulted from the second world war. Moreover, conditions in the postwar world provided a gift to Germany (and Japan for that matter), the lack of need to balance their state objective function between the military and the economic. Germany could simply pursue growth.

It can be argued that the best way to pursue growth, at least for a state that does not contain a huge internal market, is through international trade since the static and dynamic gains from trade can be expected to increase national income and growth.[29] In such a setting state policy can be directed toward freer trade. Indeed, in Germany, compared to the late nineteenth century or the interwar years, postwar policy has emphasized free trade, or openness, as an engine for growth.

Attention to the internal situation, although not required in the more classic realist vision, is able to capture some of the complexity of real-world agenda setting at the state level. It is possible to suggest that Germany's domestic interests in the postwar years were not to be at variance with the state objective of addressing growth through free trade. Labor and capital—both abundant factors of production—supported an open trading order while agriculture was declining and supported extensively through the common agricultural policy of the Community.[30]

The same conclusion appears to hold on a more narrow definition of interest. Business and financial interests that would benefit from trade, especially international banks and corporations, became increasingly powerful in the postwar years, and could be counted on at least to support a state policy of openness, if not to actively influence it in that direction.[31] Again, labor was not a concern, either because it had lost adequate power to resist (if one believes free trade was against its interests) or because it recognized its own self interest was best served by openness. Political parties, in a similar way, could be counted on for their support.

The free flow of international capital can be considered as important as unrestricted trade in goods in adding to international efficiency. From a state-centered view, free movements of capital can complement growth engendered by exports, at least at a certain stage of a nation's maturity. Net exports, adding to growth, need a balance-of-payments framework to be generally offset by capital outflows. In more than simply an accounting sense capital exports provide a way to allow other states to purchase exports, further stimulating growth. More basic than this, however, is that capital exports are often considered a form of international power in their own right (as in Frieden, 1991).

For the Germans it has been consistent state policy to encourage the free movement of capital in Europe. Movements toward integration associated with the Werner Report, the SEA, and EMU have all specified the need for free capital movements.

Exchange-rate and monetary policy are also utilized in a framework that maximizes international trade and investment and growth. The arguments above on the role of stability of exchange rates need not be repeated here, but it can be seen how the loss of the single market, even the threatened loss, through the capital controls and trade barriers that might result from the need to protect economies from competitive devaluations or extensive exchange rate fluctuations, would carry a good deal of weight to a state directed to maximizing growth through openness.[32]

The control over inflation adds to the discussion in several ways. First, there is the avoidance of social instability, which is a rationale of its own. The German aversion to inflation in reference to the events of the 1920s is well understood, even for those Germans who only are aware of these times from the study of history. Added to this, however, is the notion that inflation hampers growth, a message that Germany at least delivered to the extent that its own high rates of growth were consistent with rigid control over inflation. Another way of saying this is that for Germany avoiding inflation is not in any way costly, and involves no form of tradeoff, either economic or political. Next, it can be that exchange-rate stability coupled with price stability can result in a "virtuous circle," where, in spite of relatively high goods prices and labor remuneration, high growth and increasing exports of especially high quality goods reinforce one another over time on a positive path of expansion.[33] Finally, it is possible to bring the two objectives of low inflation and fixed exchange rates together in a theoretically important way. It will be remembered that optimum currency area theory suggests—for small open economies and even for larger relatively open economies for which avoiding inflation is judged to be of importance—fixing exchange rates with major trading partners is appropriate.

The policy considerations result is a combination of objectives that could help postwar Germany achieve the goal of maximizing noninflationary growth. They include free trade, capital mobility, fixed rates of exchange, and low money-supply growth rates (in order to achieve low inflation). Only the last of these does not require international policy coordination. But, in a sense, even monetary policy is dependent on the other three, given the inconsistency between them. Differential inflation rates resulting from uncoordinated monetary policies, of course, threaten the other objectives, and demand some form of attention to coordination. The implication of the inconsistency is that German policy has needed to be directed not only at establishing fixed exchange rates and the free flow of capital with its major trading partners, but also at coordinating monetary policies with these same countries, and insuring that these policies are directed toward price stability. Again, policy coordination of this type would help maximize the growth and, therefore, power of the German state in a realist framework, as well as foster the low inflation deemed necessary for social stability.

It is possible to see both the continued German interest in EMU and the bargaining positions of the German state at critical times of EU institution building in this perspective. It will be recalled that the "economist" position during the Werner Report discussions, which in effect constituted the German position, established the need to establish policy coordination before any serious attempt could be made to fix exchange rates. The EMS as a system of fixed-but-adjustable exchange rates was established as the result of a joint German and French initiative. The inclusion of the elimination of capital controls as part of the SEA was based on German insistence. Finally, there were the several conditions insisted upon by Germany as part of Maastricht, conditions to which that state attached as much value after as during the negotiations. They, of course, included independence and a commitment to price stability of the ECB, the elimination of all capital controls at an early stage of the process, and strict convergence criteria centered around low inflation, budgetary discipline and the maintenance of fixed exchange rates.

Needed to supplement this notion, however, are two more propositions: the instability of a quasi-monetary union in the long run and the costs involved with hegemonic stability. The first of these was apparent even before the rending of the EMS during 1992 and 1993. Even though it could be said that Germany could not have designed a better system around its own interests, and as defined here, nevertheless the system could not indefinitely continue in the way it had. When the EMS was working, Germany, in other words, could decide upon its own monetary policy, and have its trading partners maintain not only stable exchange rates but their own low inflation rates in line with those of Germany.[34] Increasing capital mobility worldwide and suspicion of the incentives underlying independent policies doomed this ideal world for German interests.[35]

The second is an alternative, to have stability encouraged through the action of a hegemon. The theory of hegemonic stability speaks to the requirement of a global hegemon to engage in those activities necessary to maintain a liberal trading order. It has been applied to England in the nineteenth century and the United States following the second world war. It is considered an important example of realist theory in that it establishes an economic outcome, a liberal trading order, on the power distribution of states, in this case a structure where there is one very strong power in a position of dominance. It has also been the source of an enormous degree of controversy, in spite of which, much like neofunctionalism and realism itself, it continues to serve as the basis for a good deal of research.[36] Again, this is undoubtedly due to its ability to add useful insights into the structure and functioning of international relations.

By extension, one could apply the theory to a region, with Germany providing the role of hegemon in Western Europe.[37] The evidence of German economic dominance within the EU is supportive. German GDP is the highest in the EU, and constitutes by itself about a quarter of total EU GDP. Germany similarly provides around a quarter of total intra-EU exports, and about the same amount of total official reserves of convertible currencies. In addition, before reunification, Germany had by far the largest trade surplus and long-term capital outflow among the EU states (European Communities, 1990).[38]

Again, the role of a hegemonic state is to ensure the conditions upon which a free trading system may flourish. Although the original thought was that it might do this out of altruism or responsibility, its application within realist models has more often emphasized the role of self-interest for the hegemon.[39] The hegemon, in other words, is willing to make some short-run sacrifices in maintaining the system against the greater long-run benefits that would accrue from the growth of the hegemon itself. Free trade is a costly public good that takes a large, powerful, and indeed, rich state to be willing to provide, especially in the face of "free riding" by other states who also benefit but do not have to share the costs.[40]

One may revisit the several original Kindleberger (1986, pp. 289–95) functions for which the leader is responsible and compare them to Germany's modern role in Europe. The first function, "maintaining a relatively open market for distress goods," applies to ensuring an open market for imports in times of stress, and is here perhaps the least applicable. The second, "providing countercyclical, or at least stable, long-term lending," on the other hand is at least partially pertinent, as German capital export has been large and continuous.[41] The third function, "policing a relatively stable system of exchange rates," speaks to the example of the German acceptance—albeit somewhat reluctant—of the new EMS rules agreed at Basle-Nyborg in 1987 regarding crisis lending to weaker currency countries to allow them to maintain their ERM parities. It is easy to understand the German acceptance of these conditions, in spite of their potential inflationary implications, when viewing Germany as a regional leader.[42] The fourth condition, "ensuring the coordination of macroeconomic policies," has been given ample reference here already. Nevertheless, the Basle-Nyborg accord was seen at the time as a French-German compromise, whereby France "forced" the expansion of the lending rules on a reluctant Germany, whereas Germany gained "a strengthening of monetary policy coordination and more active use of interest rates" in the interest of stability (Gros and Thygesen, 1992, p. 95). Again, the "compromise" is more easily understood in light of the theory. The final function, "acting as a lender of last resort by discounting or otherwise providing liquidity in financial crises," has both domestic and international dimensions. The Bundesbank, of course, performs this function internally as part of its role as a modern central bank. Externally, active German intervention during EMS exchange crises over the years, as well as a formal acceptance of this role in exchange crises (if not banking crises) at Basle-Nyborg, gave to the EMS a perception of stability it had not had before. This, in turn, led to a view of the EMS as a fixed-rate system, so much so that it became increasingly perceived as a fixed-rate stage that would provide the base for movement on to EMU. It bears reiterating that it was not until the exchange crises of 1992 and 1993 that this vision was destroyed.[43]

Part of the theory of hegemonic stability is that international institutions, difficult to develop in virtually all cases, are nonetheless easier to forge within a trading system dominated by one state. This is especially the case when it is in the interest of the leader to establish such institutions in order to help share some of the costs of maintaining stability.

The German openness toward consideration of EMU over the years is understandable in this realist framework. The single major cost involved, of course, would be giving up control of its currency to a European central bank in which it would not have sole influence. The benefits, on the other hand, would be considerable. With a serious central bank mandate for price stability as part of its charter there could ideally be a greater certainty of low inflation, and less concern for imported inflation. Likewise with the common currency, there would be the elimination of short-run exchange instability as well as long-run misalignments. Also, there would be for Germany, presented here as very much the reluctant hegemon, the ability to avoid many of the costs of economic leadership.[44] There would, for example, no longer be any need to coordinate monetary policies among independent states creating separate currencies. Again, with a serious price stability mandate the European central bank would enact the optimal policy, from the German viewpoint, for all of the members of the EMU. In addition, the need to police exchange-rate stability would be eliminated. This is a cost that may have become more of a concern in recent years, following upon fewer EMS realignments and the increased responsibility of the Bundesbank to intervene in favor of weaker currencies. The common currency would thereby eliminate any risk of possibly inflating the DM as a result of required exchange market intervention in order to maintain the ERM in times of crisis.[45] The sheer amount of intervention required to maintain the EMS, of course, had grown larger, and it is tenable that the Bundesbank, without unlimited reserves, found itself unable to push back the tide of exchange market pressures. A European central bank, on the other hand, would simultaneously not need to worry about intra-EU exchange rates (at least among those countries represented) and would have significantly increased reserves at hand better to stabilize the euro against foreign currencies. The latter would yield more stability on the larger international scene, certainly a concern of Germany for decades, and one that would become larger with the growth in trade.

A realist approach, therefore, along with generally accepted economic concepts and attention to systemic international events, can enhance a deeper understanding of Germany's motivations in seeking a liberal trading order coupled with free capital flows and fixed exchange rates. When supplemented with the notion of Germany as an albeit reluctant regional hegemon, this approach suggests why Germany might have engaged in an exercise in international institution creation that would lead to the counterintuitive conclusion of that state being willing to significantly reduce its own sovereignty. It would accept the sacrifice of one of the strongest noninflationary currencies in the world to a common central bank over which it would not have full control. Again, these results might provide insights that would not necessarily follow from such alternative visions as classic economics or neofunctionalism.

Conclusion

Certain conclusions emerge as the result of applying traditional models in the field of integration theory to inform the question of monetary integration in Europe. First, the influence of external forces is important, both for neofunctionalism and for the newer variants of realism. Second, it seems that these forces can, in sympathy with neofunctionalist thought, set up the conditions for change that imply greater integration. Spillovers, in addition, are an important part of the analysis of European integration. Third, integration can also make sense in a somewhat narrowly defined calculation of political power as refined by the realists, even, remarkably, for Germany. Finally, both theories can speak to the possibility of greater economic integration in Europe around money in ways that enhance an understanding of a process that is difficult to explain solely from an economic perspective.

There are concerns with the application of both of these theories to EMU. They both, for example, seem to leave out too many important people in their attempt to be parsimonious. This is as true for neofunctionalism, with its emphasis on international institutional and nongovernmental elites, as it is for realism, with its emphasis on states as unitary actors in intergovernmental bargaining. Some of the newer applications of both theories make this less of a problem because they allow for interests to percolate up from below, but this is still a concern if one looks at an important role of the state as representing broader community interests. European integration is no exception. Lack of representation of the people, broadly defined, is seen in the generally recognized lack of any serious transfer of loyalty, or even much attraction or enthusiasm, by individuals to the European level. The Danish rejection in the 1992 referendum alerted the Community to the problem, but it is not clear how much has been done to remedy the democratic deficit, in spite of rhetoric over subsidiarity and EPU. Labor in particular, in spite of being weakened, could find itself in such an unacceptable state that it could bring pressure to bear in very powerful ways on attempts to integrate further, much less to maintain a liberal trading order. Both the Bundesbank and the German government seem to have been the only forces suggesting the need for greater political cohesion at the European level as a condition for greater economic stability in the future, this in order to remedy the "legitimacy vacuum" rendered by an extensively integrated economic community lacking a political counterpart.

There is also the question of structural shifts and how they might affect any movement toward greater integration. German reunification took more of a toll in terms of resources and energy than originally thought, resources and energy that could have been directed toward integration. Institutions are difficult to construct even in the best circumstances, and it is a defensible hypothesis that the costs involved encouraged Germany, the natural leader, to turn inward in order to complete its own union first before returning with full enthusiasm to broader European union.[46] The question of new entrants of Eastern European states into the EU only complicates the matter, and adds to financial considerations now facing a Germany already concerned over those who look to it to be the final paymaster of Europe. Add to this a number of relatively large middle-sized European states that, in reaction to unwelcome macroeconomic conditions, could act as "spoilers" to the integration process, and it is clear that reversal is certainly a possible outcome.

Another view is conceivable. Most of the states have remained determined to make monetary unification work. The Germans as well, although steeled by events perhaps to demand even more strongly the prior conditions of full convergence before the fact, do not seem to have backed away from commitment to the task. Full reunification will, after all, take place in time, and allow for a turning back to finish the job at hand. This might be, if anything, enhanced by the felt need to bring the Eastern European states convincingly into the fold of a Europe that will need economic and political stability to be able to function well in the future.

In addition, it seems clear that many of the stronger underlying conditions that helped create the agreements at Maastricht have not changed. The external technical and economic conditions of a neofunctional analysis of EMU are still relevant. The need for access to a larger market in order to take advantage of economies of scale implies the importance of the single market as well as the need to be competitive in an increasingly competitive world. There is still a need to create an atmosphere of monetary stability in order to encourage and maintain free trade and capital flows. The technical interdependence of states still indicates little ability for countries to be able to resort to independent policies, even if they were deemed useful, as well as highlighting the inconsistency of free capital flows, fixed exchange rates, and independent monetary policies. Continued floating at the international level likewise reinforces the need for cooperation in the monetary sphere. A spillover, in other words, flows from the single market, supported by underlying external conditions, to monetary integration in Europe. Moreover, the internal interests of internationally-oriented European industrial and financial elites that benefit from an open trading order are still present, and can still be counted on to support the EU institutions in their pursuit of monetary integration.

A realist view that notably finds Germany in favor of monetary integration, is similarly not altered at heart by some of the major structural changes that have occurred in the world in the 1990s. In fact, the need for economic stability to foster growth through trade and investment might even be considered more important in a more uncertain world. In addition, the shared consensus of most of the other EU states with Germany as the best model for that growth, a belief to which they have demonstrated their commitment at no little cost to themselves, appears unaltered.

In sum, an application of integration theory to the question of monetary integration in Europe not only helps explain the attraction of EMU, but suggests deeper commitments that might not finally be overcome by momentous structural changes in the world. In other words, all of the core areas of agreement that created a felt need to integrate monetarily through the institutional structure of the Community may remain in place, suggesting that the conditions of external stimulus, spillover, interest calculation, and state power assessment that brought forth EMU continue unaltered.

ELEVEN

Money and European Union: Synopsis

Europe is integrating around money. In spite of the sometimes ago-nizing difficulties in moving forward, and often low levels of recorded public approval, the process of monetary union remains strong. The Maastricht Treaty was signed and ratified, entailing a major sac-rifice of sovereignty of the participating states to the European level. More-over, there is evidence that the conditions that brought Maastricht about, including a convergence of interests among and between the signatory states, are still in place and are unlikely to be affected even by relatively powerful negative forces and momentous external events. Prior moves to-ward economic and monetary union in Europe had not fared so well in the onslaught of similar forces and events, but in this case it appears that the convergence of interests is strong enough to resist problems of income dis-tribution, reluctant states, unenthusiastic public support, and even the de-mands created by German reunification and the breakup of Soviet dominance in Eastern Europe.

One particularly relevant form of convergence of interests in Europe in the latter part of the twentieth century was that of macroeconomic prefer-ences. It had been part of the history of monetary integration in Europe that such attempts were foredoomed if there did not exist a prior compatibility of views on how best to run an economy. Such a consensus emerged during the 1980s around monetary discipline, and for at least three reasons. The first was that economic theory at this time established the point very per-suasively that countercyclical policies could not be relied upon to improve macroeconomic performance, especially regarding unemployment, for more than short periods of time at best, and that continuing efforts to do so would only result in accelerating inflation. The second was that Europe absorbed the lesson from the attempt by France in the very early 1980s to stimulate its economy with old-style demand management methods, including devaluation and expansive monetary and fiscal policies, an attempt that quickly failed partly due to its very divergence in an increasingly interdependent world. The final reason was that Europe equally noted well the lesson being taught by Germany at this same time, that growth was best enhanced by monetary discipline. Germany was becoming increasingly strong in these years, especially in economic terms, a strength that found reflection in its representing a powerful economic model for its neighbors to emulate.

A related form of harmony of views that served to fortify movement in the monetary sphere was the general acceptance that a liberal trading order formed the best basis for growth among the European states. The United States and Japan, again during the early 1980s, were able to recover from the economic conditions of the previous decade with much greater ease than Europe. Their economies were able to respond by being more competitive, due undoubtedly to a number of factors, including productive flexibility and government structures that effectively supported growth. One important component in reducing costs, however, was taking full advantage of economies of scale, which in turn required a large market. This market might be adequate internally for the United States, but Japan clearly continued to demonstrate the power of large-scale production in an open trading network based upon export expansion. Increasingly internationally oriented industrial and financial interests in Europe could be counted on to support sympathetic ears within the European Community institutions for policies that would encourage a larger market characterized by the free movement of goods, services, capital, and labor. The single internal market, therefore, became an important statement in the answer to Eurosclerosis and Europessimism; it would help provide a genuine common market that could serve as the basis for strong economic growth.

Fixed rates of exchange were a notable supplement to the single market that was enhanced by the adoption of the measures constituting the Single European Act. Europe had shown a revealed preference for relatively fixed rates even as much of the rest of the world had seemed anxious to embrace floating as a means of achieving equilibrium in the exchange markets; the exchange-rate mechanisms of the snake and the EMS being two clear examples of this preference. The latter, by attempting to create a zone of monetary stability in an uncertain world in fact helped create an institutional model of agreement that would contribute to the possibility of success of the single market itself. The system, however, became increasingly viewed as one of truly fixed rates without the underlyling convergence of monetary policies among the member states that would convincingly encourage the foreign exchange markets of its continuance. The exchange crises of 1992 and 1993 were the result, finding the EMS so severely damaged as to call into question whether it could even any longer be called a system.

The inconsistency of fixed exchange rates, independent monetary policies, and free capital movements, however, had been recognized well before this time in the Delors Report. It was understood that the next step—no exchange rates at all following upon the creation of a common currency—was the only one that would maintain the kind of stability Europe sought in this area. Capital had become much more mobile, and governments found they could no longer control such movements across borders, without extreme measures, even if they felt that desirable. Together, then, the rise of capital mobility and the part freer capital would intrinsically play in constructing a contiguous market meant a spillover of institution building from the single market toward economic and monetary union.

This notion would, in spite of negotiation and ratification difficulties, be agreed to by all of the states of the EU, albeit with opt-outs for Denmark and the United Kingdom. Most of the states had little to lose and only more voice in decisions to gain by adopting a common currency and European central bank, as they were already captive to German monetary policy. That made the level of German acquiescence and even enthusiasm for the project especially significant and, in many ways, counterintuitive. It could be argued, however, that German power in the postwar world is based on economic growth, and that, in turn, dependent upon free trade and capital flows. Combined with a reluctance to fully assume the mantle and financial responsibilities of a hegemon on the European scene, the lack of an adequate default to maintaining a stable trading order would mean a common currency. Much the rest of Europe shared the latter concern. A common currency might be necessary because a quasi-union, such as the EMS, could not work, and the default was floating or easy access by the states to devaluations. The specter of the interwar years, with its competitive devaluations, exchange controls, and draconian protectionism, loomed to remind Europe of what would be lost if the single market were abandoned. If the threat of loss of the single market, and implied reduction in real income and growth all around, meant a single currency, so be it.

That did not mean, on the other hand, that Germany would not insist on certain conditions in order to make such a move. These would include full credibility of any European central bank, at the minimum through constitutional independence and commitment to price stability, and macroeconomic convergence of potential members. These were consistent concerns of the Germans, expressed decades earlier in the Werner Report that similarly had attempted to achieve monetary union, but with their increasing political and economic strength the Germans would now broach no compromise. The fact is that the German model was so powerful that such views, in spite of some misgivings, were now accepted virtually unaltered by the rest of Europe.

There are some problems inherent in moving to monetary union that raise questions about its efficacy. First, there is an unequal distribution of income in Europe between states and regions, and it is possible that union could only exacerbate these differences. In the past there has been a willingness by the richer states of the EU to agree to at least some degree of redistribution through the Community structures in order to encourage the poorer states to committing to greater union. The eagerness by the richer states to participate in such schemes seems to have considerably dissipated in a more constrained economic environment.

Second, not all of the members of the EU share an equal degree of enthusiasm about being part of monetary union. Optimum currency area theory—especially the variant that deals with openness among states as a criterion by which policies lose much of their effectiveness and price stability is put in jeopardy—seems applicable here. The result from this model would be a two-speed Europe, with a core of countries around the French-German axis moving forward more quickly, while others wait a time to prepare for entry. The major defector, the United Kingdom, on the other hand, seems very much isolated, and its opinions on the value of a common currency politely listened to but, finally, little heeded by the rest of Europe.

A third concern is that the people of Europe have not been adequately included as an important component of the movement. The lack of perceived public support for all of the European institutions, much less for a sacrifice of national currencies is palpable. Especially after the Danish rejection of the Maastricht Treaty in 1992, attention has been paid to both the democratic deficit in Community structures as well as the proper role for the institutions, but it remains that citizens of states do not find their loyalties being transferred in any meaningful way to the European level. This does not mean, however, that there is not at least a grudging public acceptance of the same limited choices available if growth is to be maximized around free markets in an increasingly interdependent and competitive environment, the same understanding that drives the decisions of the states themselves.

Without demeaning the importance of democratic support, it could be a great public problem if the adopted model for economic growth itself were very costly. Again there may well be no alternative, but an outcome that yields so much unemployment and so much uncertainly over job security is worrisome and potentially explosive. As a close reading of the debate prior to the 1997 French elections over restructuring in preparation for satisfying the convergence criteria demonstrates, monetary union itself may be less a problem than the need for states to alter their governmental structures in order to make them more compatible with economic flexibility and competitiveness.

Without sacrificing what might be termed a more European model, in other words, if states do accept the supply-oriented model for growth then there are certain policy changes that are necessary for them to implement, as difficult as these might be. The evidence of much of the unemployment in Europe as being structural in nature, associated with low skill levels especially, reinforces such notions, both about the proper role for government and the culpability of movements toward greater union. The latter must, however, be considered in the light of invariant convergent criteria that may not only prevent the endeavor from going forward, but may insist upon a reduction in net public spending during a time of considerable economic stress.

Finally, the momentous events associated with the last decade of the twentieth century, including the collapse of the former Soviet system and German reunification, call into question the viability of further moves toward integration in Europe. Applicable here is whether or not crises encourage or discourage such movement, and there is evidence on both sides. Some of the events surrounding the establishment of the snake in the 1970s and later Maastricht itself speak for the theory; the eventual breakup of the snake and reunification seeming to sap some of the strength of Germany to be able to lead, respectively, lend support to the other side. Perhaps another way of addressing the question is whether the resolve of members to support integration movements is strong enough to weather probably inevitable crises. Here the evidence is stronger in favor of the viability of monetary union. The exchange crises of 1992–93 apparently did not eliminate the determination of Europe to move forward, nor finally did events in the east.

A possible reason why this might be the case, in opposition to experiences two decades earlier, is the solidity of the institutional structure in place. In fact, the existence and use of a long and resilient institutional structure at the Community level could be considered another argument in support of further union. The institutions seemed to have mattered and helped Europeans to address and solve problems, and they have looked to them increasingly to do so. A mature institutional framework that is and has been functioning for some time now, in other words, seems the natural basis around which to conclude economic cooperation in this area. Such a concept, reasonable as it is, somehow still misses an important point, one that is certainly difficult to quantify but seems nonetheless valid. It is that some of the political will that built these institutions, maintained them in times of crisis, and increased their structures in order to deal with areas of common felt need, has been due to leaders, statesmen who at critical junctures decided to opt for Europe.

In spite of many important concerns and problems, a continuing convergence of economic interests coupled with an appreciation and support for existing Community structures means that the states of Europe are integrating around money.

The Werner Report of 1970

(Report to the Council and the
Commission on the Realisation by Stages of
Economic and Monetary Union in the Community)

Introduction

In accordance with the directives issued by the Conference of Heads of State
or Government held at The Hague on 1 and 2 December 1969 and in accordance with the mandate given to it by a decision of the Council of Ministers of 6 March 1970, the Group, presided over by Mr. Pierre Werner, the
Prime Minister and Minister of Finance of the Luxembourg Government,
presented to the Council of Ministers on 20 May 1970 an interim report on
the realization by stages of economic and monetary union in the Community. In response to the invitation of the Council issued during its session of
8 and 9 June 1970 the Group has the honour to present its final report
which completes and amplifies the interim report, in the light in particular
of the directives that emerged from the exchange of views that took place in
the course of the same session. The present report does not reflect the individual preferences of the members of the Group but formulates replies in
common. The ideas expressed are given on the personal responsibility of the
members of the Group.

The formulation of the plan by stages presupposes that an examination
will first be made of the present situation, facilitating a precise definition of
the starting point and the development of a common concept of the state of
economic and monetary union upon the completion of the plan by stages.
Thus, having clarified the extreme limits of the development, the report sets
out certain fundamental principles and specific proposals for starting and

developing the process which should lead the Member States to economic and monetary union.

Without neglecting in any way the final phase of the process, the Group has thought fit to place particular emphasis on the first stage which implies concrete and important measures to be taken at the outset.

Starting point

Since the signature of the Treaty of Rome, the European Economic Community has taken several steps of prime importance towards economic integration. The completion of the customs union and the definition of a common agricultural policy are the most significant landmarks.

However, the advances towards integration will have the result that general economic disequilibrium in the member countries will have direct and rapid repercussions on the global evolution of the Community. The experience of recent years has clearly shown that such disequilibrium is likely to compromise seriously the integration realized in the liberation of the movement of goods, services and capital. This is particularly true of the agricultural common market. Having regard to the marked differences existing between the member countries in the realization of the objectives of growth and stability, there is a grave danger of disequilibria arising if economic policy cannot be harmonized effectively.

The increasing interpenetration of the economies has entailed a weakening of autonomy for national economic policies. The control of economic policy has become all the more difficult because the loss of autonomy at the national level has not been compensated by the inauguration of Community policies. The inadequacies and disequilibrium that have occurred in the process of realization of the Common Market are thus thrown into relief.

The efforts expended have made it possible to achieve partial progress but they have not in fact led to the coordination or effective harmonization of economic policies in the Community, which would, however, have accorded with the spirit of the Treaty of Rome and which could have been realized to a large extent by the application of the fundamental provisions of the Treaty and in particular of the articles relating to economic and monetary policy.

Quantitative objectives sufficiently harmonized, which are one of the important conditions for effective coordination, have not been achieved in the first two medium-term programmes. Investigations that have been made into the economic situation in the Community have often not had any other result than recommendations formulated in altogether general terms, even when the Community interest calls for the assumption of a more positive position.

In general, the consultation procedures have not yielded the results expected, either because they have been of a purely formal character or because the Member States have taken refuge in escape clauses.

The extension of the liberation of movements of capital and the realization of the right of establishment and of the free rendering of services by banking and financial undertakings have not progressed far enough. The delay has been caused by the absence of sufficient coordination of economic and monetary policies and by local peculiarities of law or of fact.

The freedom of persons to circulate is not yet assured in an entirely satisfactory manner and real progress has not yet been accomplished as regards the harmonization of social policies.

In the matter of regional policy, policies for particular sectors, and transport policy the progress realized has so far been fairly modest.

In foreign relations, and more particularly in international monetary relations, the Community has not succeeded in making its personality felt by the adoption of common positions, by reason as the case may be of divergencies of policy or of concept.

While these gaps have been appearing, economic agents have been adapting themselves at least partially to the new conditions in the markets. Thus, multinational companies have been formed and the markets in Euro-currencies and Euro-currency issues have sprung up and developed considerably. Furthermore, speculative movements of capital have assumed enormous proportions. These developments, some of which have positive aspects, help nonetheless to make still more difficult the control of economic development by Member States, while the constantly increasing interdependence of the industrialized economies throws into clearer and clearer relief the problem of the individuality of the Community.

The realization of the measures advocated in the memorandum of the Commission to the Council of 12 February 1969 may give a new impulse to the efforts of coordination and harmonization of economic and monetary policies. The realization of these measures, however, only provides a basis for the construction of the economic and monetary union which it is essential to conclude as soon as possible.

The final objective

The Group has not sought to construct an ideal system in the abstract. It has set out rather to determine the elements that are indispensable to the existence of a complete economic and monetary union. The union as it is described here represents the minimum that must be done, and is a stage in a dynamic evolution which the pressure of events and political will can model in a different way.

Economic and monetary union will make it possible to realize an area within which goods and services, people and capital will circulate freely and without competitive distortions, without thereby giving rise to structural or regional disequilibrium.

The implementation of such a union will effect a lasting improvement in welfare in the Community and will reinforce the contribution of the Community to economic and monetary equilibrium in the world. It presupposes the cooperation of the various economic and social groups so that by the combined effect of the market forces and the polices elaborated and consciously applied by the authorities responsible there may be achieved simultaneously satisfactory growth, a high level of employment, and stability. In addition, the Community policy should tend to reduce the regional and social disparities and ensure the protection of the environment.

A monetary union implies inside its boundaries the total and irreversible convertibility of currencies, the elimination of margins of fluctuation in exchange rates, the irrevocable fixing of parity rates and the complete liberation of movements of capital. It may be accompanied by the maintenance of national monetary symbols or the establishment of a sole Community currency. From the technical point of view the choice between these two solutions may seem immaterial, but considerations of a psychological and political nature militate in favour of the adoption of a sole currency which would confirm the irreversibility of the venture.

For such a union only the global balance of payments of the Community vis-à-vis the outside world is of any importance. Equilibrium within the Community would be realized at this stage in the same way as within a nation's frontiers, thanks to the mobility of the factors of production and financial transfers by the public and private sectors.

To ensure the cohesion of economic and monetary union, transfers of responsibility from the national to the Community plane will be essential. These transfers will be kept within the limits necessary for the effective operation of the Community and will concern essentially the whole body of policies determining the realization of general equilibrium. In addition, it will be necessary for the instruments of economic policy to be harmonized in the various sectors.

Quantitative objectives at medium term established in the form of projections compatible with one another and with the objects of the Common Market will be fixed at the Community level for growth, employment, prices and external equilibrium. These projections will be revised periodically.

Short-term economic policy will be decided in its broad outlines at a Community level. For this purpose to appreciate and fix the conditions of operation on global supply and demand, especially by means of monetary and budgetary policy, it will be necessary to establish normative and compatible economic budgets each year and to control their realization.

It is indispensable that the principal decisions in the matter of *monetary policy* should be centralized, whether it is a question of liquidity, rates of interest, intervention in the foreign exchange market, the management of the reserves or the fixing of foreign exchange parities vis-à-vis the outside world. The Community must have at its disposal a complete range of necessary instruments, the utilization of which, however, may be different from country to country within certain limits. In addition, it will be necessary to ensure a Community policy and Community representation in monetary and financial relations with third countries and international organizations of an economic, financial and monetary nature.

For influencing the general development of the economy *budget policy* assumes great importance. The Community budget will undoubtedly be more important at the beginning of the final stage than it is today, but its economic significance will still be weak compared with that of the national budgets, the harmonized management of which will be an essential feature of cohesion in the union.

The margins within which the main budget aggregates must be held both for the annual budget and the multi-year projections will be decided at the Community level, taking account of the economic situation and the particular structural features of each country. A fundamental element will be the determination of variations in the volume of budgets, the size of the balance and the methods of financing deficits or utilizing any surpluses. In order to be able to influence the short term economic trend rapidly and effectively it will be useful to have at the national level budgetary and fiscal instruments that can be handled in accordance with Community directives.

In this field, it is necessary to guard against excessive centralization. The transfers of power to the Community organs must be effected to the extent necessary for the proper functioning of the union, and must allow for a differentiated budgetary structure operating at several levels, Community, national, etc.

To make possible the abolition of fiscal frontiers while safeguarding the elasticity necessary for fiscal policy to be able to exercise its functions at the various levels a sufficient degree of *fiscal harmonization* will be effected, notably as regards the value-added tax, taxes likely to have an influence on the movement of capital and certain excise duties.

The suppression of the obstacles of various kinds should make it possible to arrive at a true *common market for capital* free from distortions. The financial policy of the Member States must be sufficiently unified to ensure the balanced operation of this market.

The realization of global economic equilibrium may be dangerously threatened by differences of structure. Cooperation between the partners in the Community in the matter of *structural and regional policies* will help to surmount these difficulties, just as it will make it possible to eliminate the distortions of competition. The solution of the big problems in this field will be facilitated by financial measures of compensation. In an economic and monetary union, structural and regional policies will not be exclusively a matter for national budgets. Furthermore, the problems of environment raised by industrial growth and urban development must be treated at the Community level under their various technical, financial and social aspects. Finally the continuous development of intra-Community trade will find a new stimulus in a suitable transport policy.

The cohesion of the economic and monetary union will be the better safeguarded if the *social partners* are consulted prior to the formulation and the implementation of the Community policy. It is important to adopt procedures that confer on such consultations a systematic and continuous character. In this context, in order to avoid the emergence of excessive divergencies, the trend of incomes in the various member countries will be studied and discussed at the Community level with the participation of the social partners.

To resume, economic and monetary union implies the following principal consequences:

— the Community currencies will be assured of total and irreversible mutual convertibility free from fluctuations in rates and with immutable parity rates, or preferably they will be replaced by a sole Community currency;

— the creation of liquidity throughout the area and monetary and credit policy will be centralized;

— monetary policy in relation to the outside world will be within the jurisdiction of the Community;

— the policies of the Member States as regards the capital market will be unified;

— the essential features of the whole of the public budgets, and in particular variations in their volume, the size of balances and the methods of financing or utilizing them, will be decided at the Community level;

— regional and structural policies will no longer be exclusively within the jurisdiction of the member countries;

— a systematic and continuous consultation between the social partners will be ensured at the Community level.

A result of this is that on the plane of *institutional reforms* the realization of economic and monetary union demands the creation of the transformation of a certain number of Community organs to which powers until then exercised by the national authorities will have to be transferred. These transfers of responsibility represent a process of fundamental political significance which implies the progressive development of political cooperation. Economic and monetary union thus appears as a leaven for the development of political union, which in the long run it cannot do without.

The Group does not consider that it will have to formulate detailed proposals as to the institutional form to be given to the different Community organs; it nevertheless indicates the principal requirements to be observed by two organs that seem to it indispensable to the control of economic and monetary policy inside the union: a centre of decision for economic policy, and a Community system for the central banks.

The *centre of decision for economic policy* will exercise independently, in accordance with the Community interest, a decisive influence over the general economic policy of the Community. In view of the fact that the role of the Community budget as an economic instrument will be insufficient, the Community's centre of decision must be in a position to influence the national budgets, especially as regards the level and the direction of the balances and the methods for financing the deficits or utilizing the surpluses. In addition, changes in the parity of the sole currency or the whole of the national currencies will be within the competence of this centre. Finally, in order to ensure the necessary links with the general economic policy its responsibility will extend to other domains of economic and social policy which will have been transferred to the Community level. It is essential that the centre of decision for economic policy should be in a position to take rapid and effective decisions by methods to be specified, especially as regards the way in which the Member States will participate.

The transfer to the Community level of the powers exercised hitherto by national authorities will go hand-in-hand with the transfer of a corresponding Parliamentary responsibility from the national plane to that of the Community. The centre of decision of economic policy will be politically responsible to a European Parliament. The latter will have to be furnished with a status corresponding to the extension of the Community missions, not only from the point of view of the extent of its powers, but also having regard to the method of election of its members.

The constitution of the Community system for the central banks could be based on organisms of the type of the Federal Reserve System operating in the United States. This Community institution will be empowered to take decisions, according to the requirements of the economic situation in the matter of internal monetary policy as regards liquidity, rates of interest, and the granting of loans to public and private sectors. In the field of external monetary policy, it will be empowered to intervene in the foreign exchange market and the management of the monetary reserves of the Community.

The transfer of powers to the Community level from the national centres of decision raises a certain number of political problems. In this respect it is fitting to quote in particular the relationship between the centre of decision for economic policy and the Community system of central banks as well as that between the Community organs and the national authorities. While safeguarding the responsibilities proper to each it will be necessary to guarantee that the Community organ competent for economic policy and that dealing with monetary problems are aiming at the same objectives.

A deeper study of the institutional problems thus raised is outside the framework of the mission of the Group, which has, however, thought it necessary to raise the essential aspects.

The implementation of economic and monetary union demands institutional reforms which presuppose a modification of the Treaties of Rome. Certainly, the present provisions already allow substantial progress to be made towards economic and monetary union, but a modification of the treaties will be necessary eventually to make possible a more advanced development of transfers of responsibility and the progressive establishment of the final institutions.

The Group considers that economic and monetary union is an objective realizable in the course of the present decade, provided the political will of the Member States to realize this objective, solemnly declared at the Conference at The Hague, is present.

The principles of realization of the plan by stages

In describing the desired result the Group intended to establish with clarity and precision the final objective aimed at. It is essential that there should be no misunderstanding in this matter, for economic and monetary unification is an irreversible process which must be approached with the firm intention to pursue it to its conclusion in the acceptance of all the implications contained in it on the economic and political plane.

The Group in no way wishes to suggest that economic and monetary union are realizable without transition. The union must, on the contrary, be developed progressively by the prolongation of the measures already taken for the reinforcement of the coordination of economic policies and monetary cooperation.

In every field the steps to be taken will be interdependent and will reinforce one another, in particular the development of monetary unification must be based on sufficient progress in the field of convergence and then in that of the unification of economic policies. Parallel to the limitation of the autonomy of the Member States in the matter of economic policy it will be necessary to develop corresponding powers at the Community level.

While pursuing its economic and monetary unification the Community will have to declare, vis-à-vis the outside world, its own objectives of international political economy. It is important that in adapting its internal structures it should continue to participate through the member countries or by itself in the measures for the liberation of trade, economic and monetary cooperation, and aid to developing countries that are decided on at the world level. Under these conditions, economic and monetary union will have served to reinforce the international division of labour and not to establish a new autarkic bloc within the world economy.

The Communiqué from The Hague envisages that the plan by stages for economic and monetary union will be formulated "on the basis of the memorandum presented by the Commission on 12 February 1969." The Group therefore considers that the actions advocated in the memorandum constitute the starting point for the whole process and that it is essential in consequence that the Council should pronounce before the end of 1970 on the only elements still outstanding in the memorandum, that is to say, on the one hand, the third medium-term programme setting out guidelines supported by figures and structural measures and, on the other hand financial aid at medium term.

On the basis of these principles, the Group has first of all set out to clarify the principal measures to be considered in the course of the first stage for the purpose of reinforcing the common working practices of the national authorities and of providing the indispensable structures and mechanisms.

The first stage

The measures proposed for the first stage at once call for a substantial effort on the part of the Member States and the Community. It is necessary to guard against any excessive precipitateness, but the credibility and the smooth progress of the undertaking demand that a specific period should be fixed; the Group considers that a period of three years would be appropriate.

GENERAL ARRANGEMENTS

The reinforcement of the coordination of economic policies during the first stage seems one of the principal measures to be taken. One of the essential objectives to be attained will be to develop a rapid reciprocal exchange of information and to make possible the determination in common of the fundamental guidelines of economic and monetary policy.

A certain number of requirements and limits must be set. The coordination of economic policies necessarily entails constraint, but this can only be applied progressively. The arrangements to be adopted and the actions to be undertaken must aim at efficiency, and take account of the final concept of economic and monetary union. During the first stage the mechanisms and institutions necessary will be established and will function on the basis of the present provisions of the Treaty. However, the decisions taken must already be recorded in the progress of evolution that must end in the structure envisaged for the conclusion of the plan by stages.

PROCEDURE

The coordination of the economic policies must be based on *at least three annual surveys* in depth of the economic situation in the Community that will make it possible to decide on guidelines in common.

The timetable indicated below has been deliberately left fairly flexible. Nevertheless, the surveys will be made on fixed dates. At the outset, these dates will be chosen in such a way as to ensure the best possible adaptation to the deadlines now in force in the Member States for the establishment and adoption of their budgets. Subsequently the deadlines will be synchronized so as to permit greater efficiency in the coordination of policies.

A *first survey* in the spring will provide an opportunity for drawing up a balance sheet for economic policy in the previous year and possibly for adapting that relating to the current year to the requirements of economic development. At the same time a first exchange of views will take place to prepare for the following meeting. In addition, the quantitative medium-term objectives will be revised according to the procedure laid down for drawing up the medium-term programmes of economic policy.

In order to arrive at the determination of quantitative guidelines for the principal elements of the whole of the public budgets for the following year and to enable governments to take note of the Community reactions before they draw up their budget plans, ordinary and extraordinary, on a definitive basis, a *second survey,* a little before the middle of the year will make an initial selection of the guidelines for the policy to be implemented in the following year and will review the policy to be followed during the current year. This analysis will be effected within the framework of the economic accounts and will make it possible to establish preliminary economic budgets.

Finally, a *survey carried out in the autumn* will make it possible to lay down in greater detail the guidelines arrived at in the course of the year. Economic budgets compatible with one another will then be drawn up. They will contain as regards budget policy the same elements as at the previous survey completed by additional data which would not have been available previously. The guidelines given in the economic budgets will serve as a point of reference for the authorities responsible for the determination of monetary and credit policy. On the occasion of this survey the Council will draw up, on the proposal of the Commission, an *"annual report on the economic situation of the Community,"* indicating in particular the guidelines for economic policy at short term in the following year.

These regular examinations will make it possible to proceed to a permanent surveillance of the situation. However, as was foreseen also in the decision of the Council of 17 July 1969, *ad hoc* surveys may prove to be necessary for recommending or deciding on specific measures; they will be undertaken at the request of a Member State or of the Commission. In order to facilitate the detection of dangerous situations, a system of Community indicators will be worked out.

The recommendations regarding the guidelines for the economic policy to be followed will be addressed in a specific and detailed manner to each member country. Also, it is possible to envisage an arrangement of general import providing that in the event of such recommendations having to be put to the vote the country concerned would abstain.

The procedures for consultation will be reinforced by the abandonment of any previous obligatory restriction as to their character. These consultations will cover economic policy at medium term, short term economic policy, budget policy and monetary policy; they should lead to the formulation of national decisions in accordance with the points of view arrived at in common.

To ensure the necessary effectiveness, rapidity and discretion, special procedures must be envisaged for the preparation of the work, its development, and the conclusions. The procedures now in force are not adapted to the requirements of the case. The Group is fully conscious of the very heavy labours entailed in the proposed procedure. They demand great effort on the part of all the participants and assume that in both the Member States and the Community institutions the necessary conditions from the personal and organizational point of view will be fulfilled.

ORGANS

The coordination of economic policies during the first stage will depend on increased activity by the Community organs, in particular the Council and the Commission as well as the Committee of Governors of the central banks.

During the first stage the Council will be the central organ of decision for general economic policy. It will fix the objectives at medium term and within this framework will work out annual programmes. More generally, it will follow and direct economic policy throughout the year. In particular the Council will translate the intentions of general policy while defining the broad lines of budget policy.

The Council will be composed of the ministers responsible in each Member State for economic and financial matters, with the participation of the competent members of the Commission; the Governors of the central banks should attend the meetings. The meetings will be limited in number and will take place on the date fixed for the regular surveys mentioned above.

In order to ensure the effectiveness of the Council's labours on the basis of reports as up-to-date as possible and to guarantee a sufficient measure of coordination it must be possible to assemble rapidly persons of high standing representing Governments and central banks. These persons, who will thus not be sitting as independent experts, will have sufficient powers to facilitate the taking of decisions. Furthermore, they will be able to proceed to the consultations rendered obligatory by the decisions of the Council of 17 July 1969 and of 16 February 1970.

Important responsibilities will have to be assumed by the Commission, which will be entitled in particular within the framework of the powers laid down in the Treaties to make any proposal to the Council in order that the latter may rule on the matters in question. The Commission will make all necessary contacts with the competent national administrations, either direct or through Committees or groups of experts.

Greater activity will also be exercised by the different committees responsible for the problems of economic policy.

Finally, the Committee of Governors of the central banks will play an increasingly important role as regards problems of monetary policy both internal and external. The frequency of the meetings and the competence of the Committee will be adapted to ensure the preparation of the monetary aspects of the meetings of the Council envisaged above, to bring about current consultation and in particular to make it possible to define the general guidelines of monetary and credit policy within the Community.

The Committee of Governors will be able to express opinions or make recommendations to the central banks of the member countries when it wishes to give a particular direction to the action of the latter. It will be able to make recommendations to the Council and the Commission suggesting the Community measures that seem to it to be called for.

The proposals outlined above will help to ensure the coordination of economic policies, but it is advisable that at least once a year this should be the subject of a more formal approach. For this purpose the "annual report on the economic situation in the Community" brought out at the time of the survey scheduled for the autumn will be presented to the European Parliament and to the Economic and Social Committee, and the governments will bring it to the notice of the national parliaments for the latter to take into account in the debates on the budget proposals. An analogous procedure will be followed for the quantitative objectives at medium term determined at Community level.

"CONCERTATION" WITH THE SOCIAL PARTNERS

For the successful realization of economic and monetary union it is essential to bring the social partners into the preparations for the Community economic policy. It is therefore necessary that major guidelines on economic policy should not be adopted until they have been consulted. For this purpose it will be necessary to establish at the outset procedures for regular "concertation" at the Community level between the Commission and the social partners.

POLICIES

Budget policy

Within the framework of the procedures already described special emphasis must be placed on the efforts to be made with a view to the coordination and harmonization of budget policies.

According to the economic situation in each country quantitative guidelines will be given on the principal elements of the public budgets, notably on global receipts and expenditure, the distribution of the latter between investment and consumption, and the direction and amount of the balance. Finally, special attention will be paid to the method of financing deficits or utilizing surpluses.

To facilitate the harmonization of budget policies, searching comparisons will be made of the budgets of the Member States from both quantitative and qualitative points of view. From the quantitative point of view the comparison will embrace the total of the public budgets, including local authorities and social security. It will be necessary to evaluate the whole of the fiscal pressure and the weight of public expenditure in the different countries of the Community and the effects that public receipts and expenditure have on global internal demand and on monetary stability. It will also be necessary to devise a method of calculation enabling an assessment to be made of the impulses that the whole of the public budgets impart to the economy.

From the practical point of view, it will be necessary to effect a harmonization of timetables for the presentation and adoption of the budget proposals.

Finally, from the very outset, efforts will be made to introduce and develop homologous instruments in each country; examples are, on the revenue side, the "fiscal regulators" and on the expenditure side, "cyclical budgets." Fiscal regulators authorize rapid adjustments in the rates of tax up to a limited amount and for a limited period; cyclical budgets permit the addition or reduction of final budget figures by a certain percentage of expenditure.

Fiscal policy

In order to permit the progressive and complete suppression of fiscal frontiers in the Community, while respecting the elasticity that is necessary in order that fiscal policy may have its effect at different levels, it will be necessary to realize in the various fiscal fields the measures enumerated below.

As regards indirect taxes, the system of the value-added tax will be made general and a programme for the alignment of rates adopted. Similarly, as regards excise duties, a programme leading to a sufficient alignment of the rates will be formulated for those that have a direct bearing on free movement across the frontiers.

The programmes of alignment will be carried out in a parallel manner and the rate of implementation will be such that as from the end of the first stage the controls on private individuals at intra-Community frontiers can be suppressed.

In the field of direct taxes, it will be necessary to standardize certain types of tax which are likely to have a direct influence on the movement of capital within the Community. In practice it is mainly a question of the harmonization of the fiscal regime applied to interest payments on fixed interest securities and dividends. It will also be necessary to initiate and actively promote the harmonization of the structure of taxes on corporations.

The policy for financial markets

The freedom of movement of capital within the Common Market has fallen short of the objectives fixed in the Treaty: in a certain number of countries there still exist exchange restrictions on important transactions; and in addition internal legislation and practices prevent the free circulation of capital within the Community. Disparities in the cost of credit and the conditions of access to credit resulting therefrom falsify competition and conflict with the institution of economic and monetary union.

To remedy this state of affairs, it seems necessary to take prompt action in two directions: the abolition of obstacles to capital movements, in particular residual exchange control regulations, and a coordination of policies as regards financial markets. This double action seems necessary so that the opening of markets can have its full effect and contribute to the smooth operation of the Common Market.

As regards the abolition of obstacles, it will be necessary as a first step to fix ceilings up to which issues of bonds by residents in other member countries may be authorized without discrimination resulting from exchange control regulations or administrative practices. These ceilings will be raised progressively until all the markets have been opened completely. Similar actions will be taken for the financing of investments by credit at medium and long term.

The introduction on the stock exchange of securities emanating from other member countries will be freed from all discrimination. In addition, it will be necessary to adapt the regulations governing institutional investors so as to enable them to effect placings throughout the Community.

As regards the coordination of policies in relation to financial markets a distinction must be made between current aspects and structural aspects. For the current aspects the member countries will proceed to regular consultations concerning the policy of equilibrium in the markets and the problems raised within and outside the Community by movements of capital; and they will initiate the concertation of national policies in these domains. As regards the structural aspect, it is necessary to carry out measures of "technical" harmonization in a series of fields, as for example regulations governing the activities of credit institutions and institutional investors, the notification and protection of holders of securities, conditions for the operation of stock exchanges, the encouragement of saving and certain forms of investment, and the legal instruments of financial transactions.

Domestic monetary and credit policy

The general lines of monetary and credit policy will be defined on a common basis. In this context it is necessary to introduce progressively a measure of conformity between the instruments of monetary and credit policy at the disposal of the member countries.

In order to ensure the coordination of domestic monetary and credit policies, prior obligatory consultations will be held within the Committee of Governors. These consultations will be effected in the following way: the Committee of Governors will examine periodically, and at least twice a year, the situation and policies in each member country in the monetary field. At the end of each scrutiny, and having regard to the conclusions arrived at by the Council for economic policy, guidelines will be laid down concerning the conduct of monetary and credit policy, principally as regards the level of interest rates, the evolution of bank liquidity and the granting of credit to the private and public sectors.

The measures to be taken should correspond to the guidelines formulated by the Committee of Governors and should be the subject of mutual reports prior to their application. If the competent authorities in one or several Member States, or the Commission, consider that the measures to be put into force are not in accordance with the guidelines given they may demand a consultation. In the event of dispositions departing from the guidelines given being contemplated by a Member State, the latter must arrange a consultation beforehand.

The harmonization of the instruments of monetary policy is one of the necessary conditions for ensuring the complete effectiveness of coordination and joint maintenance of the monetary policies. For this reason it will be necessary to establish without delay a programme for action in this field. In addition it is essential to press on with harmonization in order to ensure a better adaptation of the structures and statutes of the credit institutions to the requirements of a unified market.

External monetary policy

The process for the realization of economic and monetary union demands from the outset an intensification of cooperation in the matter of external monetary policy.

It is desirable that the solidarity of the member countries in the determination of their exchange parities should be supported by a reinforcement of the consultation procedures in the matter.

The reinforcement of concertation in the matter of monetary policy will concern the utilization and the granting of credits, as for example drawings from the International Monetary Fund and swap credits, the creation of new liquidity in the form of an increase in the quotas or a further development of Special Drawing Rights, as well as the foreign exchange position of the banks. It will be necessary to take a first step towards the progressive institution of a representative unit for the EEC at the IMF and other international financial undertakings.

In accordance with the decision of the Council of 8 and 9 June 1970, the Community must progressively adopt common positions in its monetary relations with third countries and international organizations; in particular it must not avail itself in foreign exchange relations between member countries of any provisions allowing greater flexibility in the international foreign exchange system.

As regards foreign exchange relations within the Community itself, the Group advocates for the first stage a certain number of measures the realization of which will be conditioned for each one by the result of the previous measure, so as to permit a constant adaptation of the process according to the circumstances:

— From the start of the first stage, by the way of experiment, the central banks acting in concert will limit *de facto* the fluctuations in the rates of exchange between their currencies to narrower margins than those resulting from the application of the margins in force for the dollar at the time of the adoption of the system. This objective will be achieved by concerted action in relation to the dollar.

— After this experimental period the limitation of the margins can be officially announced.

— The concerted action in relation to the dollar can be completed by interventions in Community currencies, first at the limit of the margins and later within them. These interventions should be so arranged, however, that during the first stage the credit facilities to which they might give rise do not go beyond those provided for in the mechanism of monetary support at short term.

— Further reductions in the margins of fluctuation in the rates of exchange between Community currencies can be decided upon.

The first of the measures referred to above should be taken at the beginning of the first stage, when the Council will have adopted the plan for the realization of economic and monetary union; for the subsequent steps the Group thinks it better not to suggest a rigid timetable. For this reason it proposes that the Committee of Governors should twice a year make a report to the Council and to the Commission on the development of the measures being taken and on the advisability of adopting new measures. On this basis and according to the progress realized towards the harmonization of economic policies, the Council or the Member States assembled in the Council will take the appropriate decisions. Nevertheless, this procedure will not be necessary for reductions *de facto* in the intra-community margins resulting from the concerted action of the central banks.

In order to facilitate the development of the operations advocated it will be advisable to entrust to an agent the task of recording the balances of the operations effected in the foreign exchange markets of the member countries of the Community, to inform each central bank of them periodically and if the need arises to suggest transfers or possible offsets in Community currencies and in dollars.

It is necessary, finally, to undertake a study in depth of the conditions of creation and operation, and of the statutes of the "European Fund for monetary cooperation" outlined in chapter VI below and intended to ensure the necessary transition towards the Community system for central banks contemplated for the final phase.

The other fields

It is essential to pursue the measures undertaken in the various fields, for example the suppression of the residual obstacles to intra-community trade; an inventory of the aid and grants the standardization of which is necessary, on the one hand to ensure the free play of competition, and on the other hand to develop common industrial and regional policies; the formulation of a transport policy; the application of a common commercial policy in conformity with the treaty; the implementation of a common policy in the matter of insurance and credit for exports and aid to countries in course of development; and the formulation and adoption of statutes for a European company.

The statistical apparatus of the Member States is still far from being satisfactory and presents gaps. To facilitate the coordination of economic policies it is essential that the efforts already made in this field should be renewed.

THE INSTITUTIONAL ARRANGEMENTS

In the course of this stage it will be necessary to complete the preparatory work designed to adapt and complete the Treaty, in order to permit, a sufficient interval before the end of the first stage and following the procedures laid down in Article 236 of the Treaty of Rome, the convocation in good time of an intergovernmental conference which will be apprised of the proposals formulated in the matter. In this way procedures will be adopted making it possible to establish the necessary legal bases for the transition to the complete realization of economic and monetary union and the implementation of the essential institutional reforms implied by the latter.

In the light of a balance sheet making it possible to measure the progress realized in all fields, the Council will then be in a position to establish a new programme of action containing measures that could be undertaken on the basis of the Treaty and others which would have to await its revision before they could be realized.

The transition towards the final objective

In the course of this final phase, action will have to be taken on a number of fronts. The action will entail, first further coordination of national policies, then their harmonization by the adoption of directives or common decisions, and finally the transfer of responsibility from the national authorities to Community authorities. As progress is made, Community instruments will be created to carry on or complete the action of the national instruments.

The coordination of economic and monetary policies will already have advanced to a point at which its fundamental elements are in place; subsequently it will have to be strengthened by ever closer regard for the common interest.

This will first have to be done in relation to *short-term economic policy.* To do this it will be necessary to isolate the conflicts and the lines of convergence in national policies. It will then be essential to define strategies aiming at the realization of a Community optimum which will not necessarily be a simple juxtaposition of national optimums. At the same time it will be necessary progressively to make the definition and general guidelines of economic policy more binding and ensure a sufficient degree of harmonization in monetary and budget policies.

The programmes of *economic policy at medium term* will have to be more and more closely geared to Community objectives, the realization of which will be ensured by policies conducted on the one hand at the national level and on the other hand at the Community level, the emphasis shifting gradually from the former to the latter.

In the matter of *budgetary policy,* the norms fixed for the variation in the volume, and for the direction and size of the balances on the public budgets, will be made increasingly restrictive. The homologous instruments of budget policy developed during the first stage will be applied progressively on a common basis.

The suppression of the obstacles of various kinds and the harmonization of the financial structures should make it possible to arrive at a true *common capital market* by the progressive interpenetration of the national markets.

In the framework of an economic and monetary union it is not enough to pay attention to policies of global economic equilibrium alone. It will also be necessary to envisage measures bearing on *structural problems* the essence of which will be profoundly modified by the realization of this process. In this context the Community measures should primarily concern regional policy and employment policy. Their realization would be facilitated by an increase in financial intervention effected at Community level. In addition, it will be necessary to arrive progressively at Community guidance for policies on industry, transport, power, housing, and the environment.

The reinforcement of intra-community links in the *monetary field* must be so formulated as to facilitate the transition to economic and monetary union, in which equilibrium between the economies of the Member States will be ensured by the free circulation of the factors of production and by financial transfers in the public and private sectors.

Progress in the convergence of economic and monetary policies should be such in the course of the second stage that the member States no longer have to resort on an autonomous basis to the instrument of parity adjustment. In any case, it will be necessary further to reinforce the consultation procedures laid down for the first stage. Only at the moment of transition to the final stage will autonomous parity adjustments be totally excluded.

In order to prepare the final stage in good time, it will be necessary to set up as soon as possible a "European Fund for monetary cooperation" under the control of the Governors of the central banks. To the extent that the techniques of intervention in the foreign exchange markets laid down for the first stage and described on pages 22 and 23 have functioned normally and without friction and that sufficient harmonization has been achieved in economic policies it may well be possible to establish the fund in the course of the first stage. In any event it will have to be established during the second stage. This fund will have to absorb the mechanisms for monetary support at short term and for financial aid at medium term. As progress is achieved towards economic and monetary union the fund will gradually become an organ of management of the reserves at the Community level and be integrated at the final stage in the Community system of central banks which will then be set up. Furthermore, it will be necessary to bring about the harmonization of the instruments of monetary policy in order to facilitate the reinforcement of Community policy in this field.

Conclusions

The Group, recalling that the Council adopted on 8 and 9 June 1970 the conclusions presented by the Group in its interim report, suggests to the Council that it should accept the contents of the present report and approve the following conclusions:

A. Economic and monetary union is an objective realizable in the course of the present decade provided only that the political will of the Member States to realize this objective, as solemnly declared at the Conference at The Hague, is present. The union will make it possible to ensure growth and stability within the Community and reinforce the contribution it can make to economic and monetary equilibrium in the world and make it a pillar of stability.

B. Economic and monetary union means that the principal decisions of economic policy will be taken at Community level and therefore that the necessary powers will be transferred from the national plane to the Community plane. These transfers of responsibility and the creation of the corresponding Community institutions represent a process of fundamental political significance which entails the progressive development of political cooperation. The economic and monetary union thus appears as a leaven for the development of political union which in the long run it will be unable to do without.

C. A monetary union implies, internally, the total and irreversible convertibility of currencies, the elimination of margins of fluctuation in rates of exchange, the irrevocable fixing of parity ratios and the total liberation of movements of capital. It may be accompanied by the maintenance of national monetary symbols, but considerations of a psychological and political order militate in favour of the adoption of a single currency which would guarantee the irreversibility of the undertaking.

D. On the institutional plane, in the final stage, two Community organs are indispensable: a centre of decision for economic policy and a Community system for the central banks. These institutions, while safeguarding their own responsibilities, must be furnished with effective powers of decision and must work together for the realization of the same objectives. The centre of economic decision will be politically responsible to a European Parliament.

E. Throughout the process, as progress is achieved Community instruments will be created to carry out or complete the action of the national instruments. In all fields the steps to be taken will be interdependent and will reinforce one another; in particular the development of monetary unification will have to be combined with parallel progress towards the harmonization and finally the unification of economic policies.

F. At this stage the laying down of a precise and rigid timetable for the whole of the plan by stages does not seem feasible. It is necessary in fact to maintain a measure of flexibility to permit any adaptations that the experience acquired during the first stage may suggest. Particular emphasis should therefore be placed on the first stage, for which a package of concrete measures is presented. The decisions on the details of the final stages and the future timetable will have to be taken at the end of the first stage.

G. The first stage will commence on 1 January 1971 and will cover a period of three years. In addition to the action approved by the Council in its decision of 8 and 9 June 1970 it will entail the adoption of the following measures:

1. The consultation procedures will have a preliminary and obligatory character and will call for increased activity by the Community organs, in particular the Council and the Commission, as well as the Committee of Governors of the central banks. These consultations will principally concern

economic policy at medium term, short-term economic policy, budget policy and monetary policy.

2. The Council will meet at least three times a year to lay down, on the proposal of the Commission, the broad lines of economic policy at Community level and quantitative guidelines for the principal elements of the whole of the public budgets. Once a year, in the autumn, the economic policy in the Community will be the subject of recommendations contained in an annual report on the economic situation of the Community which will be transmitted to the European Parliament and to the Economic and Social Committee and which the Governments will bring to the notice of the national parliaments.

3. In order to promote efficiency in the Council's labours and to ensure sufficient coordination, the Council must be in a position to assemble rapidly persons of high standing representing Governments and central banks, who will be able to hold prior consultations.

4. Before the adoption of the broad lines of economic policy at the Community level, consultations will take place between the Commission and the social partners in accordance with procedures to be laid down.

5. The budget policy of the Member States will be conducted in accordance with Community objectives. For this purpose, within the framework of the meetings of the Council referred to in paragraph 2 above, a Community survey will be effected before the Governments draw up their budget proposals on a definitive basis. The national budget procedures will be synchronized. In the fiscal field, countries will adopt the harmonization advocated in the present report and the integration of financial markets will be intensified.

6. The Committee of Governors will play an increasingly important role in the coordination of monetary and credit policy; in particular it will lay down in this field general guidelines for the Community. It will be able to express opinions and make recommendations to the central banks of the member countries and express opinions to the Council and the Commission.

7. To reinforce solidarity within the Community in the matter of foreign exchange, the central banks are invited, from the beginning of the first stage, to restrict on an experimental basis the fluctuations of rates between Community currencies within narrower bands than those resulting from the application of the margins in force in relation to the dollar. This objective would be achieved by concerted action in relation to the dollar. According to circumstances and to the results achieved in the standardization of economic policies new measures may be taken. These will consist of a transition from a *de facto* regime to a *de jure* regime of intervention in Community currencies and the progressive narrowing of the margins of fluctuation between Community currencies.

8. The actions foreseen in the foreign exchange field will be facilitated by the intervention of an agent charged with the tasks of statistical registration, information, and advice.

9. The rapid harmonization of the instruments of monetary policy is necessary. For this reason it will be necessary as soon as possible to undertake the preparatory work in this field.

10. The modifications to be made in the Treaty of Rome in order to make possible the final realization of economic and monetary union must be prepared in good time during the first stage.

11. In accordance with Article 236 of the Treaty of Rome, an intergovernmental conference will be called in good time before the end of the first stage with a view to drawing up the necessary modifications for the complete realization of economic and monetary union. A special meeting of the Council will be called to draw up a balance sheet of progress achieved in the first stage and lay down a programme for specific action in the years to come.

H. The *second stage* will be characterized by the promotion on a number of fronts and on ever more restrictive lines of the action undertaken during the first stage: the laying down of global economic guidelines, the coordination of short-term economic policies by monetary and credit measures, and budget and fiscal measures, the adoption of Community policies in the matter of structures, the integration of financial markets and the progressive elimination of exchange rate fluctuations between Community currencies.

The reinforcement of the intra-Community links in monetary matters must be effected as soon as possible by the establishment of a European Fund for monetary cooperation as a forerunner of the Community system of central banks for the final stage. In accordance with the experience acquired in the matter of the reduction of margins and the convergence of economic policies it may well be possible to establish the Fund during the first stage and in any event in the course of the second stage. The preparatory work for this purpose must be put in hand as soon as possible.

The Group expresses the wish that the Council should approve the suggestions contained in the present report and should make, on the proposal of the Commission, all the arrangements needed for the realization of the plan by stages, and in particular before the end of the year any that may be necessary to put the first stage into operation on 1 January 1971.

The Delors Report

(Report on Economic and Monetary
Union in the European Community)

Chapter 1: Past and present developments in economic and monetary integration in the Community

Section 1: The objective of economic and monetary union

1. In 1969 the Heads of State or Government, meeting in The Hague, agreed that a plan should be drawn up with a view to the creation, in stages, of an economic and monetary union within the Community. This initiative was taken against the background of major achievements by the Community in the 1960s: the early completion of the transition period leading to a full customs union, the establishment of the common agricultural policy and the creation of a system of own resources. At the same time the Bretton Woods system was showing signs of decline. The *Werner Report,* prepared in 1970, presented a plan for the attainment of economic and monetary union. In March 1971, following the Werner Report, Member States expressed 'their political will to establish an economic and monetary union'.

2. Several important *moves followed:* in 1972 the 'snake' was created; in 1973 the European Monetary Cooperation Fund (EMCF) was set up; and in 1974 the Council Decision on the attainment of a high degree of convergence in the Community and the Directive on stability, growth and full employment were adopted. Yet, by the mid-1970s the process of integration

had lost momentum under the pressure of divergent policy responses to the economic shocks of the period.

3. In 1979 the process of monetary integration was relaunched with the creation of the *European Monetary System* (EMS) and the European Currency Unit (ECU). The success of the EMS in promoting its objectives of internal and external monetary stability has contributed in recent years to further progress, as reflected in the adoption, in 1985, of the internal market programme and the signing of the Single European Act.

Section 2: The European Monetary System and the ECU

4. The *European Monetary System* was created by a Resolution of the European Council followed by a Decision of the Council of Ministers and an Agreement between the participating central banks.

5. Within the framework of the EMS the participants in the exchange rate mechanism have succeeded in creating *a zone of increasing monetary stability* at the same time as gradually relaxing capital controls. The exchange rate constraint has greatly helped those participating countries with relatively high rates of inflation in gearing their policies, notably monetary policy, to the objective of price stability, thereby laying the foundations for both a downward convergence of inflation rates and the attainment of a high degree of exchange rate stability. This, in turn, has helped moderate cost increases in many countries, and has led to an improvement in overall economic performance. Moreover, reduced uncertainty regarding exchange rate developments and the fact that the parities of the participating currencies have not been allowed to depart significantly from what is appropriate in the light of economic fundamentals have protected intra-European trade from excessive exchange rate volatility.

The EMS has served as the focal point for improved monetary policy coordination and has provided a basis for multilateral surveillance within the Community. In part, its success can be attributed to the participants' willingness to opt for a strong currency stance. Also important has been the flexible and pragmatic way in which the System has been managed, with increasingly close cooperation among central banks. Moreover, the System has benefited from the role played by the Deutschmark as an 'anchor' for participants' monetary and intervention policies. The EMS has evolved in response to changes in the economic and financial environment, and on two occasions (Palermo 1985 and Basle/Nyborg 1987) its mechanisms have been extended and strengthened.

At the same time, the EMS has not fulfilled its full potential. Firstly, a number of Community countries have not yet joined the exchange rate mechanism and one country participates with wider fluctuation margins. Secondly, the lack of sufficient convergence of fiscal policies as reflected in large and persistent budget deficits in certain countries has remained a source of tensions and has put a disproportionate burden on monetary policy. Thirdly, the transition to the second stage of the EMS and the establishment of the European Monetary Fund, as foreseen by the Resolution of the European Council adopted in 1978, have not been accomplished.

6. In launching the EMS, the European Council declared in 1978 that '*a European Currency Unit (ECU)* will be at the centre of the EMS'. Apart from being used as the numeraire of the exchange rate mechanism and to denominate operations in both the intervention and credit mechanisms, the ECU serves primarily as a reserve asset and a means of settlement for EMS central banks. Although it is an integral part of the EMS, the ECU has for a number of reasons played only a limited role in the operating mechanisms of the EMS. One reason is that central banks have preferred to intervene intra-marginally; therefore, compulsory interventions and the build-up of intervention balances to be settled in ECUs have remained rather limited.

By contrast, the ECU has gained considerable popularity in the market place, where its use as a denominator for financial transactions has spread significantly. It ranks fifth in international bond issues, with a 6% market share. The expansion of financial market activity in ECUs reflects in part a growing issuance of ECU-denominated debt instruments by the Community institutions and public-sector authorities of some member countries, and in part the ECU's attractiveness as a means of portfolio diversification and as a hedge against currency risks.

International banking business in ECUs grew vigorously in the first half of this decade, but has moderated since then, although the creation of an ECU clearing system has contributed to the development and liquidity of the market, as has the issue of short-term bills by the UK Treasury. The lion's share of banking business represents interbank transactions, whereas direct business with non-banks has remained relatively limited and appears to have been driven primarily by officially encouraged borrowing demand in a few countries. ECU-denominated deposits by the non-bank sector have stagnated since 1985, suggesting that the ECU's appeal as a near money substitute and store of liquidity is modest. In addition, in the nonfinancial sphere the use of the ECU for the invoicing and settlement of commercial transactions has remained limited, covering at present only about 1% of the Community countries' external trade.

Section 3: The Single European Act and the internal market programme

7. In January 1985 the Commission proposed realizing the objective of a market without internal frontiers by the end of 1992. The detailed measures for the removal of physical, technical and fiscal barriers were set out in a White Paper, which specified the precise programme, timetable and methods for creating a unified economic area in which persons, goods, services and capital would be able to move freely. This objective was embodied in December 1985 in the *Single European Act*.

8. The Single European Act marked the first significant revision of the Treaty of Rome. It introduced *four important changes* in the Community's strategy for advancing the integration process. Firstly, it greatly simplified the requirements of harmonizing national law by limiting harmonization to the essential standards and by systematic adoption of mutual recognition of national norms and regulations. Secondly, it established a faster and more efficient decision-making process by extending the scope of qualified majority voting. Thirdly, it gave the European Parliament a greater role in the legislative process. Fourthly, it reaffirmed the need to strengthen the Community's economic and social cohesion, to enhance the Community's monetary capacity with a view to economic and monetary union, to reinforce the Community's scientific and technological base, to harmonize working conditions with respect to health and safety standards, to promote the dialogue between management and labour and to initiate action to protect the environment.

9. Over the last three years considerable progress has been made in implementing the internal market programme. In particular, it has been decided that eight member countries will have fully liberalized capital movements by 1 July 1990 and that the other member countries will follow suit after a period of transition.

In December 1988 the European Council, meeting in Rhodes, noted that 'at the halfway stage towards the deadline of December 1992, half of the legislative programme necessary for the establishment of the large market is already nearly complete' and underlined 'the *irreversible nature* of the movement towards a Europe without internal frontiers'. There is, indeed, widespread evidence that the objective of a single market enjoys the broad support of consumers and producers and that their economic decisions are increasingly influenced by the prospects of 1992. The anticipation of a market without internal frontiers has generated a new dynamism and has contributed to the recent acceleration of economic growth in the Community.

Section 4: Problems and perspectives

10. The completion of the single market will link national economies much more closely together and significantly *increase the degree of economic integration* within the Community. It will also entail profound structural changes in the economies of the member countries. These changes offer considerable opportunities for economic advancement, but many of the potential gains can only materialize if economic policy—at both national and Community levels—responds adequately to the structural changes.

By greatly strengthening economic interdependence between member countries, the single market will reduce the room for independent policy manoeuvre and amplify the cross-border effects of developments originating in each member country. It will, therefore, necessitate a more effective coordination of policy between separate national authorities. Furthermore, Community policies in support of a broadly balanced development are an indispensable complement to a single market. Indeed, the need to back up the removal of market barriers with a strengthening of common regional and structural policies was clearly recognized in the Brussels package of measures agreed in February 1988.

11. Although substantial progress has been made, the process of integration has been uneven. *Greater convergence of economic performance is needed.* Despite a marked downward trend in the average rate of price and wage inflation, considerable national differences remain. There are also still notable divergences in budgetary positions and external imbalances have become markedly greater in the recent past. The existence of these disequilibria indicates that there are areas where economic performances will have to be made more convergent.

12. With full freedom of capital movements and integrated financial markets incompatible national policies would quickly translate into exchange rate tensions and put an increasing and undue burden on monetary policy. The integration process thus requires *more intensive and effective policy coordination,* even within the framework of the present exchange rate arrangements, not only in the monetary field but also in areas of national economic management affecting aggregate demand, prices and costs of production.

A tighter coordination of economic policy-making is required. In the monetary field, the problems of the EMS referred to above continue to exist. In the economic field, policy coordination remains insufficient. Especially in the area of fiscal policy, the 1974 Decision on economic convergence has not succeeded in establishing an effective foundation for policy coordination. The pressure for mutually consistent macroeconomic policies has stemmed from the growing reluctance to change exchange rate parities. Such pressure has hitherto been lessened to some extent by the existence of capital controls in some countries and by the segmentation of markets through various types of non-tariff barriers, but as capital movements are liberalized and as the internal market programme is implemented, each country will be less and less shielded from developments elsewhere in the Community. The attainment of national economic objectives will become more dependent on a cooperative approach to policy-making.

13. Decision-making authorities are subject to many pressures and institutional constraints and even best efforts to take into account the international repercussions of their policies are likely to fail at certain times. While *voluntary cooperation* should be relied upon as much as possible to arrive at increasingly consistent national policies, thus taking account of divergent constitutional situations in member countries, there is also likely to be a need for more binding procedures.

14. The success of the internal market programme hinges to a decisive extent on a much closer coordination of national economic policies, as well as on more effective Community policies. This implies that in essence a number of the steps towards economic and monetary union will already have to be taken in the course of establishing a single market in Europe.

Although in many respects a natural consequence of the commitment to create a market without internal frontiers, the move towards economic and monetary union represents a quantum jump which could secure a significant increase in economic welfare in the Community. Indeed, *economic and monetary union implies far more than the single market programme* and, as is discussed in the following two chapters of this Report, will require further major steps in all areas of economic policy-making. A particular role would have to be assigned to common policies aimed at developing a more balanced economic structure throughout the Community. This would help to prevent the emergence or aggravation of regional and sectoral imbalances which could threaten the viability of an economic and monetary union. This is especially important because the adoption of permanently fixed exchange rates would eliminate an important indicator of policy inconsistencies among Community countries and remove the exchange rate as an instrument of adjustment from the member countries' set of economic tools. Economic imbalances among member countries would have to be corrected by policies affecting the structure of their economies and costs of production if major regional disparities in output and employment were to be avoided.

15. At its meeting on 27 and 28 June 1988 the European Council confirmed the objective of economic and monetary union for the Community. In accordance with its mandate, the Committee has focused its attention on the task of studying and proposing concrete stages leading to-

wards the *progressive realization of economic and monetary union.* In investigating how to achieve economic and monetary union the Committee has examined the conditions under which such a union could be viable and successful. The Committee feels that concrete proposals towards attaining this objective can only be made if there is a clear understanding of the implications and requirements of economic and monetary union and if due account is taken of past experience with and developments in economic and monetary integration in the Community. Hence, Chapter II of this Report examines the principal features and implications of an economic and monetary union. Chapter III then presents a pragmatic step-by-step approach which could lead in three stages to the final objective. The question of when these stages should be implemented is a matter for political decision.

Chapter II: The final stage of economic and monetary union

Section 1: General considerations

16. *Economic and monetary union* in Europe would imply complete freedom of movement for persons, goods, services and capital, as well as irrevocably fixed exchange rates between national currencies and, finally, a single currency. This, in turn, would imply a common monetary policy and require a high degree of compatibility of economic policies and consistency in a number of other policy areas, particularly in the fiscal field. These policies should be geared to price stability, balanced growth, converging standards of living, high employment and external equilibrium. Economic and monetary union would represent the final result of the process of progressive economic integration in Europe.

17. Even after attaining economic and monetary union the Community would continue to consist of individual nations with differing economic, social, cultural and political characteristics. The existence and preservation of this *plurality* would require a degree of autonomy in economic decision-making to remain with individual member countries and a balance to be struck between national and Community competences. For this reason it would not be possible simply to follow the example of existing federal States; it would be necessary to develop an innovative and unique approach.

18. The Treaty of Rome, as amended by the Single European Act, provides the legal foundation for many of the necessary steps towards economic integration, but does not suffice for the creation of an economic and monetary union. The realization of this objective would call for new arrangements which could only be established on the basis of *a Treaty change* and consequent changes in national legislations. For this reason the union would have to be embodied in a Treaty which clearly laid down the basic functional and institutional arrangements, as well as provisions governing their step-by-step implementation.

19. Taking into account what is already provided for in the EC Treaties, the need for *a transfer of decision-making power* from Member States to the Community as a whole would arise primarily in the fields of monetary policy and macroeconomic management. A monetary union would require a single monetary policy and responsibility for the formulation of this policy would consequently have to be vested in one decision-making body. In the economic field a wide range of decisions would remain the preserve of national and regional authorities. However, given their potential impact on the overall domestic and external economic situation of the Community and their implications for the conduct of a common monetary policy, such decisions would have to be placed within an agreed macroeconomic framework and be subject to binding procedures and rules. This would permit the determination of an overall policy stance for the Community as a whole, avoid unsustainable differences between individual member countries in public-sector borrowing requirements and place binding constraints on the size and the financing of budget deficits.

20. An essential element in defining the appropriate balance of power within the Community would be adherence to the *'principle of subsidiarity'*, according to which the functions of higher levels of government should be as limited as possible and should be subsidiary to those of lower levels. Thus, the attribution of competences to the Community would have to be confined specifically to those areas in which collective decision-making was necessary. All policy functions which could be carried out at national (and regional and local) levels without adverse repercussions on the cohesion and functioning of the economic and monetary union would remain within the competence of the member countries.

21. Economic union and monetary union form *two integral parts of a single whole* and would therefore have to be implemented in parallel. It is only for reasons of expositional clarity that the following sections look separately at an economic and a monetary union. The description begins with monetary union, chiefly because the principal features of an economic union depend significantly on the agreed monetary arrangements and constraints. But the Committee is fully aware that the process of achieving

monetary union is only conceivable if a high degree of economic convergence is attained.

Section 2: The principal features of monetary union

22. A *monetary union* constitutes a currency area in which policies are managed jointly with a view to attaining common macroeconomic objectives. As already stated in the 1970 Werner Report, there are three necessary conditions for a monetary union:

— the assurance of total and irreversible convertibility of currencies;
— the complete liberalization of capital transactions and full integration of banking and other financial markets; and
— the elimination of margins of fluctuation and the irrevocable locking of exchange rate parities.

The first two of these requirements have already been met, or will be with the completion of the internal market programme. The single most important condition for a monetary union would, however, be fulfilled only when the decisive step was taken to lock exchange rates irrevocably.

As a result of this step, national currencies would become increasingly close substitutes and their interest rates would tend to converge. The pace with which these developments took place would depend critically on the extent to which firms, households, labour unions and other economic agents were convinced that the decision to lock exchange rates would not be reversed. Both coherent monetary management and convincing evidence of an effective coordination of non-monetary policies would be crucial.

23. The three abovementioned requirements define a single currency area, but their fulfillment would not necessarily mark the end of the process of monetary unification in the Community. The adoption of *a single currency*, while not strictly necessary for the creation of a monetary union, might be seen—for economic as well as psychological and political reasons—as a natural and desirable further development of the monetary union. A single currency would clearly demonstrate the irreversibility of the move to monetary union, considerably facilitate the monetary management of the Community and avoid the transactions costs of converting currencies. A single currency, provided that its stability is ensured, would also have a much greater weight relative to other major currencies than any individual Community currency. The replacement of national currencies by a single currency should therefore take place as soon as possible after the locking of parities.

24. The establishment of a monetary union would have far-reaching implications for the formulation and execution of monetary policy in the Community. Once permanently fixed exchange rates had been adopted, there would be *a need for a common monetary policy*, which would be carried out through new operating procedures. The coordination of as many national monetary policies as there were currencies participating in the union would not be sufficient. The responsibility for the single monetary policy would have to be vested in a new institution, in which centralized and collective decisions would be taken on the supply of money and credit as well as on other instruments of monetary policy, including interest rates.

This shift from national monetary policies to a single monetary policy is an inescapable consequence of monetary union and constitutes one of the principal institutional changes. Although a progressively intensified coordination of national monetary policies would in many respects have prepared the way for the move to a single monetary policy, the implications of such a move would be far-reaching. The permanent fixing of exchange rates would deprive individual countries of an important instrument for the correction of economic imbalances and for independent action in the pursuit of national objectives, especially price stability.

Well before the decision to fix exchange rates permanently, the full liberalization of capital movements and financial market integration would have created a situation in which the coordination of monetary policy would have to be strengthened progressively. Once every banking institution in the Community is free to accept deposits from, and to grant loans to, any customer in the Community and in any of the national currencies, the large degree of territorial coincidence between a national central bank's area of jurisdiction, the area in which its currency is used and the area in which 'its' banking system operates will be lost. In these circumstances the effectiveness of national monetary policies will become increasingly dependent on cooperation among central banks. Indeed, the growing coordination of monetary policies will make a positive contribution to financial market integration and will help central banks gain the experience that would be necessary to move to a single monetary policy.

Section 3: The principal features of economic union

25. *Economic union*—in conjunction with a monetary union—combines the characteristics of an unrestricted common market with a set of rules which are indispensable to its proper working. In this sense economic union can be described in terms of four basic elements:

— the single market within which persons, goods, services and capital can move freely;

— competition policy and other measures aimed at strengthening market mechanisms;

— common policies aimed at structural change and regional development; and

— macroeconomic policy coordination, including binding rules for budgetary policies.

In defining specific rules and arrangements governing an economic union, the Community should be guided by two considerations.

Firstly, the economic union should be based on the same market-oriented economic principles that underlie the economic order of its member countries. Differences in policy choices may exist between member countries or, within the same country, in different periods. However, beyond such differences, a distinctive common feature of economic systems in Europe is the combination of a large degree of freedom for market behaviour and private economic initiative with public intervention in the provision of certain social services and public goods.

Secondly, an appropriate balance between the economic and monetary components would have to be ensured for the union to be viable. This would be essential because of the close interactions between economic and monetary developments and policies. A coherent set of economic policies at the Community and national levels would be necessary to maintain permanently fixed exchange rates between Community currencies and, conversely, a common monetary policy, in support of a single currency area, would be necessary for the Community to develop into an economic union.

26. The creation of a single currency area would add to the potential benefits of an enlarged economic area because it would remove intra-Community exchange rate uncertainties and reduce transactions costs, eliminate exchange rate variability and reduce the susceptibility of the Community to external shocks.

At the same time, however, exchange rate adjustments would no longer be available as an instrument to correct economic imbalances within the Community. Such *imbalances might arise* because the process of adjustment and restructuring set in motion by the removal of physical, technical and fiscal barriers is unlikely to have an even impact on different regions or always produce satisfactory results within reasonable periods of time. Imbalances might also emanate from labour and other cost developments, external shocks with differing repercussions on individual economies, or divergent economic policies pursued at national level.

With parities irrevocably fixed, foreign exchange markets would cease to be a source of pressure for national policy corrections when national economic disequilibria developed and persisted. Moreover, the statistical measurement and the interpretation of economic imbalances might become more difficult because in a fully integrated market balance-of-payments figures, which are currently a highly visible and sensitive indicator of economic disequilibria, would no longer play such a significant role as a guidepost for policy-making. None the less, such imbalances, if left uncorrected, would manifest themselves as regional disequilibria. Measures designed to strengthen the mobility of factors of production and the flexibility of prices would help to deal with such imbalances.

27. In order to create an economic and monetary union the single market would have to be complemented with *action in three interrelated areas:* competition policy and other measures aimed at strengthening market mechanisms; common policies to enhance the process of resource allocation in those economic sectors and geographical areas where the working of the market forces needed to be reinforced or complemented; macroeconomic coordination, including binding rules in the budgetary field; and other arrangements both to limit the scope for divergences between member countries and to design an overall economic policy framework for the Community as a whole.

28. *Competition policy*—conducted at the Community level—would have to operate in such a way that access to markets would not be impeded and market functioning not be distorted by the behaviour of private or public economic agents. Such policies would not only have to address conventional forms of restrictive practices and the abuse of dominant market positions, but would also have to deal with new aspects of antitrust laws, especially in the field of merger and takeover activities. The use of government subsidies to assist particular industries should be strictly circumscribed because they distort competition and cause an inefficient use and allocation of scarce economic resources.

29. *Community policies in the regional and structural field* would be necessary in order to promote an optimum allocation of resources and to spread welfare gains throughout the Community. If sufficient consideration were not given to regional imbalances, the economic union would be faced with grave economic and political risks. For this reason particular attention would have to be paid to an effective Community policy aimed at narrowing regional and structural disparities and promoting a balanced development throughout the Community. In this context the regional dimension of other Community policies would have to be taken into account.

Economic and monetary integration may have beneficial effects on the less developed regions of the Community. For example, regions with lower wage levels would have an opportunity to attract modern and rapidly growing service and manufacturing industries for which the choice of location would not necessarily be determined by transport costs, labour skills and market proximity. Historical experience suggests, however, that in the absence of countervailing policies, the overall impact on peripheral regions could be negative. Transport costs and economies of scale would tend to favour a shift in economic activity away from less developed regions, especially if they were at the periphery of the Community, to the highly developed areas at its centre. The economic and monetary union would have to encourage and guide structural adjustment which would help poorer regions to catch up with the wealthier ones.

A step in this direction was taken in February 1988 when the European Council decided to strengthen and reorganize the Community's regional and structural policies in several respects: the size of structural funds will be doubled over the period up to 1993, emphasis will be shifted from project to programme financing, and a new form of partnership will be established between the Community and the recipient regions. Depending upon the speed of progress, such policies might have to be strengthened further after 1993 in the process of creating economic and monetary union.

At the same time, excessive reliance on financial assistance through regional and structural policies could cause tensions. The principal objective of regional policies should not be to subsidize incomes and simply offset inequalities in standards of living, but to help to equalize production conditions through investment programmes in such areas as physical infrastructure, communications, transportation and education so that large-scale movements of labour do not become the major adjustment factor. The success of these policies will hinge not only on the size of the available financial resources, but to a decisive extent also on their efficient use and on the private and social return on the investment programmes.

Apart from regional policies, the Treaty of Rome, as amended by the Single European Act, has established the basis for Community policies in areas such as infrastructure, research and technological development, and the environment. Such policies would not only enhance market efficiency and offset market imperfections, but could also contribute to regional development. While respecting the principle of subsidiarity, such policies would have to be developed further in the process towards economic and monetary union.

Wage flexibility and labour mobility are necessary to eliminate differences in competitiveness in different regions and countries of the Community. Otherwise there could be relatively large declines in output and employment in areas with lower productivity. In order to reduce adjustment burdens temporarily, it might be necessary in certain circumstances to provide financing flows through official channels. Such financial support would be additional to what might come from spontaneous capital flows or external borrowing and should be granted on terms and conditions that would prompt the recipient to intensify its adjustment efforts.

30. *Macroeconomic policy* is the third area in which action would be necessary for a viable economic and monetary union. This would require an appropriate definition of the role of the Community in promoting price stability and economic growth through the coordination of economic policies.

Many developments in macroeconomic conditions would continue to be determined by factors and decisions operating at the national or local level. This would include not only wage negotiations and other economic decisions in the fields of production, saving and investment, but also the action of public authorities in the economic and social spheres. Apart from the system of binding rules governing the size and the financing of national budget deficits, decisions on the main components of public policy in such areas as internal and external security, justice, social security, education, and hence on the level and composition of government spending, as well as many revenue measures, would remain the preserve of Member States even at the final stage of economic and monetary union.

However, an economic and monetary union could only operate on the basis of mutually consistent and sound behaviour by governments and other economic agents in all member countries. In particular, uncoordinated and divergent national budgetary policies would undermine monetary stability and generate imbalances in the real and financial sectors of the Community. Moreover, the fact that the centrally managed Community budget is likely to remain a very small part of total public-sector spending and that much of this budget will not be available for cyclical adjustments will mean that the task of setting a Community-wide fiscal policy stance will have to be performed through the coordination of national budgetary policies. Without such coordination it would be impossible for the Community as a whole to establish a fiscal/monetary policy mix appropriate for the preservation of internal balance, or for the Community to play its part in the international adjustment process. Monetary policy alone cannot be expected to perform these functions. Moreover, strong divergences in wage levels and developments, not justified by different trends in productivity, would produce economic tensions and pressure for monetary expansion.

To some extent market forces can exert a disciplinary influence. Financial markets, consumers and investors would respond to differences in macroeconomic developments in individual countries and regions, assess their budgetary and financial positions, penalize deviations from commonly agreed budgetary guidelines or wage settlements, and thus exert pressure for sounder policies. However, experience suggests that market perceptions do not necessarily provide strong and compelling signals and that access to a large capital market may for some time even facilitate the financing of economic imbalances. Rather than leading to a gradual adaptation of borrowing costs, market views about the creditworthiness of official borrowers tend to change abruptly and result in the closure of access to market financing. The constraints imposed by market forces might either be too slow and weak or too sudden and disruptive. Hence counties would have to accept that sharing a common market and a single currency area imposed policy constraints.

In the general macroeconomic field, a common overall assessment of the short-term and medium-term economic developments in the Community would need to be agreed periodically and would constitute the framework for a better coordination of national economic policies. The Community would need to be in a position to monitor its overall economic situation, to assess the consistency of developments in individual countries with regard to common objectives and to formulate guidelines for policy.

As regards wage formation and industrial relations the autonomous negotiating process would need to be preserved, but efforts would have to be made to convince European management and labour of the advantages of gearing wage policies largely to improvements in productivity. Governments, for their part, would refrain from direct intervention in the wage and price formation process.

In the budgetary field, binding rules are required that would: firstly, impose effective upper limits on budget deficits of individual member countries of the Community, although in setting these limits the situation of each member country might have to be taken into consideration; secondly, exclude access to direct central bank credit and other forms of monetary financing while, however, permitting open market operations in government securities; thirdly, limit recourse to external borrowing in non-Community currencies. Moreover, the arrangements in the budgetary field should enable the Community to conduct a coherent mix of fiscal and monetary policies.

Section 4: Institutional arrangements

31. Management of the economic and monetary union would call for *an institutional framework* which would allow policy to be decided and executed at the Community level in those economic areas that were of direct relevance for the functioning of the union. This framework would have to promote efficient economic management, properly embedded in the democratic process. Economic and monetary union would require the creation of a new monetary institution, placed in the constellation of Community institutions (European Parliament, European Council, Council of Ministers, Commission and Court of Justice). The formulation and

implementation of common policies in non-monetary fields and the coordination of policies remaining within the competence of national authorities would not necessarily require a new institution; but a revision and, possibly, some restructuring of the existing Community bodies, including an appropriate delegation of authority, could be necessary.

32. A new monetary institution would be needed because a single monetary policy cannot result from independent decisions and actions by different central banks. Moreover, day-to-day monetary policy operations cannot respond quickly to changing market conditions unless they are decided centrally. Considering the political structure of the Community and the advantages of making existing central banks part of a new system, the domestic and international monetary policy-making of the Community should be organized in a federal form in what might be called a *European System of Central Banks* (ESCB). This new System would have to be given the full status of an autonomous Community institution. It would operate in accordance with the provisions of the Treaty, and could consist of a central institution (with its own balance sheet) and the national central banks. At the final stage the ESCB—acting through its Council—would be responsible for formulating and implementing monetary policy as well as managing the Community's exchange rate policy *vis-à-vis* third currencies. The national central banks would be entrusted with the implementation of policies in conformity with guidelines established by the Council of the ESCB and in accordance with instructions from the central institution.

The European System of Central Banks would be based on the following principles:

MANDATE AND FUNCTIONS

— The System would be committed to the objective of price stability;
— subject to the foregoing, the System should support the general economic policy set at the Community level by the competent bodies;
— the System would be responsible for the formulation and implementation of monetary policy, exchange rate and reserve management, and the maintenance of a properly functioning payment system;
— the System would participate in the coordination of banking supervision policies of the supervisory authorities.

POLICY INSTRUMENTS

— The policy instruments available to the System, together with a procedure for amending them, would be specified in its Statutes; the instruments would enable the System to conduct central banking operations in financial and foreign exchange markets as well as to exercise regulatory power;

— while complying with the provision not to lend to public-sector authorities, the System could buy and sell government securities on the market as a means of conducting monetary policy.

STRUCTURE AND ORGANIZATION

— A federative structure, since this would correspond best to the political diversity of the Community;

— establishment of an ESCB Council (composed of the Governors of the central banks and the members of the Board, the latter to be appointed by European Council), which would be responsible for the formulation of and decisions on the thrust of monetary policy; modalities of voting procedures would have to be provided for in the Treaty;

— establishment of a Board (with supporting staff) which would monitor monetary developments and oversee the implementation of the common monetary policy;

— national central banks, which would execute operations in accordance with the decisions taken by the ESCB Council.

STATUS

— Independence: the ESCB Council should be independent of instructions from national governments and Community authorities; to that effect the members of the ESCB Council, both Governors and the Board members should have appropriate security of tenure;

— accountability: reporting would be in the form of submission of an annual report by the ESCB to the European Parliament and the European Council; moreover, the Chairman of the ESCB could be invited to report to these institutions. Supervision of the administration of the System would be carried out independently of the Community bodies, for example by a supervisory council or a committee of independent auditors.

33. In the *economic field,* in contrast to the monetary field, an institutional framework for performing policy tasks was already established under the Treaty of Rome, with different and complementary functions conferred on the European Parliament, the Council of Ministers, the Monetary Committee, the Commission and the Court of Justice. The new Treaty would therefore not have to determine the mandate, status and structure of a new institution but would have to provide for additional or changed roles for the

existing bodies in the light of the policy functions they would have to fulfil in an economic and monetary union. It would have to specifically define these changes and determine the areas in which decision-making authority would have to be transferred from the national to the Community level.

GENERAL CRITERIA

In order to ensure the flexible and effective conduct of policies in those economic areas in which the Community would be involved, several basic requirements would have to be fulfilled:

— Where policies were decided and enacted at the Community level there would have to be a clear distribution of responsibilities among the existing Community institutions, a distinction being made as to whether decisions related to the setting of broad policy directions or to day-to-day operations. By analogy with the structure of the European System of Central Banks, where the ESCB Council would determine the broad lines of monetary policy and the Board would be responsible for its day-to-day execution, a similar division of responsibilities could be envisaged in the economic field. The Council of Ministers would determine the broad lines of economic policy, while the implementation would be left to the national governments and the Commission in their respective areas of competence.

— in the event of non-compliance by Member States, the Commission, or another appropriately delegated authority as envisaged in paragraph 31, would be responsible for taking effective action to ensure compliance; the nature of such action would have to be explored.

SINGLE MARKET AND COMPETITION POLICY

In these two areas, the necessary procedures and arrangements have already been established by the Treaty of Rome and the Single European Act, which confer the requisite legislative, executive and judicial authority on the Community. The completion of the internal market will result in a marked easing of the overall burden of regulation for economic agents, but for the Community institutions it will mean a substantial addition to their executive and policing functions.

COMMUNITY POLICIES IN THE
REGIONAL AND STRUCTURAL FIELD

The foundations for a more effective Community role in regional and structural development have recently been established, with both a doubling of the resources of structural funds and a reorganization of policies as described earlier in this Report. These mechanisms would perhaps have to be further extended and made more effective as part of the process leading to economic and monetary union.

MACROECONOMIC POLICY

The broad *objective* of economic policy coordination would be to promote growth, employment and external balance in an environment of price stability and economic cohesion. For this purpose coordination would involve defining a medium-term framework for budgetary policy within the economic and monetary union; managing common policies with a view to structural and regional development; formulating in cooperation with the ESCB Council the Community's exchange rate policy and participating in policy coordination at the international level.

New *procedures* required for this purpose would have to strike a balance between reliance on binding rules, where necessary, to ensure effective implementation and discretionary coordination adapted to particular situations.

In particular it would seem necessary to develop both binding rules and procedures for *budgetary policy,* involving respectively:

— effective upper limits on budget deficits of individual member countries; exclusion of access to direct central bank credit and other forms of monetary financing; limits on borrowing in non-Community currencies;
— the definition of the overall stance of fiscal policy over the medium term, including the size and financing of the aggregate budgetary balance, comprising both the national and the Community positions.

34. The new Treaty laying down the objectives, features, requirements, procedures and organs of the economic and monetary union would add to the existing Community institutions (European Parliament, European Council, Council of Ministers, Commission and Court of Justice) a new institution of comparable status, the European System of Central Banks. With due respect for the independent status of the ESCB, as defined elsewhere in this Report, appropriate consultation procedures would have to be set up to allow for effective *coordination between budgetary and monetary policy.* This might involve attendance by the President of the Council and the President of the Commission at meetings of the ESCB Council, without power to vote or to block decisions taken in accordance with the rules laid down by the ESCB Council. Equally, the Chairman of the ESCB Council might attend meetings of the Council of Ministers, especially on matters of relevance to

the conduct of monetary policy. Consideration would also have to be given to the role of the European Parliament, especially in relation to the new policy functions exercised by various Community bodies.

Section 5: Economic and monetary union in the context of the world economy

35. The establishment of an economic and monetary union would give *the Community a greater say in international negotiations* and enhance its capacity to influence economic relations between industrial and developing countries.

36. The responsibility for *external trade policy* has been assigned to the Community in the Treaty of Rome, and the Commission acting as the Community's spokesman, represents all the member countries in multilateral trade negotiations. This role will be strengthened with the completion of the single market, which has the potential to stimulate multilateral trade and economic growth at the global level. However, this potential can only be exploited to the full in an open trading system, which guarantees foreign suppliers free access to the Community market and conversely, guarantees exporters from the Community free access to foreign markets. The removal of internal trade barriers within the Community should constitute a step towards a more liberal trading system on a worldwide scale.

37. The creation of an economic and monetary union would increase the role of the Community in the process of *international policy concertation*. In the monetary field this would involve short-term cooperation between central banks in interest rate management and exchange market interventions as well as the search for solutions to issues relating to the international monetary system. In the economic field, the formulation of a policy mix would allow the Community to contribute more effectively to world economic management.

38. The institutional *arrangements* which would enable the Community to fulfil the new responsibilities implied by its increased weight in the world economy are partly in place or would be implemented in the process of creating an economic and monetary union. In the area of external trade policies and, to some extent, in the field of cooperation with developing countries, the responsibilities have already been attributed to the Community. With the establishment of the European System of Central Banks the Community would also have created an institution through which it could participate in all aspects of international monetary management. As far as macroeconomic policy coordination at the international level is concerned, the Community as such is currently represented only at the summit meetings of the major industrial countries. In order to make full use of its posi-

tion in the world economy and to exert influence on the functioning of the international economic system, the Community would have to be able to speak with one voice. This emphasizes the need for an effective mechanism for macroeconomic policy coordination within the economic and monetary union.

Chapter III: Steps towards economic and monetary union

39. After defining the main features of an economic and monetary union, the Committee has undertaken the 'task of studying and proposing concrete stages leading towards this union'. The Committee agreed that the *creation of an economic and monetary union must be viewed as a single process.* Although this process is set out in stages which guide the progressive movement to the final objective, the decision to enter upon the first stage should be a decision to embark on the entire process.

A clear political commitment to the final stage, as described in Chapter II of this Report, would lend credibility to the intention that the measures which constitute stage one should represent not just a useful end in themselves but a firm first step on the road towards economic and monetary union. It would be a strong expression of such a commitment if all members of the Community became full members of the EMS in the course of stage one and undertook the obligation to formulate a convergent economic policy within the existing institutions.

Given that background, commitment by the political authorities to enter into negotiations on a new Treaty would ensure the continuity of the process. Preparatory work for these negotiations would start immediately. At the end of this Report suggestions are made regarding the procedures to be followed for the further development of economic and monetary union.

Section 1: Principles governing a step-by-step approach

40. In *designing a step-by-step approach* along the path to economic and monetary union the general principle of subsidiarity, referred to earlier in

this Report, as well as a number of further considerations, would have to be taken into account.

41. *Discrete but evolutionary steps.* The process of implementing economic and monetary union would have to be divided into a limited number of clearly defined stages. Each stage would have to represent a significant change with respect to the preceding one. New arrangements coming into force at the beginning of each stage would gradually develop their effects and bring about a change in economic circumstances so as to pave the way for the next stage. This evolutionary development would apply to both functional and institutional arrangements.

42. *Parallelism.* As has been argued in Chapter II, monetary union without a sufficient degree of convergence of economic policies is unlikely to be durable and could be damaging to the Community. Parallel advancement in economic and monetary integration would be indispensable in order to avoid imbalances which could cause economic strains and loss of political support for developing the Community further into an economic and monetary union. Perfect parallelism at each and every point of time would be impossible and could even be counter-productive. Already in the past the advancement of the Community in certain areas has taken place with temporary standstill in others, so that parallelism has been only partial. Some temporary deviations from parallelism are part of the dynamic process of the Community. But bearing in mind the need to achieve a substantial degree of economic union if monetary union is to be successful, and given the degree of monetary coordination already achieved, it is clear that material progress on the economic policy front would be necessary for further progress on the monetary policy front. Parallelism would have to be maintained in the medium term and also before proceeding from one stage to the next.

43. *Calendar.* The conditions for moving from stage to stage cannot be defined precisely in advance; nor is it possible to foresee today when these conditions will be realized. The setting of explicit deadlines is therefore not advisable. This observation applies to the passage from stage one to stage two and, most importantly, to the move to irrevocably fixed exchange rates. The timing of both these moves would involve an appraisal by the Council, and from stage two to stage three also by the European System of Central Banks in the light of the experience gained in the preceding stage. However, there should be a clear indication of the timing of the first stage, which should start no later than 1 July 1990 when the Directive for the full liberalization of capital movements comes into force.

44. *Participation.* There is one Community, but not all the members have participated fully in all its aspects from the outset. A consensus on the final objectives of the Community, as well as participation in the same set of in-

stitutions, should be maintained, while allowing for a degree of flexibility concerning the date and conditions on which some member countries would join certain arrangements. Pending the full participation of all member countries—which is of prime importance—influence on the management of each set of arrangements would have to be related to the degree of participation by Member States. However, this management would have to keep in mind the need to facilitate the integration of the other members.

Section 2: The ECU

45. The Committee investigated *various aspects of the role* that the ECU might play in the process of economic and monetary integration in Europe.

46. Firstly, the Committee examined the role of the ECU in connection with an eventual move to a single currency. Although a monetary union does not necessarily require a single currency, it would be a desirable feature of a monetary union. The Committee was of the opinion that the ECU has the potential to be developed into such a *common currency*. This would imply that the ECU would be transformed from a basket of currencies into a genuine currency. The irrevocable fixing of exchange rates would imply that there would be no discontinuity between the ECU and the single currency of the union and that ECU obligations would be payable at face value in ECUs if the transition to the single currency had been made by the time the contract matured.

47. Secondly, the Committee considered the possibility of adopting a *parallel currency strategy* as a means of accelerating the pace of the monetary union process. Under this approach the definition of the ECU as a basket of currencies would be abandoned at an early stage and the new fully-fledged currency, called the ECU, would be created autonomously and issued in addition to the existing Community currencies, competing with them. The proponents of this strategy expect that the gradual crowding-out of national currencies by the ECU would make it possible to circumvent the institutional and economic difficulties of establishing a monetary union. The Committee felt that this strategy was not to be recommended for two main reasons. Firstly, an additional source of money creation without a precise linkage to economic activity could jeopardize price stability. Secondly, the addition of a new currency, with its own independent monetary implications, would further complicate the already difficult endeavour of coordinating different national monetary policies.

48. Thirdly, the Committee examined the possibility of using the official ECU as an instrument *in the conduct of a common monetary policy*. The main features of possible schemes are described in the Collection of papers submitted to the Committee, which represent personal contributions.

49. Fourthly, the Committee agreed that there should be no discrimination against the *private use of the ECU* and that existing administrative obstacles should be removed.

Section 3: The principal steps in stage one

50. Stage one represents the *initiation of the process* of creating an economic and monetary union. It would aim at a greater convergence of economic performance through the strengthening of economic and monetary policy coordination within the existing institutional framework. In the institutional field, by the time of the transition to stage two, it would be necessary to have prepared and ratified the Treaty change.

51. *In the economic field* the steps would centre on the completion of the internal market and the reduction of existing disparities through programmes of budgetary consolidation in those countries concerned and more effective structural and regional policies. In particular, there would be action in three directions.

Firstly, there would be a complete removal of physical, technical and fiscal barriers within the Community, in line with the internal market programme. The completion of the internal market would be accompanied by a strengthening of Community competition policy.

Secondly, the reform of the structural Funds and doubling of their resources would be fully implemented in order to enhance the ability of Community policies to promote regional development and to correct economic imbalances.

Thirdly, the 1974 Council Decision on economic convergence would be replaced by a new procedure that would strengthen economic and fiscal policy coordination and would, in addition, provide a comprehensive framework for an assessment of the consequences and consistency of the overall policies of Member States. On the basis of this assessment, recommendations would be made aimed at achieving a more effective coordination of economic policies, taking due account of the views of the Committee of Central Bank Governors. The task of economic policy coordination should be the primary responsibility of the Council of Economic and Finance Ministers (Ecofin). Consistency between monetary and economic policies would be facilitated by the participation of the Chairman of the Committee of Central Bank Governors in appropriate Council meetings. In particular, the revised 1974 Decision on convergence would:

— establish a process of multilateral surveillance of economic developments and policies based on agreed indicators. Where performances were judged inadequate or detrimental to commonly set objectives,

policy consultations would take place at Community level and recommendations would be formulated with a view to promoting the necessary corrections in national policies;
— set up a new procedure for budgetary policy coordination, with precise quantitative guidelines and medium-term orientations;
— provide for concerted budgetary action by the member countries.

52. *In the monetary field* the focus would be on removing all obstacles to financial integration and on intensifying cooperation and the coordination of monetary policies. In this connection consideration should be given to extending the scope of central banks' autonomy. Realignments of exchange rates would still be possible, but an effort would be made by every country to make the functioning of other adjustment mechanisms more effective. Action would be taken along several lines.

Firstly, through the approval and enforcement of the necessary Community Directives, the objective of a single financial area in which all monetary and financial instruments circulate freely and banking, securities and insurance services are offered uniformly throughout the area would be fully implemented.

Secondly, it would be important to include all Community currencies in the EMS exchange rate mechanism. The same rules would apply to all the participants in the exchange rate mechanism.

Thirdly, all impediments to the private use of the ECU would be removed.

Fourthly, the 1964 Council Decision defining the mandate of the Committee of Central Bank Governors would be replaced by a new Decision. According to this Decision the Committee of Central Bank Governors should:

— formulate opinions on the overall orientation of monetary and exchange rate policy, as well as on measures taken in these fields by individual countries. In particular, the Committee would normally be consulted in advance of national decisions on the course of monetary policy, such as the setting of annual domestic monetary and credit targets;
— express opinions to individual governments and the Council of Ministers on policies that could affect the internal and external monetary situation in the Community, especially the functioning of the EMS. The outcome of the Committee's deliberations could be made public by the Chairman of the Committee;

— submit an annual report on its activities and on the monetary situation of the Community to the European Parliament and the European Council.

The Committee could express majority opinions, although at this stage they would not be binding. In order to make its policy coordination function more effective, the Committee would set up three sub-committees, with a greater research and advisory role than those existing hitherto, and provide them with a permanent research staff:

— a monetary policy committee would define common surveillance indicators, propose harmonized objectives and instruments and help to gradually bring about a change from *ex post* to an *ex ante* approach to monetary policy cooperation;
— a foreign exchange policy committee would monitor and analyse exchange market developments and assist in the search for effective intervention strategies;
— an advisory committee would hold regular consultations on matters of common interest in the field of banking supervision policy.

53. A number of Committee members advocated the creation of a *European Reserve Fund (ERF)* that would foreshadow the future European System of Central Banks. The main objectives of the ERF would be:

— to serve as a training ground for implementing a better coordination of monetary analysis and decisions;
— to facilitate, from a Community point of view, the concerted management of exchange rates and possibly to intervene visibly (in third and participating currencies) on the foreign exchange market at the request of the participating central banks;
— to be the symbol of the political will of the European countries and thus reinforce the credibility of the process towards economic and monetary union.

The resources of the fund would be provided by the pooling of a limited amount of reserves (for instance 10% at the start) by participating central banks. The Fund would, moreover, require a permanent structure and staff in order to carry out its tasks, namely:

— managing the pooled reserves;
— intervening on the exchange markets as decided by the members;
— analysing monetary trends, from a collective perspective, in order to enhance policy coordination.

All EC central banks would be eligible to join the Fund. However, membership would be subject to their participation in the exchange rate mechanism, the reason being that the EMS implies specific constraints on monetary policy and foreign exchange interventions, both of which require a common approach on the part of the central banks concerned.

The ERF would consist of:

— a Board of Directors, which would comprise, ex officio, the Governors of all the central banks participating in the ERF;
— an Executive Committee, whose members would be selected by the Committee of Governors on the basis of competence. This Executive Committee would be small in size, consisting of three or four members who would have direct responsibility for the different departments of the ERF;
— three committees, namely the Foreign Exchange Policy Committee, the Monetary Policy Committee and the Committee on Banking Supervision policy;
— two departments: a Foreign Exchange and Reserve Management Department and a Monetary Policy Department.

54. Other members of the Committee felt that the creation of an ERF was not opportune at this stage. Their reservations stem from the following considerations:

— too much emphasis is placed on external considerations; common interventions by such a Fund cannot be a substitute for economic adjustment to correct imbalances within the Community;
— the proposal involves an institutional change which, in accordance with Article 102a of the amended Treaty of Rome, would fall under the procedure stipulated in Article 236 and require a new Treaty; the setting-up of a Fund under the same procedures as those applied in establishing the EMS is not considered possible;
— they consider that some functions of the Fund could be performed by the Committee of Governors if it were given wider powers; thus there is no need to set up a new institution immediately;
— what, in the view of these members, is essential is coordination of intervention policies rather than the technique of common interventions. Such coordination can provide the necessary training ground while avoiding the unnecessary complication of instituting an additional intervention window.

Section 4: The principal steps in stage two

55. The *second stage* could begin only when the new Treaty had come into force. In this stage the basic organs and structure of the economic and monetary union would be set up, involving both the revision of existing institutions and the establishment of new ones. The institutional framework would gradually take over operational functions, serve as the centre for monitoring and analysing macroeconomic developments and promote a process of common decision-making with certain operational decisions taken by majority vote. Stage two must be seen as a period of transition to the final stage and would thus primarily constitute a training process leading to collective decision-making, while the ultimate responsibility for policy decisions would remain at this stage with national authorities. The precise operating procedures to be applied in stage two would be developed in the light of the prevailing economic conditions and the experience gained in the previous stage.

56. *In the economic field,* the European Parliament, the Council of Ministers, the Monetary Committee and the Commission would reinforce their action along three lines.

Firstly, in the area of the single market and competition policy the results achieved through the implementation of the single market programme would be reviewed and, wherever necessary, consolidated.

Secondly, the performance of structural and regional policies would be evaluated and, if necessary, be adapted in the light of experience. The resources for supporting the structural policies of the Member States might have to be enlarged. Community programmes for investment in research and infrastructure would be strengthened.

Thirdly, in the area of macroeconomic policy, the procedures set up in the first stage through the revision of the 1974 Decision on convergence would be further strengthened and extended on the basis of the new Treaty. Policy guidelines would be adopted by majority decision. On this basis the Community would:

— set a medium-term framework for key economic objectives aimed at achieving stable growth, with a follow-up procedure for monitoring performances and intervening when significant deviations occurred;

— set precise, although not yet binding, rules relating to the size of annual budget deficits and their financing; the Commission should be responsible for bringing any instance of non-compliance by Member States to the Council's attention and should propose action as necessary;

— assume a more active role as a single entity in the discussion of questions arising in the economic and exchange rate field, on the basis of its present representation (through the Member States or the Commission) in the various forums for international policy coordination.

57. *In the monetary field,* the most important feature of this stage would be that the European System of Central Banks would be set up and would absorb the previously existing institutional monetary arrangements (the EMCF, the Committee of Central Bank Governors, the sub-committees for monetary policy analysis, foreign exchange policy and banking supervision, and the permanent secretariat). The functions of the ESCB in the formulation and operation of a common monetary policy would gradually evolve as experience was gained. Some possible schemes for coordinating monetary policies in the course of this stage are discussed in the *Collection of papers submitted to the Committee.* Exchange rate realignments would not be excluded as an instrument of adjustment, but there would be an understanding that they would be made only in exceptional circumstances.

The key task for the European System of Central Banks during this stage would be to begin the transition from the coordination of independent national monetary policies by the Committee of Central Bank Governors in stage one to the formulation and implementation of a common monetary policy by the ESCB itself scheduled to take place in the final stage.

The fundamental difficulty inherent in this transition would lie in the organization of a gradual transfer of decision-making power from national authorities to a Community institution. At this juncture, the Committee does not consider it possible to propose a detailed blueprint for accomplishing this transition, as this would depend on the effectiveness of the policy coordination achieved during the first stage, on the provisions of the Treaty, and on decisions to be taken by the new institutions. Account would also have to be taken of the continued impact of financial innovation on monetary control techniques (which are at present undergoing radical changes in most industrial countries), of the degree of integration reached in European financial markets, of the constellation of financial and banking centres in Europe and of the development of the private, and in particular banking, use of the ECU.

The transition that characterizes this second stage would involve a certain number of actions. For instance, general monetary orientations would be set for the Community as a whole, with an understanding that national monetary policy would be executed in accordance with these global guidelines. Moreover, while the ultimate responsibility for monetary policy decisions would remain with national authorities, the operational framework necessary for deciding and implementing a common monetary policy would be created and experimented with. Also, a certain amount of exchange reserves would be pooled and would be used to conduct exchange market interventions in accordance with guidelines established by the ESCB Council. Finally, regulatory functions would be exercised by the ESCB in the monetary and banking field in order to achieve a minimum harmonization of provisions (such as reserve requirements or payment arrangements) necessary for the future conduct of a common monetary policy.

As circumstances permitted and in the light of progress made in the process of economic convergence, the margins of fluctuation within the exchange rate mechanism would be narrowed as a move towards the final stage of the monetary union, in which they would be reduced to zero.

Section 5: The principal steps in stage three

58. The *final stage* would commence with the move to irrevocably locked exchange rates and the attribution to Community institutions of the full monetary and economic competences described in Chapter II of this Report. In the course of the final stage the national currencies would eventually be replaced by a single Community currency.

59. *In the economic field,* the transition to this final stage would be marked by three developments.

Firstly, there might need to be a further strengthening of Community structural and regional policies. Instruments and resources would be adapted to the needs of the economic and monetary union.

Secondly, the rules and procedures of the Community in the macroeconomic and budgetary field would become binding. In particular, the Council of Ministers, in cooperation with the European Parliament, would have the authority to take directly enforceable decisions, i.e.:

— to impose constraints on national budgets to the extent to which this was necessary to prevent imbalances that might threaten monetary stability;
— to make discretionary changes in Community resources (through a procedure to be defined) to supplement structural transfers to Member States or to influence the overall policy stance in the Community;
— to apply to existing Community structural policies and to Community loans (as a substitute for the present medium-term financial assistance facility) terms and conditions that would prompt member countries to intensify their adjustment efforts.

Thirdly, the Community would assume its full role in the process of international policy-cooperation, and a new form of representation in arrangements for international policy coordination and in international monetary negotiations would be adopted.

60. *In the monetary field,* the irrevocable locking of exchange rates would come into effect and the transition to a single monetary policy would be made, with the ESCB assuming all its responsibilities as foreseen in the Treaty and described in Chapter II of this Report. In particular:

— concurrently with the announcement of the irrevocable fixing of parities between the Community currencies, the responsibility for the formulation and implementation of monetary policy in the Community would be transferred to the ESCB with its Council and Board exercising their statutory functions;

— decisions on exchange market interventions in third currencies would be made on the sole responsibility of the ESCB Council in accordance with Community exchange rate policy; the execution of interventions would be entrusted either to national central banks or to the European System of Central Banks;

— official reserves would be pooled and managed by the ESCB;

— preparations of a technical or regulatory nature would be made for the transition to a single Community currency.

The change-over to the single currency would take place during this stage.

Section 6: One or several Treaties

61. *Legal basis.* The Committee has examined the scope for progress in economic and monetary integration under the present legal provisions in force in each member country. This investigation has shown that under present national legislations no member country is able to transfer decision-making power to a Community body, nor is it possible for many countries to participate in arrangements for a binding *ex ante* coordination of policies.

As has been pointed out in paragraph 18 of this Report, the Treaty of Rome, as amended by the Single European Act, is insufficient for the full realisation of economic and monetary union. There is at present no transfer of responsibility for economic and monetary policy from Member States to the Community. The rules governing the EMS are based on agreements between the central banks concerned and are not an integral part of Community legislation. Without a new Treaty it would not be possible to take major additional steps towards economic and monetary union. The process of integration based on a step-by-step approach requires, however, a clear understanding of its content and final objective, its basic functional and institutional arrangements and the provisions governing its gradual implementation. A new political and legal basis would accordingly be needed. A new Treaty would establish not only the objective but also the stages by which it is to be achieved and the procedures and institutions required to move forward at each stage along the way. Political agreement would be required for each move to be implemented.

A new Treaty would also be required to ensure parallel progress in the economic and in the monetary fields. The appropriate institutional and procedural arrangements to that effect should also be set out in the Treaty.

62. The Committee has not investigated in detail the possible approaches by means of which the objective of economic and monetary union and its implementation would be embodied in the new Treaty. There would be basically two options. One procedure would be to conclude *a new Treaty for each stage*. The advantage of this procedure would be that it would explicitly reaffirm the political consensus at each stage and would allow for modification of the form the following stage should take in the light of experience with the current stage. At the same time, this approach might prove unwieldy and slow, it might not safeguard the overall consistency of the process sufficiently and it might carry the risk that parallel progress on the monetary and non-monetary sides might not be respected. In any event, if this procedure were chosen it would be crucial that the first Treaty laid down clearly the principal features of the ultimate objective of economic and monetary union.

63. Alternatively, it could be decided to conclude *a single comprehensive Treaty* formulating the essential features and institutional arrangements of economic and monetary union and the steps by which it could be achieved. Such a Treaty should indicate the procedures by which the decision would be taken to move from stage to stage. Each move would require an appraisal of the situation and a decision by the European Council.

Section 7: Suggested follow-up procedure

64. If the European Council can accept this Report as a basis for further development towards economic and monetary union, the following procedure is suggested.

65. The Council and the Committee of Governors should be invited to take the decisions necessary to implement the first stage.

66. Preparatory work for the negotiations on the new Treaty would start immediately. The competent Community bodies should be invited to make concrete proposals on the basis of this Report concerning the second and the final stages, to be embodied in a revised Treaty. These proposals should contain a further elaboration and concretization, where necessary, of the present Report. They should serve as the basis for future negotiations on a revised Treaty at an inter-governmental conference to be called by the European Council.

APPENDIX 3

Maastricht Treaty

(Treaty on European Union,
text dated February 7, 1992)

TITLE I
COMMON PROVISIONS

Article A

By this Treaty, the High Contracting Parties establish among themselves a European Union, hereinafter called 'the Union'.

This Treaty marks a new stage in the process of creating an ever closer union among the peoples of Europe, in which decisions are taken as closely as possible to the citizen.

The Union shall be founded on the European Communities, supplemented by the policies and forms of cooperation established by this Treaty. Its task shall be to organize, in a manner demonstrating consistency and solidarity, relations between the Member States and between their peoples.

Article B

The Union shall set itself the following objectives:

— to promote economic and social progress which is balanced and sustainable, in particular through the creation of an area without internal frontiers, through the strengthening of economic and social cohesion and through the establishment of economic and monetary union, ultimately including a single currency in accordance with the provisions of this Treaty;

— to assert its identity on the international scene, in particular through the implementation of a common foreign and security policy including the eventual framing of a common defence policy, which might in time lead to a common defence;

— to strengthen the protection of the rights and interests of the nationals of its Member States through the introduction of a citizenship of the Union;

— to develop close cooperation on justice and home affairs;

— to maintain in full the *acquis communautaire* and build on it with a view to considering, through the procedure referred to in Article N (2), to what extent the policies and forms of cooperation introduced by this Treaty may need to be revised with the aim of ensuring the effectiveness of the mechanisms and the institutions of the Community.

The objectives of the Union shall be achieved as provided in this Treaty and in accordance with the conditions and the timetable set out therein while respecting the principle of subsidiarity as defined in Article 3b of the Treaty establishing the European Community.

TITLE II

PROVISIONS AMENDING THE TREATY ESTABLISHING THE EUROPEAN ECONOMIC COMMUNITY WITH A VIEW TO ESTABLISHING THE EUROPEAN COMMUNITY

Article G

The Treaty establishing the European Economic Community shall be amended in accordance with the provisions of this Article, in order to establish a European Community.

A—THROUGHOUT THE TREATY:

(1) The term "European Economic Community" shall be replaced by the term "European Community."

B—IN PART ONE 'PRINCIPLES':

(2) Article 2 shall be replaced by the following:

Article 2

The Community shall have as its task, by establishing a common market and an economic and monetary union and by implementing the common policies or activities referred to in Articles 3 and 3a, to promote throughout the Community a harmonious and balanced development of economic activities, sustainable and non-inflationary growth respecting the environment, a high degree of convergence of economic performance, a high level of employment and of social protection, the raising of the standard of living and quality of life, and economic and social cohesion and solidarity among Member States.'

(4) The following Article shall be inserted:

Article 3a

1. For the purposes set out in Article 2, the activities of the Member States and the Community shall include, as provided in this Treaty and in accordance with the timetable set out therein, the adoption of an economic policy which is based on the close coordination of Member States' economic policies, on the internal market and on the definition of common objectives, and conducted in accordance with the principle of an open market economy with free competition.

2. Concurrently with the foregoing, and as provided in this Treaty and in accordance with the timetable and the procedures set out therein, these activities shall include the irrevocable fixing of exchange rates leading to the introduction of a single currency, the ecu, and the definition and conduct of a single monetary policy and exchange-rate policy the primary objective of both of which shall be to maintain price stability and, without prejudice to this objective, to support the general economic policies in the Community, in accordance with the principle of an open market economy with free competition.

3. These activities of the Member States and the Community shall entail compliance with the following guiding principles: stable prices, sound public finances and monetary conditions and a sustainable balance of payments.'

(5) The following Article shall be inserted:

Article 3b

The community shall act within the limits of the powers conferred upon it by this Treaty and of the objectives assigned to it therein.

In areas which do not fall within its exclusive competence, the Community shall take action, in accordance with the principle of subsidiarity, only if and in so far as the objectives of the proposed action cannot be sufficiently achieved by the Member States and can therefore, by reason of the scale or effects of the proposed action be better achieved by the Community.

Any action by the Community shall not go beyond what is necessary to achieve the objectives of this Treaty'.

(7) The following Articles shall be inserted:

'Article 4a

A European System of Central Banks (hereinafter referred to as "ESCB") and a European Central Bank (hereinafter referred to as "ECB") shall be established in accordance with the procedures laid down in this Treaty; they shall act within the limits of the powers conferred upon them by this Treaty and by the Statute of the ESCB and of the ECB (hereinafter referred to as "Statute of the ESCB") annexed thereto.

'Article 4b

A European Investment Bank is hereby established, which shall act within the limits of the powers conferred upon it by this Treaty and the Statute annexed thereto.'

'CHAPTER 4
CAPITAL AND PAYMENTS'

(15) The following Articles shall be inserted:

'Article 73b

1. Within the framework of the provisions set out in this Chapter, all restrictions on the movement of capital between Member States and between Member States and third countries shall be prohibited.

2. Within the framework of the provisions set out in this Chapter, all restrictions on payments between Member States and between Member States and third countries shall be prohibited.

'Article 73c

1. The provisions of Article 73b shall be without prejudice to the application to third countries of any restrictions which exist on 31 December 1993 under national or Community law adopted in respect of the move-

ment of capital to or from third countries involving direct investment—including investment in real estate—establishment, the provision of financial services or the admission of securities to capital markets.

2. Whilst endeavouring to achieve the objective of free movement of capital between Member States and third countries to the greatest extent possible and without prejudice to the other Chapters of this Treaty, the Council may, acting by a qualified majority on a proposal from the Commission, adopt measures on the movement of capital to or from third countries involving direct investment—including investment in real estate—establishment, the provision of financial services or the admission of securities to capital markets. Unanimity shall be required for measures under this paragraph which constitute a step back in Community law as regards the liberalization of the movement of capital to or from third countries.

'Article 73f

Where, in exceptional circumstances, movements of capital to or from third countries cause, or threaten to cause, serious difficulties for the operation of economic and monetary union, the Council, acting by a qualified majority on a proposal from the Commission and after consulting the ECB may take safeguard measures with regard to third countries for a period not exceeding six months if such measures are strictly necessary.

'Article 73g

1. If, in the cases envisaged in Article 228a, action by the Community is deemed necessary, the Council may, in accordance with the procedure provided for in Article 228a, take the necessary urgent measures on the movement of capital and on payments as regards the third countries concerned.

2. Without prejudice to Article 224 and as long as the Council has not taken measures pursuant to paragraph 1, a Member State may, for serious political reasons and on grounds of urgency, take unilateral measures against a third country with regard to capital movements and payments. The Commission and the other Member Sates shall be informed of such measures by the date of their entry into force at the latest. The Council may, acting by a qualified majority on a proposal from the Commission, decide that the Member State concerned shall amend or abolish such measures. The President of the Council shall inform the European Parliament of any such decision taken by the Council.

TITLE VI
ECONOMIC AND MONETARY POLICY

CHAPTER 1
Economic policy

Article 102a

Member States shall conduct their economic policies with a view to contributing to the achievement of the objectives of the Community, as defined in Article 2 and in the context of the broad guidelines referred to in Article 103(2). The Member States and the Community shall act in accordance with the principle of an open market economy with free competition, favouring an efficient allocation of resources, and in compliance with the principles set out in Article 3a.

Article 103

1. Member States shall regard their economic policies as a matter of common concern and shall coordinate them within the Council, in accordance with the provisions of Article 102a.

2. The Council shall, acting by a qualified majority on a recommendation from the Commission, formulate a draft for the broad guidelines of the economic policies of the Member States and of the Community, and shall report its findings to the European Council.

The European Council shall, acting on the basis of the report from the Council, discuss a conclusion on the broad guidelines of the economic policies of the Member States and of the Community.

On the basis of this conclusion, the Council shall, acting by a qualified majority, adopt a recommendation setting out these broad guidelines. The Council shall inform the European Parliament of its recommendation.

3. In order to ensure closer coordination of economic policies and sustained convergence of the economic performances of the Member States, the Council shall, on the basis of reports submitted by the Commission, monitor economic developments in each of the Member States and in the Community as well as the consistency of economic policies with the broad guidelines referred to in paragraph 2, and regularly carry out an overall assessment.

For the purpose of this multilateral surveillance, Member States shall forward information to the Commission about important measures taken by them in the field of their economic policy and such other information as they deem necessary.

4. Where it is established, under the procedure referred to in paragraph 3, that the economic policies of a Member State are not consistent with the

broad guidelines referred to in paragraph 2 or that they risk jeopardizing the proper functioning of economic and monetary union, the Council may, acting by a qualified majority on a recommendation from the Commission, make the necessary recommendations to the Member State concerned. The Council may, acting by a qualified majority on a proposal from the Commission, decide to make its recommendations public.

The President of the Council and the Commission shall report to the European Parliament on the results of multilateral surveillance. The President of the Council may be invited to appear before the competent Committee of the European Parliament if the Council has made its recommendations public.

5. The Council, acting in accordance with the procedure referred to in Article 189c, may adopt detailed rules for the multilateral surveillance procedure referred to in paragraphs 3 and 4 of this Article.

Article 103a

1. Without prejudice to any other procedures provided for in this Treaty the Council may, acting unanimously on a proposal from the Commission, decide upon the measures appropriate to the economic situation, in particular if severe difficulties arise in the supply of certain products.

2. Where a Member State is in difficulties or is seriously threatened with severe difficulties caused by exceptional occurrences beyond its control the Council may, acting unanimously on a proposal from the Commission, grant, under certain conditions, Community financial assistance to the Member State concerned. Where the severe difficulties are caused by natural disasters, the Council shall act by qualified majority. The President of the Council shall inform the European Parliament of the decision taken.

Article 104

1. Overdraft facilities or any other type of credit facility with the ECB or with the central banks of the Member States (hereinafter referred to as "national central banks") in favour of Community institutions or bodies, central governments, regional, local or other public authorities, other bodies governed by public law, or public undertakings of Member States shall be prohibited, as shall the purchase directly from them by the ECB or national central banks of debt instruments.

Article 104a

1. Any measure, not based on prudential considerations, establishing privileged access by Community institutions or bodies, central governments, regional, local or other public authorities, other bodies governed by public

law, or public undertakings of Member States to financial institutions shall be prohibited.

Article 104b

1. The Community shall not be liable for or assume the commitments of central governments, regional, local or other public authorities, other bodies governed by public law, or public undertakings of any Member State, without prejudice to mutual financial guarantees for the joint execution of a specific project. A Member State shall not be liable for or assume the commitments of central governments, regional, local or other public authorities, other bodies governed by public law or public undertakings of another Member State, without prejudice to mutual guarantees for the joint execution of a specific project.

Article 104c

1. Member States shall avoid excessive government deficits.

2. The Commission shall monitor the development of the budgetary situation and of the stock of government debt in the Member States with a view to identifying gross errors. In particular it shall examine compliance with budgetary discipline on the basis of the following two criteria:

(a) whether the ratio of the planned or actual government deficit to gross domestic product exceeds a reference value, unless

— either the ratio has declined substantially and continuously and reached a level that comes close to the reference value;
— or, alternatively, the excess over the reference value is only exceptional and temporary and the ratio remains close to the reference value;

(b) whether the ratio of government debt to gross domestic product exceeds a reference value, unless the ratio is sufficiently diminishing and approaching the reference value at a satisfactory pace. The reference values are specified in the Protocol on the excessive deficit procedure annexed to this Treaty.

3. If a Member State does not fulfil the requirements under one or both of these criteria, the Commission shall prepare a report. The report of the Commission shall also take into account whether the government deficit exceeds government investment expenditure and take into account all other relevant factors, including the medium-term economic and budgetary position of the Member State. The Commission may also prepare a report if, notwithstanding the fulfilment of the requirements under the criteria, it is of the opinion that there is a risk of an excessive deficit in a Member State.

4. The Committee provided for in Article 109c shall formulate an opinion on the report of the Commission.

5. If the Commission considers that an excessive deficit in a Member State exists or may occur, the Commission shall address an opinion to the Council.

6. The Council shall, acting by a qualified majority on a recommendation from the Commission, and having considered any observations which the Member State concerned may wish to make, decide after an overall assessment whether an excessive deficit exists.

7. Where the existence of an excessive deficit is decided according to paragraph 6, the Council shall make recommendations to the Member State concerned with a view to bringing that situation to an end within a given period. Subject to the provisions of paragraph 8, these recommendations shall not be made public.

8. Where it establishes that there has been no effective action in response to its recommendations within the period laid down, the Council may make its recommendations public.

9. If a Member State persists in failing to put into practice the recommendations of the Council, the Council may decide to give notice to the Member State to take, within a specified time-limit, measures for the deficit reduction which is judged necessary by the Council in order to remedy the situation. In such a case, the Council may request the Member State concerned to submit reports in accordance with a specific timetable in order to examine the adjustment efforts of that Member State.

10. The rights to bring actions provided for in Articles 169 and 170 may not be exercised within the framework of paragraphs 1 to 9 of this article.

11. As long as a Member State fails to comply with a decision taken in accordance with paragraph 9, the Council may decide to apply or, as the case may be, intensify one or more of the following measures:

— to require the Member State concerned to publish additional information, to be specified by the Council, before issuing bonds and securities;
— to invite the European Investment Bank to reconsider its lending policy towards the Member State concerned;
— to require the Member State concerned to make a non-interest-bearing deposit of an appropriate size with the Community until the excessive deficit has in the view of the Council, been corrected;
— to impose fines of an appropriate size. The President of the Council shall inform the European Parliament of the decisions taken.

12. The Council shall abrogate some or all of its decisions referred to in paragraphs 6 and 9 and 11 to the extent that the excessive deficit in the Member State concerned has, in the view of the Council, been corrected.

If the Council has previously made public recommendations, it shall as soon as the decision under paragraph 8 has been abrogated, make a public statement that an excessive deficit in the Member State concerned no longer exists.

13. When taking the decisions referred to in paragraphs 7 to 9, 11 and 12, the Council shall act on a recommendation from the Commission by a majority of two-thirds of the votes of its members weighted in accordance with Article 148(2) excluding the votes of the representative of the Member State concerned.

14. Further provisions relating to the implementation of the procedure described in this Article are set out in the Protocol on the excessive deficit procedure annexed to this Treaty.

The Council shall, acting unanimously on a proposal from the Commission and after consulting the European Parliament and the ECB, adopt the appropriate provisions which shall then replace the said Protocol.

Subject to the other provisions of this paragraph the Council shall, before 1 January 1994 acting by a qualified majority on a proposal from the Commission and after consulting the European Parliament, lay down detailed rules and definitions for the application of the provisions of the said Protocol.

CHAPTER 2
Monetary policy

Article 105

1. The primary objective of the ESCB shall be to maintain price stability. Without prejudice to the objective of price stability, the ESCB shall support the general economic policies in the Community with a view to contributing to the achievement of the objectives of the Community as laid down in Article 2. The ESCB shall act in accordance with the principle of an open market economy with free competition, favouring an efficient allocation of resources, and in compliance with the principles set out in Article 3a.

2. The basic tasks to be carried out through the ESCB shall be:

— to define and implement the monetary policy of the Community;
— to conduct foreign-exchange operations consistent with the provisions of Article 109;
— to hold and manage the official foreign reserves of the Member States;
— to promote the smooth operation of payment systems.

3. The third indent of paragraph 2 shall be without prejudice to the holding and management by the governments of Member Sates of foreign exchange working balances.

4. The ECB shall be consulted:

— on any proposed Community act in its fields of competence;
— by national authorities regarding any draft legislative provision in its fields of competence, but within the limits and under the conditions set out by the Council in accordance with the procedure laid down in Article 106(6).

The ECB may submit opinions to the appropriate Community institutions or bodies or to national authorities on matters in its fields of competence.

5. The ESCB shall contribute to the smooth conduct of policies pursued by the competent authorities relating to the prudential supervision of credit institutions and the stability of the financial system.

6. The Council may, acting unanimously on a proposal from the Commission and after consulting the ECB and after receiving the assent of the European Parliament, confer upon the ECB specific tasks concerning policies relating to the prudential supervision of credit institutions and other financial institutions with the exception of insurance undertakings.

Article 105a

1. The ECB shall have the exclusive right to authorize the issue of bank notes within the Community. The ECB and the national central banks may issue such notes. The bank notes issued by the ECB and the national central banks shall be the only such notes to have the status of legal tender within the Community.

2. Member States may issue coins subject to approval by the ECB of the volume of the issue. The Council may, acting in accordance with the procedure referred to in Article 189c and after consulting the ECB, adopt measures to harmonize the denominations and technical specifications of all coins intended for circulation to the extent necessary to permit their smooth circulation within the Community.

Article 106

1. The ESCB shall be composed of the ECB and of the national central banks.

2. The ECB shall have legal personality.

3. The ESCB shall be governed by the decision-making bodies of the ECB which shall be the Governing Council and Executive Board.

4. The Statute of the ESCB is laid down in a Protocol annexed to this Treaty.

5. Articles 5.1, 5.2, 5.3, 17, 18, 19.1, 22, 23, 24, 26, 32.2, 32.3, 32.4, 32.6, 33.1 (a) and 36 of the Statute of the ESCB may be amended by the Council, acting either by a qualified majority on a recommendation from the ECB and after consulting the Commission or unanimously on a proposal from the Commission and after consulting the ECB. In either case, the assent of the European Parliament shall be required.

6. The Council, acting by a qualified majority either on a proposal from the Commission and after consulting the European Parliament and the Commission, shall adopt the provision referred to in Articles 4, 5.4, 19.2, 20, 28.1, 29.2, 30.4 and 34.3 of the Statute of the ESCB.

Article 107

When exercising the powers and carrying out the tasks and duties conferred upon them by this Treaty and the Statute of the ESCB, neither the ECB, nor a national central bank, nor any member of their decision-making bodies shall seek or take instructions from Community institutions or bodies, from any government of a Member State or from any other body. The Community institutions and bodies and the governments of the Member States undertake to respect this principle and not to seek to influence the members of the decision-making bodies of the ECB or of the national central banks in the performance of their tasks.

Article 108

Each Member State shall ensure, at the latest at the date of the establishment of the ESCB, that its national legislation including the statutes of its national central bank is compatible with this Treaty and the Statute of the ESCB.

Article 109

1. By way of derogation from Article 228, the Council may, acting unanimously on a recommendation from the ECB or from the Commission, and after consulting the ECB in an endeavour to reach a consensus consistent with the objective of price stability, after consulting the European Parliament, in accordance with the procedure in paragraph 3 for determining the arrangements, conclude formal agreements on an exchange-rate system for the ecu in relation to non-Community currencies. The Council may, acting

by a qualified majority on a recommendation from the ECB or from the Commission, and after consulting the ECB in an endeavour to reach a consensus consistent with the objective of price stability, adopt, adjust or abandon the central rates of the ecu within the exchange-rate system. The President of the Council shall inform the European Parliament of the adoption, adjustment or abandonment of the ecu central rates.

2. In the absence of an exchange-rate system in relation to one or more non-Community currencies as referred to in paragraph 1, the Council, acting by a qualified majority either on a recommendation from the Commission and after consulting the ECB or on a recommendation from the ECB, may formulate general orientations for exchange-rate policy in relation to these currencies. These general orientations shall be without prejudice to the primary objective of the ESCB to maintain price stability.

3. By way of derogation from Article 228, where agreements concerning monetary or foreign-exchange regime matters need to be negotiated by the Community with one or more States or international organizations, the Council, acting by a qualified majority on a recommendation from the Commission and after consulting the ECB, shall decide the arrangements for the negotiation and for the conclusion of such agreements. These arrangements shall ensure that the Community expresses a single position. The Commission shall be fully associated with the negotiations.

Agreements concluded in accordance with this paragraph shall be binding on the institutions of the Community, on the ECB and on Member States.

4. Subject to paragraph 1, the Council shall, on a proposal from the Commission and after consulting the ECB, acting by a qualified majority decide on the position of the Community at international level as regards issues of particular relevance to economic and monetary union and, acting unanimously, decide its representation in compliance with the allocation of powers laid down in Articles 103 and 105.

5. Without prejudice to Community competence and Community agreements as regards economic and monetary union, Member States may negotiate in international bodies and conclude international agreements.

CHAPTER 3
Institutional provisions

Article 109a

1. The Governing Council of the ECB shall comprise the members of the Executive Board of the ECB and the Governors of the national central banks.

2. (a) The Executive Board shall comprise the President, the Vice-President and four other members.

(b) The President, the Vice-President and the other members of the Executive Board shall be appointed from among persons of recognized standing and professional experience in monetary or banking matters by common accord of the Governments of the Member States at the level of Heads of State or of Government, on a recommendation from the Council, after it has consulted the European Parliament and the Governing Council of the ECB.

Their term of office shall be eight years and shall not be renewable.

Only nationals of Member States may be members of the Executive Board.

Article 109b

1. The President of the Council and a member of the Commission may participate, without having the right to vote, in meetings of the Governing Council of the ECB.

The President of the Council may submit a motion for deliberation to the Governing Council of the ECB.

2. The President of the ECB shall be invited to participate in Council meetings when the Council is discussing matters relating to the objectives and tasks of the ESCB.

3. The ECB shall address an annual report on the activities of the ESCB and on the monetary policy of both the previous and current year to the European Parliament, the Council and the Commission, and also to the European Council. The President of the ECB shall present this report to the Council and to the European Parliament, which may hold a general debate on that basis.

The President of the ECB and the other members of the Executive Board may, at the request of the European Parliament or on their own initiative, be heard by the competent Committees of the European Parliament.

CHAPTER 4
Transitional provisions

Article 109e

1. The second stage for achieving economic and monetary union shall begin on 1 January 1994.

2. Before that date

(a) each Member State shall:

— adopt, where necessary, appropriate measures to comply with the prohibitions laid down in Article 73b, without prejudice to Article 73e, and in Articles 104 and 104a(1);

— adopt, if necessary, with a view to permitting the assessment provided for in subparagraph (b), multiannual programmes intended to ensure the lasting convergence necessary for the achievement of economic and monetary union, in particular with regard to price stability and sound public finances;

(b) the Council shall, on the basis of a report from the Commission, assess the progress made with regard to economic and monetary convergence, in particular with regard to price stability and sound public finances, and the progress made with the implementation of Community law concerning the internal market.

3. The provisions of Articles 104, 104a(1) and 104c with the exception of paragraphs 1, 9, 11 and 14 shall apply from the beginning of the second stage.

The provisions of Articles 103a(2), 104c(1), (9) and (11), 105, 105a, 107, 109, 109a, 109b and 109c(2) and (4) shall apply from the beginning of the third stage.

4. In the second stage, Member States shall endeavour to avoid excessive government deficits.

5. During the second stage, each Member State shall, as appropriate, start the process leading to the independence of its central bank, in accordance with Article 108.

Article 109f

1. At the start of the second stage, a European Monetary Institute (hereinafter referred to as "EMI") shall be established and take up its duties; it shall have legal personality and be directed and managed by a Council, consisting of a President and the Governors of the national central banks, one of whom shall be Vice-President.

The President shall be appointed by common accord of the Governments of the Member States at the level of Heads of State or of Government, on a recommendation from, as the case may be, the Committee of Governors of the central banks of the Member States (hereinafter referred to as "Committee of Governors") or the Council of the EMI, and after consulting the European Parliament and the Council. The President shall be selected from among persons of recognized standing and professional experience in monetary or banking matters. Only nationals of Member States may be President of the EMI. The Council of the EMI shall appoint the Vice-President.

The Statute of the EMI is laid down in a Protocol annexed to this Treaty.

The Committee of Governors shall be dissolved at the start of the second stage.

2. The EMI shall:

— strengthen cooperation between the national central banks;
— strengthen the coordination of the monetary policies of the Member States, with the aim of ensuring price stability;
— monitor the functioning of the European Monetary System;
— hold consultations concerning issues falling within the competence of the national central banks and affecting the stability of financial institutions and markets;
— take over the tasks of the European Monetary Cooperation Fund, which shall be dissolved; the modalities of dissolution are laid down in the Statute of the EMI;
— facilitate the use of the ecu and oversee its development, including the smooth functioning of the ecu clearing system.

3. For the preparation of the third stage, the EMI shall:

— prepare the instruments and the procedures necessary for carrying out a single monetary policy in the third stage;
— promote the harmonization, where necessary, of the rules and practices governing the collection, compilation and distribution of statistics in the areas within its field of competence;
— prepare the rules for operations to be undertaken by the national central banks within the framework of the ESCB;
— promote the efficiency of cross-border payments;
— supervise the technical preparation of ecu bank notes.

At the latest by 31 December 1996, the EMI shall specify the regulatory, organizational and logistical framework necessary for the ESCB to perform its tasks in the third stage. This framework shall be submitted for decision to the ECB at the date of its establishment.

4. The EMI, acting by a majority of two thirds of the members of its Council, may:

— formulate opinions or recommendations on the overall orientation of monetary policy and exchange-rate policy as well as on related measures introduced in each Member State;

— submit opinions or recommendations to Governments and to the Council on policies which might affect the internal or external monetary situation in the Community and, in particular, the functioning of the European Monetary System;

— make recommendations to the monetary authorities of the Member States concerning the conduct of their monetary policy.

5. The EMI, acting unanimously, may decide to publish its opinions and its recommendations.

6. The EMI shall be consulted by the Council regarding any proposed Community act within its field of competence.

Within the limits and under the conditions set out by the Council, acting by a qualified majority on a proposal from the Commission and after consulting the European Parliament and the EMI, the EMI shall be consulted by the authorities of the Member States on any draft legislative provision within its field of competence.

7. The Council may, acting unanimously on a proposal from the Commission and after consulting the European Parliament and the EMI, confer upon the EMI other tasks for the preparation of the third stage.

Article 109g

The currency composition of the ecu basket shall not be changed.

From the start of the third state, the value of the ecu shall be irrevocably fixed in accordance with Article 1091(4).

Article 109h

1. Where a Member State is in difficulties or is seriously threatened with difficulties as regards its balance of payments either as a result of an overall disequilibrium in its balance of payments, or as a result of the type of currency at its disposal, and where such difficulties are liable in particular to jeopardize the functioning of the common market or the progressive implementation of the common commercial policy, the Commission shall immediately investigate the position of the State in question and the action which, making use of all the means at its disposal, that State has taken or may take in accordance with the provisions of this Treaty. The Commission shall state what measures it recommends the State concerned to take.

If the action taken by a Member State and the measures suggested by the Commission do not prove sufficient to overcome the difficulties, which have arisen or which threaten, the Commission shall, after consulting the Committee referred to in Article 109c, recommend to the Council the granting of mutual assistance and appropriate methods therefor.

The Commission shall keep the Council regularly informed of the situation and of how it is developing.

2. The Council, acting by a qualified majority, shall grant such mutual assistance; it shall adopt directives or decisions laying down the conditions and details of such assistance, which may take such forms as:

(a) a concerted approach to or within any other international organizations to which Member States may have recourse;

(b) measures needed to avoid deflection of trade where the State which is in difficulties maintains or reintroduces quantitative restrictions against third countries;

(c) the granting of limited credits by other Member States, subject to their agreement.

3. If the mutual assistance recommended by the Commission is not granted by the Council or if the mutual assistance granted and the measures taken are insufficient, the Commission shall authorize the State, which is in difficulties to take protective measures, the conditions and details of which the Commission shall determine.

Such authorization may be revoked and such conditions and details may be changed by the Council acting by a qualified majority.

4. Subject to Article 109k(6) this Article shall cease to apply from the beginning of the third stage.

Article 109i

1. Where a sudden crisis in the balance of payments occurs and a decision within the meaning of Article 109h(2) is not immediately taken, the Member State concerned may, as a precaution, take the necessary protective measures. Such measures must cause the least possible disturbance in the functioning of the common market and must not be wider in scope than is strictly necessary to remedy the sudden difficulties which have arisen.

2. The Commission and the other Member States shall be informed of such protective measures not later than when they enter into force. The Commission may recommend to the Council the granting of mutual assistance under Article 109h.

3. After the Commission has delivered an opinion and the Committee referred to in Article 109c has been consulted, the Council may, acting by a qualified majority, decide that the State concerned shall amend, suspend or abolish the protective measures referred to above.

4. Subject to Article 109(k) this article shall cease to apply from the beginning of the third stage.

Article 109j

1. The Commission and the EMI shall report to the Council on the progress made in the fulfilment by the Member States of their obligations regarding the achievement of economic and monetary union. These reports shall include an examination of the compatibility between each Member State's national legislation, including the statutes of its national central bank, and Articles 107 and 108 of this Treaty and the Statute of the ESCB. The reports shall also examine the achievement of a high degree of sustainable convergence by reference to the fulfilment by each Member State of the following criteria:

— the achievement of a high degree of price stability; this will be apparent from a rate of inflation which is close to that of, at most, the three best performing Member States in terms of price stability;

— the sustainability of the government financial position; this will be apparent from having achieved a government budgetary position without a deficit that is excessive as determined in accordance with Article 104c(6);

— the observance of the normal fluctuation margins provided for by the exchange-rate mechanism of the European Monetary System, for at least two years, without devaluing against the currency of any other Member State;

— the durability of convergence achieved by the Member State and of its participation in the Exchange Rate Mechanism of the European Monetary System being reflected in the long-term interest rate levels.

The four criteria in this paragraph and the relevant periods over which they are to be respected are developed further in a Protocol annexed to this Treaty. The reports of the Commission and the EMI shall also take account of the development of the ecu, the results of the integration of markets, the situation and development of the balances of payments on current account and an examination of the development of unit labour costs and other price indices.

2. On the basis of these reports, the Council, acting by a qualified majority on a recommendation from the Commission, shall assess:

— for each Member State, whether it fulfils the necessary conditions for the adoption of a single currency;

— whether a majority of the Member States fulfil the necessary conditions for the adoption of a single currency, and recommend its findings to the Council, meeting in the composition of the Heads of State or of Government. The European Parliament shall be consulted and forward its opinion to the Council, meeting in the composition of Heads of State or of Government.

3. Taking due account of the reports referred to in paragraph 1 and the opinion of the European Parliament referred to in paragraph 2, the Council, meeting in the composition of Heads of State or of Government, shall, acting by a qualified majority, not later than 31 December 1996:

— decide, on the basis of the recommendations of the Council referred to in paragraph 2, whether a majority of the Member States fulfil the necessary conditions for the adoption of a single currency;
— decide whether it is appropriate for the Community to enter the third stage,

and if so

— set the date for the beginning of the third stage.

4. If by the end of 1997 the date for the beginning of the third stage has not been set, the third stage shall start on 1 January 1999. Before 1 July 1998, the Council, meeting in the composition of Heads of State or of Government, after a repetition of the procedure provided for in paragraphs 1 and 2, with the exception of the second indent of paragraph 2, taking into account the reports as referred to in paragraph 1 and the opinion of the European Parliament, shall, acting by a qualified majority and on the basis of the recommendations of the Council referred to in paragraph 2, confirm which Member States fulfil the necessary conditions for the adoption of a single currency.

Article 109k

1. If the decision has been taken to set the date in accordance with Article 109j(3), the Council shall, on the basis of its recommendations referred to in Article 109j(2), acting by a qualified majority on a recommendation from the Commission, decide whether any, and if so which, Member States shall have a derogation as defined in paragraph 3 of this Article. Such Member States shall in this Treaty be referred to as "Member States with a derogation."

If the Council has confirmed which Member States fulfil the necessary conditions for the adoption of a single currency, in accordance with Article 109j(4), those Member States which do not fulfil the conditions shall have a derogation as defined in paragraph 3 of this Article. Such Member States shall in this Treaty be referred to as "Member States with a derogation."

2. At least once every two years, or at the request of a Member State with a derogation, the Commission and the ECB shall report to the Council in accordance with the procedure laid down in Article 109j(1). After consulting the European Parliament and after discussion in the Council meeting in the composition of the Heads of State or of Government, the Council shall, acting by a qualified majority on a proposal from the Commission, decide which Member States with a derogation fulfil the necessary conditions on the basis of the criteria set out in Article 109j(1), and abrogate the derogations of the Member States concerned.

3. A derogation referred to in paragraph 1 shall entail that the following Articles do not apply to the Member State concerned: Articles 104c(9) and (11), 105(1), (2), (3) and (5), 105a, 108a, 109 and 109a(2)(b). The exclusion of such a Member State and its national central bank from rights and obligations within the ESCB is laid down in Chapter IX of the Statute of the ESCB.

4. In Articles 105(1), (2) and (3), 105a, 108a, 109 and 109a(2)(b), "Member States" shall be read as "Member States without a derogation."

5. The voting rights of Member States with a derogation shall be suspended for the Council decisions referred to in the Articles of this Treaty mentioned in paragraph 3. In that case, by way of derogation from Articles 148 and 189a(1), a qualified majority shall be defined as two-thirds of the votes of the representatives of the Member States without a derogation weighted in accordance with Article 148(2), and unanimity of those Member States shall be required for an act requiring unanimity.

6. Articles 109h and 109i shall continue to apply to a Member State with a derogation.

Article 109l

1. Immediately after the decision on the date for the beginning of the third stage has been taken in accordance with Article 109j(3), or, as the case may be, immediately after 1 July 1998:

— the Council shall adopt the provisions referred to in Article 106(6);
— the governments of the Member States without a derogation shall appoint, in accordance with the procedure set out in Article 50 of the Statute of the ESCB, the President, the Vice-President and the other members of the Executive Board of the ECB. If there are Member States with a derogation, the number of members of the Executive Board may be smaller than provided for in Article 11.1 of the Statute of the ESCB, but in no circumstances shall it be less than four.

As soon as the Executive Board is appointed, the ESCB and the ECB shall be established and shall prepare for their full operation as described in this Treaty and the Statute of the ESCB. The full exercise of their powers shall start from the first day of the third stage.

2. As soon as the ECB is established, it shall, if necessary, take over tasks of the EMI. The EMI shall go into liquidation upon the establishment of the ECB; the modalities of liquidation are laid down in the Statue of the EMI.

3. If and as long as there are Member States with a derogation, and without prejudice to Article 106(3) of this Treaty, the General Council of the ECB referred to in Article 45 of the Statute of the ESCB shall be constituted as a third decision-making body of the ECB.

4. At the starting date of the third stage, the Council shall, acting with the unanimity of the Member States without a derogation, on a proposal from the Commission and after consulting the ECB, adopt the conversion rates at which their currencies shall be irrevocably fixed and at which irrevocably fixed rate the ecu shall be substituted for these currencies, and the ecu will become a currency in its own right. This measure shall by itself not modify the external value of the ecu. The Council shall, acting according to the same procedure, also take the other measures necessary for the rapid introduction of the ecu as the single currency of those Member States.

5. If it is decided, according to the procedure set out in Article 109k(2), to abrogate a derogation, the Council shall, acting with the unanimity of the Member States without a derogation and the Member State concerned on a proposal from the Commission and after consulting the ECB, adopt the rate at which the ecu shall be substituted for the currency of the Member State concerned, and take the other measures necessary for the introduction of the ecu as the single currency in the Member State concerned.

Article 109m

1. Until the beginning of the third stage, each Member State shall treat its exchange-rate policy as a matter of common interest. In so doing, member States shall take account of the experience acquired in cooperation within the framework of the European Monetary System (EMS) and in developing the ecu, and shall respect existing powers in this field.

2. From the beginning of the third stage and for as long as a Member State has a derogation, paragraph 1 shall apply by analogy to the exchange-rate policy of that Member State.

PROTOCOL
ON THE EXCESSIVE DEFICIT PROCEDURE

THE HIGH CONTRACTING PARTIES,

DESIRING to lay down the details of the excessive deficit procedure referred to in Article 104c of the Treaty establishing the European Community,

HAVE AGREED upon the following provisions, which shall be annexed to the Treaty establishing the European Community:

Article 1

The reference values referred to in Article 104c(2) of this Treaty are:

— 3% for the ratio of the planned or actual government deficit to gross domestic product at market prices;
— 60% for the ratio of government debt to gross domestic product at market prices.

Article 2

In Article 104c of this Treaty and in this Protocol:

— government means general government, that is central government, regional or local government and social security funds, to the exclusion of commercial operations, as defined in the European System of Integrated Economic Accounts;
— deficit means net borrowing as defined in the European System of Integrated Economic Accounts;
— investment means gross fixed capital formation as defined in the European System of Integrated Economic Accounts;
— debt means total gross debt at nominal value outstanding at the end of the year and consolidated between and within the sectors of general government as defined in the first indent.

Article 3

In order to ensure the effectiveness of the excessive deficit procedure, the governments of the Member States shall be responsible under this procedure for the deficits of general government as defined in the first indent of Article 2. The Member States shall ensure that national procedures in the budgetary area enable them to meet their obligations in this area deriving from this Treaty. The Member States shall report their planned and actual deficits and the levels of their debt promptly and regularly to the Commission.

Article 4

The statistical data to be used for the application of this Protocol shall be provided by the Commission.

PROTOCOL

ON THE CONVERGENCE CRITERIA REFERRED TO IN ARTICLE 109j OF THE TREATY ESTABLISHING THE EUROPEAN COMMUNITY

THE HIGH CONTRACTING PARTIES,

DESIRING to lay down the details of the convergence criteria which shall guide the Community in taking decisions on the passage to the third stage of economic and monetary union, referred to in Article 109j(1) of this Treaty,

HAVE AGREED upon the following provisions, which shall be annexed to the Treaty establishing the European Community:

Article 1

The criterion on price stability referred to in the first indent of Article 109j(1) of this Treaty shall mean that a Member State has a price performance that is sustainable and an average rate of inflation, observed over a period of one year before the examination, that does not exceed by more than 1 1/2 percentage points that of, at most, the three best performing Member States in terms of price stability. Inflation shall be measured by means of the consumer price index on a comparable basis, taking into account differences in national definitions.

Article 2

The criterion on the government budgetary position referred to in the second indent of Article 109j(1) of this Treaty shall mean that at the time of the examination the Member State is not the subject of a Council decision under Article 104c(6) of this Treaty that an excessive deficit exists.

Article 3

The criterion on participation in the exchange-rate mechanism of the European Monetary System referred to in the third indent of Article 109j(1) of this Treaty shall mean that a Member State has respected the normal fluctuation margins provided for by the exchange-rate mechanism of the European Monetary System without severe tensions for at least the last two years before the examination. In particular, the Member State shall not have devalued its currency's bilateral central rate against any other Member State's currency on its own initiative for the same period.

Article 4

The criterion on the convergence of interest rates referred to in the fourth indent of Article 109j(1) of this Treaty shall mean that, observed over a period of one year before the examination, a Member State has had an average nominal long-term interest rate that does not exceed by more than 2 percentage points that of, at most, the three best performing Member States in terms of price stability. Interest rates shall be measured on the basis of long-term government bonds or comparable securities, taking into account differences in national definitions.

Article 5

The statistical data to be used for the application of this protocol shall be provided by the Commission.

Article 6

The Council shall, acting unanimously on a proposal from the Commission and after consulting the European Parliament, the EMI or the ECB as the case maybe, and the Committee referred to in Article 109c, adopt appropriate provisions to lay down the details of the convergence criteria referred to in Article 109j of this Treaty, which shall then replace this Protocol.

Notes

Chapter 1

1. See Machlup (1977) for a full appraisal of the terms, such as "common market" and "customs union," that are associated with economic integration.

2. West Germany, France, Italy, Belgium, the Netherlands, and Luxembourg.

3. Bloomfield (1973, p. 7) seems to disagree with this, noting that the revaluations "did not seem to cause any great anxiety within the Community despite their backwash on the exchange markets." On the other hand he quotes the March 1962 report of the Monetary Committee, set up by the treaty, as reflecting that "the final decisions on these changes were not preceded by perfect coordination within the Community."

4. In his comments on Bloomfield (1973), Benjamin Cohen states, "It seems to me that we can ignore the historical role of the personalist government of France in the mid-1960s only at our own peril. The general [de Gaulle] was directly responsible for France's stubborn resistance to any hint of supranationalism in those years, in the monetary sphere no less than in any other" (p. 31).

5. See Overturf (1986, Chapter 7) for a description of the impact of exchange-rate changes on the Common Agricultural Policy.

6. It is amusing to read in official documents that the "prior" consultations to the announced August 8, 1969 French devaluation in fact took place on August 10.

7. Kruse (1980, p. 60) says that "for the authorities in Paris, acting 'in common' meant making decisions in a very restricted set of areas on the basis of unanimous agreement among national governments. They opposed the transfer of authority to Community institutions not only because of a doctrinal antipathy to supranationalism, but also because of pragmatic determination to maintain the greatest possible national freedom of action." It is instructive that the Werner Report (1970) speaks to keeping this transfer of power "within the limits necessary for the effective operation of the Community."

8. It is significant that this reducing of the margins of fluctuation is just that; it does not imply any reduction in the ability of states to alter the established rates.

9. Tsoukalis (1977, p. 106) notes that "M. Pompidou's initiatives at the Hague Summit less than a year ago had backfired at him. He had either not expected that his endorsement of EMU in the final objective would lead to such a plethora of plans with politically far-reaching proposals or that the Gaullists would not be prepared to concede some transfer of powers to the Community level. The former explanation sounds more plausible."

10. By prior agreement, they had not previously been using the full Bretton Woods 1 percent.

11. Significantly, the credit facility was to be operated between the central banks and not through a Community institution.

12. It was then that the lira left the snake.

Chapter 2

1. If the United Kingdom, France, and Italy had remained in, certainly this last point would not have been considered very important.

2. It bears emphasis that what have become described as classic Keynesian policies might not have been entirely recognized by Keynes himself as such, especially in a more inflationary environment.

3. The terms ERM and EMS will be used interchangeably in this work when there is no confusion introduced by doing so.

4. It also bears pointing out, however, that if Helmut Schmidt had not taken such a strong position of leadership, the forces within that country would surely have spelled defeat for the EMS at an early stage.

Chapter 3

1. France, Germany, the Netherlands, Belgium and Luxembourg, Denmark, Ireland, Italy, and the United Kingdom.

2. That is, if 1 DM = 1 ECU and 2 FF = 1 ECU, the bilateral central rate is 1 DM = 2 FF, and the FF cannot go beyond either 2.045 or 1.955 FF per DM.

3. The formula in this case is $(1 - w)$ times (plus or minus) 2.25 percent, or, when the DM was 37.38 percent of the ECU, the currency could rise or fall by 1.40895 percent before the divergence limit was reached. See Harrop (1989), p. 137.

4. Small, medium, or large, associated with quotas in the short-term monetary support mechanism. Again, see Swann (1988, p. 192).

5. Padoa-Schioppa (1985, p. 38). This quote is from a paper written by an important contributor to monetary integration in Europe in 1981, under the title "The ECU and the European Monetary System."

6. See McCulloch (1983) for what became an especially influential piece speaking to this question.

7. It is notable that the Netherlands, although a significant natural gas producer, had not found it a problem to remain within the structure of the EMS.

8. For example, when two currencies would move sharply in different directions.

9. See Ungerer et al. (1983) for an early analysis of these issues.

10. Although there had been several interesting suggestions floated for feasible ways to allow for this to happen without involving major institutional changes.

11. Although Belgium took the symbolic step of issuing ECU coins.

12. In addition, Lomax (1989), p. 128, was "not aware of any work which has had the effect of proving that the ECU is an inefficient portfolio." Christie (1989),

in his comments on Lomax, on the other hand, was skeptical. He asked why the actual structure of portfolios differed from Masera's results, and proceeded to question the robustness of those results.

13. Total public bond issues denominated in ECUs dropped from 1985 to 1986, and again from 1986 to 1987. There was a strong rebound, however, from 1987 to 1988. See Folkerts-Landau and Mathieson (1989).

14. The demand for ECUs in advance of an uncertain transition to monetary union is, of course, a different problem, and one that received much attention in the financial press during the middle part of 1990s.

15. See Guitián (1988) for a discussion of standards of measurement.

16. See, for example, Guitián (1988), De Grauwe and Verfaille (1988), and Weber (1990).

17. Artis and Taylor (1988) applied non-parametric tests for shifts in volatility due to the establishment of the EMS, as it has been found that exchange rate changes do not fit the standard normal distribution. Their conclusion is of (p. 195) "strong evidence of reduced intra-ERM exchange-rate volatility post-March 1979, and of increased volatility in dollar and (to a slightly lesser extent) sterling rates. These results hold, moreover, for both real and nominal exchange rates."

18. Rogoff (1985) chooses, for example, the forward exchange rate as representing the market's best prediction of the future actual "spot" exchange rate. It has also been suggested that the current spot rate is actually a better predictor of the future spot rate than is the forward rate. Artis and Taylor (1988) reinforce the other findings on conditional variance reduction by presuming the exchange rate is a random walk with a disturbance. In fact, however, the very unpredictability of exchange rates has encouraged the use of the standard measures of exchange rate variance as the best estimates of unexpected exchange rate changes. See Weber (1990).

19. "When realignments have taken place, they have at times provided for less than complete offsetting of past inflation differentials; by so doing, a message has been sent to wage and price setters in relatively high-inflation countries that the ERM will not bail out inflationary settlements for their output and employment consequences." Folkerts-Landau and Mathieson (1989, p. 13).

20. Also, strikes in France were said to have contributed to the 1987 realignment.

21. With the exception of a technical resetting of the lira within its band in January 1990.

22. Collins (1988, p. 130), for example, finds "no existence of any average reduction or convergence of inflation among EMS members during the first three years (1979–82)."

23. See Russo and Tullio (1988) and Guitián (1988).

24. Using a dummy variable for EMS membership in inflation explanation of EMS and non-EMS countries, and coming to different conclusions than Ungerer, et al. (1986).

25. Of course the size of the state and a form of economic dominance (as occurred with the United States under the Bretton Woods standard) is also an issue, one that will be dealt with later. For a contrary view in this context, however, see Russo and Tullio (1988).

26. As in Mastropasqua, et al. (1988). This interpretation, again generally accepted, owed much to Giavazzi and Giovannini (1987, for example).

27. See, for example, again, Mastropasqua, et al. (1988), Weber (1990) and MacDonald and Taylor (1990). The evidence was hardly one-sided, however. See Herz and Röger (1992) for a review of this literature and, nevertheless, an addition to the theoretical and empirical justification of the hypothesis.

Chapter 4

1. The remarks above may explain why Padoa-Schioppa (1988, p. 373) broadens this "inconsistency trinity" (independent monetary policy, international capital market integration, and nominal exchange rate targets) to become an "inconsistent quartet" by including free trade.

2. See, for example, Taylor (1989). In comparison, also see Lodge (1989).

3. The concept of uncovered interest parity seems not to hold particularly well in a "system" of floating rates, but holds considerably closer among rates that are, even only more-or-less, fixed.

4. See Gibson and Tsakalotos (1990) and the discussion in Giavazzi and Pagano (1988), in which onshore interest rates are compared with offshore ("Euro-") rates to gain some sense of the strength of the "wedge."

5. Except perhaps, for Germany.

6. Spain, as indicated, was a country that had been singled out as indicative of the regime shift. Viñals (1990), nevertheless, found that that country had been attempting to maintain independent policies—i.e., a tight monetary policy combined with easy fiscal policy—and had engaged in extensive sterilization in order to do so. But he also notes that, in spite of entry into the ERM in June 1989 at the 6-percent band, that capital controls on inflows had been used extensively as to allow for the divergent policy (p. 13):

> Clearly, once capital controls are fully removed [by end 1992], the Spanish authorities will find it impossible to simultaneously achieve money and exchange rate targets. As a result, domestic inflation targets and exchange rate stability may not be so readily reconciled as under the current policy framework. Without capital controls, domestic and foreign interest rates will have to be closely linked, especially inside the EMS. This means that fiscal policy should be tighter than at present so as to facilitate lowering the domestic interest rate.

In other words, it appears that he recognized that policies must converge, without the tool of capital controls.

Chapter 5

1. The report is included here as Appendix 2.

2. Compare the Delors Report (p. 18) with the Werner Report (p. 10).

3. Here the Werner Report (p. 10) uses much the same language: " . . . considerations of a psychological and political nature militate in favour of the adoption of a sole currency which would confirm the irreversibility of the venture."

4. For more on this see Machlup (1977).

5. Instead, emphasis is placed on investment to equalize income in the longer run.

6. If other states responded by increasing their budget deficits and interest rates a "race for the bottom" could be created, only one result of which would be that the Community exchange rate could become artificially altered.

7. Composed of member-state central-bank governors plus members of a board that would oversee policy implementation.

8. Although they would probably not have stood in the way of committed governments.

9. Thygesen (1989) also notes that EMU would bring down France's interest rates (in line with those of Germany) and would mean they would no longer need to raise them to defend the franc, as they had had to do in the past. De Cecco (1989, pp. 89–90) adds the importance of currency stability for French agriculture.

10. Hasse (1990) also draws attention to the effects of the Basle-Nyborg agreements—by making intramarginal intervention more open to creditor financing—on reducing Germany's ability to insulate its money supply (via sterilization) from intra-ERM interventions.

11. De Cecco (1989, p. 89) highlights especially the chemical, steel, machine-tool, and automobile industries which, together, represent "a very large share of industrial employment in Germany." German light industry is even more dependent.

12. Another economic motivation of Germany might have been to devise a truly EC external exchange-rate policy toward other currencies, especially, of course, the dollar and the yen.

Chapter 6

1. See, for example, Sommer (1991, p. 38), who says "I expected a solution—or an agreed non-solution—to result from slow, incremental, almost-geological change, certainly not from revolutionary upheaval."

2. Sommer (1991), again, feels that Germans "were carried to unity by the same tide of history that swept the subjugated nations of Eastern Europe to the shores of liberty." He also feels that "reunification came not as a triumph of narrow nationalism; it followed the victory of freedom all over the Old World."

3. For more along these lines see Overturf (1992).

4. See, for example, the *Economist*, July 27, 1991, p. 50. "Some countries want political union because they fear the dominance of a united Germany; we should exploit that fear before it diminishes." This a quote from the then foreign affairs spokesman for the Christian Democrats.

5. See Woolley (1993) on the linkage between monetary and political union and domestic politics within Germany.

6. In a similar vein see Overturf (1994a) and chapter 10 below.

7. See Hyde (1991) for a description and analysis of these events.

8. Other conditions were that the single market be complete, the greatest number of EC currencies possible participating in the ERM of the EMS, and that the treaty be ratified by member country parliaments. A decision on stage three, introduction of the single currency, would be decided upon no later than the beginning of 1997.

9. Directorate-General for Economic and Financial Affairs (1990).

10. Remembering that Spain had joined in June of 1989, also at the wider band.

11. Brittan (1991) encouraged the United Kingdom in this speech to move on to the 2.25-percent band for even further beneficial results.

12. Implicit in this statement must be that a single currency is simply harder to revoke than "irrevocable" exchange rates.

13. See, for example, Marsh, et al. (1991). Also, as early as the Working Document, any attempt to base EMU "on competition between monetary policies" was rejected, at least by the Commission, because "it would lead either to one of the national monetary policies playing a dominant role or to the maintenance of a number of different policies, which would then rule out irrevocably fixed exchange rates. . . . Furthermore, there are no guarantees that a system based on such competition would lead to monetary stability and to greater cohesion between national policies."

14. It is only after adhering to price stability that the bank could support, as the Working Document puts it, "the objectives of general economic policy defined at the Community level." This is very similar to language in the Bundesbank charter. Other features of the bank included its access to the whole range of monetary instruments, including open market operations. Of course, the bank would control the issue of the common currency and the payments system. The national central banks, much like regional Federal Reserve banks in the United States, would be responsible for smooth payment operations, and relations with national financial institutions.

15. Also, see the argument below on shift from currency to credit risk, a point well taken by the Germans at this time.

Chapter 7

1. See Dinan (1994) for a complete discussion of the parallel EPU discussions, compromises, and results. In this there was what many considered minimal results, at least in any sense of transferring sovereignty of these issues to the Community level, due to the lack of serious motivation of any beyond the Germans. It will be remembered that it was at their insistence that EPU, attempting to deal with a "democratic deficit" in Europe as an antidote to greater sovereignty transfer in the monetary sphere, had been on the table.

2. An exception was to be the need for a two-thirds majority for the use of other "operational methods of monetary control."

3. Exchange-rate agreements were designed to be taken by the Council with unanimity, after consultation with the ESCB. For outside formal arrangements, only "general orientations" were to issued by the Council to the bank. Again, the price stability mandate was always to take precedence. See Henning (1994).

4. This last was a concession awarded the French.

5. Sandholtz (1993) reinforces the concern of Kohl and Genscher regarding the need to associate Germany closer to Europe given reunification. He also gives a paragraph (p. 137) of description of the agreement on final date that is worth repeating here in its entirety:

> At the summit, the French introduced a new wrinkle: if the two-step procedure did not produce a decision to start stage three, it would begin automatically on January 1, 1999. Perhaps the most surprising aspect of the proposal was that the Germans accepted it. Two German officials involved in the negotiations told me that Kohl's support for the final deadline was 'very surprising to all of us.' The same officials stressed that it was a personal decision by Kohl, and that nobody knew why he took it. They surmised that the chancellor wanted EMU to be irreversible, and the deadline would accomplish that. A British official shared that interpretation. However, Dutch participants offered another explanation: the deadline was accepted because it was proposed at 3:00 AM and everyone was exhausted.

6. Crockett (1994) points out that if a country keeps its budget deficit below 3 percent this implies, arithmetically, maintaining its debt to GDP ratio below 60 percent.

7. The treaty language does not necessarily rule out such a last realignment, but the emphasis is hardly there. The words are "the observance of the normal fluctuation margins provided for by the exchange-rate mechanism of the European Monetary System, for at least two years, without devaluing against the currency of any other Member State."

8. See Glick and Hutchinson (1992) and the sources referenced there.

9. See Dinan (1994) and Henning (1994).

10. One structural problem with EMU itself was how to deal with the non-participating states in terms of exchange-rate stability during the period when they were supposedly converging toward entry. This issue will be dealt with below.

Chapter 8

1. In a conversation in a private home over dinner, a middle class, middle-aged Dane responded to the question, "It's finally the Germans, isn't it?" with a simple "Yes."

2. Olsen (1992, p. 10) notes that "many Danes also wanted to teach the establishment a lesson. They were fed up with the Eurocrats in Brussels and tired of most of their own politicians." The Olsen article, incidentally, nicely outlines (p. 7) the major groups in Denmark that were in opposition, including a high percentage against "for females, for persons between 39 and 49 years of age, for citizens of the capital [Copenhagen], for those with either a short or a long education, for unskilled workers and for public sector salaried employees, and for

persons with little or no interest in politics." In addition the article identifies many of the concerns of Danish voters that might be considered reasons for the negative vote, including, among many of those noted in the text here, the lack of perception of any clear economic benefits to outweigh the loss of some political sovereignty.

3. There was a similar instance in history when New York had threatened to keep the rest of the United States from going forward with their Constitution.

4. With the addition of a question of the ability of the state to continue to outlaw abortion. This example alone would serve to demonstrate how broad a series of concerns were brought to bear on a treaty basically concerned with monetary union.

5. On the pro side, Françoise Laurent calls attention to the importance for many French voters of broader security issues, both to the final outcome of the French vote and to continuing support for monetary union.

6. As the crises continued the krona was finally allowed to float in November of 1992.

7. Attention being paid especially to sterling and the lira, but also perhaps the franc. At Bath "neither Mr. Lamont [for the United Kingdom] nor Mr. Sapin [France] would contemplate any devaluation of their currencies." See Norman and Barber (1992).

8. The amount was DM 24 billion. See Henning (1994).

9. Hans Tietmeyer (1994), a subsequent president of the Bundesbank, reports that bank's financing during September 1992 as totaling DM 80 billion. Henning (1994) reports DM 92.7 billion for the same period, including DM 36 billion on September 16 alone.

10. John Major announced the United Kingdom would not reenter the ERM until its "fault lines" were corrected; and was roundly criticized for what turned out to be a prophetic remark.

11. Later British recriminations followed regarding the divergent enthusiasm with which the Bundesbank handled interventions in the different currencies, but the amounts spent alone lend less credence to this as being a conspiracy against sterling and in favor of the franc. Nevertheless, it is undoubtedly true that the Bundesbank considered France to have been playing the game and deserving of support while Britain, in keeping interest rates too low, had not and was not.

12. It bears repeating that the Danish EMU opt-out is unconditional, save another referendum, while the U.K. opt-out allows for a later vote by Parliament on the desire of that state to enter the last stage of monetary union.

13. One with a sense of irony might probe, therefore, exactly in what it was that the Danes had approved participation when voting positively for this version of Maastricht.

14. That this choice was very important to the Germans is amply demonstrated by an incident related in Kaufmann (1995), where Kohl had objected to the former Dutch foreign minister Ruud Lubbers succeeding Delors as Commission president because Lubbers had earlier opposed Frankfurt as the seat of the EMI and the ECB.

15. Article 109 l 4, for example, had it that at the start of the third stage, "the ecu will become a currency in its own right."

16. Tietmeyer (1994) suggests DM 60 billion in Bundesbank intervention in July of 1993.

17. Except for the Dutch guilder–DM link, which remained at 2.25 percent.

18. The capital markets, in addition, could bring in such huge sums against a currency that it was increasingly understood that even the substantial resources of the central banks would be inadequate to the purpose of maintaining parities by intervention. See Andrews (1995).

19. See the arguments provided by Velis (1995), for example.

20. Part of this hypothesis is that as EMU approached the reputational costs of (perhaps a final) devaluation would drop, making a realignment more likely. See Froot and Rogoff (1991) and Craig (1992).

21. Not including, of course, the potentially significant financing charges that might be involved in "betting" the money of others through investing on margin, or even the opportunity cost of having to accept a lower rate of return on assets denominated in another currency than one's own.

22. Gilibert (1994, p. 135) suggests that "markets thus came to believe that the unemployment situation represented an obstacle to be removed at all costs by the incumbent [French] government whose austere polices, however credibly and consistently pursued, appeared insufficient for this task."

23. Gilibert (1994). There is, incidentally, an interesting parallel with the reentry of the United Kingdom to the gold standard in 1925 at what most concede was too high a rate, the old prewar rate, only to find itself forced to go off gold in 1931 by domestic conditions.

24. Thygesen (1994a), however, seems to argue that history might have been different if the member states, both creditors and debtors, had followed policies of unsterilized interventions, with implications on allowing interest rates to diverge in such a way as better to be able to maintain parities.

25. Brittan (1993), at the time, said "but it usually takes a shock . . . to shatter a system of pegged exchange rates. In the case of the ERM, the shock had been the costs of German unification and the German government's unwillingness or inability to finance these costs through normal budgetary means. As a result an interest rate policy which suited German needs has been prohibitively tight for other countries concerned to fight recession." Similarly, no less an authority than a president of the Bundesbank, Hans Tietmeyer (1994, pp. 34–5), remarked that "as regards German unification, nobody will want to deny that the real and financial burden imposed on the richer part of Germany with its implications for inflation and interest rates affected the functioning of the EMS. This is especially true because of the inappropriate policy mix in the early 1990s between fiscal and wage policy, on the one hand, and monetary policy, on the other." Filc (1994), incidentally, assigned a good deal of independent blame for the "policy mistakes" by Germany to the monetary authorities.

26. Davidson (1993) had it that "the ERM crisis is a political, not a technical problem. Experts may disagree over how, or whether, to revise the details of the EMU programme. But the basic problem is that there is no political consensus on the objective of monetary union."

27. Lionel Barber at the 1995 European Community Studies Association Conference in Charleston, South Carolina.

28. For more on these considerations, see Thygesen (1994a and 1994b), and Artus and Bourginat (1994).

29. Boyer (1994, p. 83) suggested that

> The Danish and French referendums, and the opinion polls conducted in their countries, show that the enthusiasm of a very substantial proportion of European citizens for the extent of economic and political integration involved by the Union has cooled considerably and the momentum of the late 1980s had become fraught with doubts. This split between public opinion and the political elites, who continue everywhere to show their backing for the form of European Union defined by the Maastricht Treaty, has resulted in a divorce whose consequences have been serious and could have been more serious still.

30. What David Aaron, U.S. ambassador to the OECD, referred to as "raising the bar." Hoffmeyer (1996), governor of the Danish central bank from 1965 to 1995, suggested that "we are in a situation where the political establishments in France and Germany have badly misjudged the opinions of their electorates. The resentment is too strong to be ignored. The result is that Germany's attitude is becoming more and more cautious—and its demands on other countries tougher—as it seeks to defuse domestic opposition to Emu." The other side of the ledger was represented in the French elections of May and June, 1997. Here the Socialists (joined in government by the Communist and Green parties) took control over the National Assembly, at least partially, by attacking the austerity measures seen as necessary to satisfy the convergence criteria.

31. See Thygesen (1995) for an appraisal of the interests of the parties involved and possible exchange rate scenarios of interaction between those inside monetary union and the "outsiders." From the viewpoint of the outsiders, for example, one objective for those willing to enter would be to have an exchange-rate mechanism that would allow them to demonstrate their commitment to the macroeconomic goals of EMU, while another would be to have a system that could provide a degree of stability in the transition. For the insiders, they would also value a system that did both of these, perhaps even especially the latter in the sense of avoiding competitive devaluations against the euro. In contrast, however, the insiders would value less a prior commitment by the ECB to intervene in support of an outsider's currency because of the implications of this for the price stability objective of the union. This latter would probably hold even if sterilization were guaranteed for the insiders and full nonsterilization guaranteed by the outsiders. It was decided in Dublin in 1996 that an ERM-like structure for the outsiders would continue to operate as those countries prepared themselves for eventual entry. Currencies could fluctuate relatively widely against the euro, but countries could also adopt narrower limits. Intervention by the ECB could be limited if the price stability goal were jeopardized. Participation in the system, however, bowing to U.K. demands, would be voluntary.

32. On the easy ride, including the low "pass-though" of the devaluations to inflation rates and the circumstances surrounding, see De Grauwe and Tullio (1994).

33. See Gilibert (1994) and Maystadt (1994) on these points.

34. As reinforced by Papadia and Saccomanni (1994).

Chapter 9

1. Feldstein (1992), in a relatively famous article, for example, says the proper question is not whether the political drawbacks of a federal structure that could follow on the adoption of a common currency are sufficient to counteract the economic benefits, but rather "would the political advantages of adopting a single currency outweigh the economic disadvantages?" See also Velis (1995).

2. It should be noted that the study from the Directorate-General for Economic and Financial Affairs (1990), called "One market, one money," also generally follows an economic goal format. In a sense this, too, may have contributed to the problem, for that report, which was commissioned to serve something of the same public relations function that the famous Cecchini Report did for the single market, was seemingly biased; it was generally considered a promotion vehicle for EMU. There is also the criticism of the report that it was to serve to quiet some of the critics of the Delors Report that that former document was not a "proper cost-benefit" study.

3. See Edison and Melvin (1990) on both nominal and real exchange rates being more variable under floating than under fixed-rate regimes.

4. See Bessembinder (1991), Melvin and Tan (1991), and Costa (1990).

5. Some have argued, perhaps not entirely seriously, that the loss of business implied in this area by the banking sector is enough to have it lobby, albeit somewhat quietly, against the adoption of EMU.

6. Bean (1992, p. 39) suggests that "since short-term volatility can be insured against through forward markets, only sustained misalignments which cannot easily be insured against present real problems." Connecting the two, however, is the reduction in quality of price signals, again affecting efficient allocation, arising from both short run volatility and longer term misalignments. See also Costa (1990).

7. See Edison and Melvin (1990) for some of the difficulties involved in the measurement of misalignments, especially against an equilibrium that is neither observable nor presently empirically determinable based on any agreed model. However, also see the long discussion in Copeland (1989), with the generally agreed result (p. 68) that

> there is not even much sign of a tendency toward PPP in the long run. All that can be said is that the long swings in real exchange rates which have characterized the 1970s and 1980s have eventually been reversed, so that long periods of overvaluation relative to PPP have invariably been followed by long periods of undervaluation. As a result, the times when PPP has obtained have been few and far between and, with the benefit of hindsight, look like chance encounters on the way from one extreme disequilibrium to an opposite one of more or less equal scale.

8. See Cushman (1988), but also the conclusions in Edison and Melvin (1990).

9. The question of price and wage adjustment, and by implication real exchange-rate change, is an important question, and one dealt with below in regard to adjustment to asymmetric shocks. Here the point is merely that with monetary union, traders at least know the nominal exchange rate is truly fixed, and hence are operating under a different sense of risk than when states have differing currencies and exchange rates. The empirical results noted on regime choice, therefore, cannot be expected to directly apply.

10. It being remembered that both nominal and real-exchange rates are more variable under both fixed and flexible rates than real exchange rates in monetary unions.

11. This is presumably what is meant when Costa (1990), for example, posits that "exchange-rate volatility will fragment the single market as it increases the uncertainty of prices and weakens the quality of price mechanisms for resource-allocation purposes." Similarly, De Grauwe, (1992, p. 69) feels that "a decline in real exchange rate uncertainty, due for example to the introduction of a common currency, can reduce these adjustment costs [due to misalignments]. As a result, the price system becomes a better guide to make the right economic decisions. These efficiency gains are difficult to quantify. They are no less important for this." He adds that errors based upon misalignments occur, and that "after a while these productions and investments have to be abandoned. Massive amounts of resources are wasted in the process."

12. At least there is this perception among businesspeople. The chairman of Deutsche Morgan Grenfell Bank, R. Schmitz, was quoted by Gawith (1996) as saying that "the economic benefits of a single currency were obvious, as exchange rate risk was a barrier to the growth of intra-European trade and investment."

13. Goodhart (1995, p. 478) on this point says that

> it is much less certain . . . that the EC countries would be prepared to continue with a single market if some participants were viewed as engaging unilaterally in competitive devaluations. Few doubt the overall benefits of a single market within the EC, but there is reason to doubt that a single market, with no exchange controls, and with free movement of factors, will be compatible with the ability of its constituent members to vary exchange rates autonomously and sharply. If exchange rates can be shifted independently of the desires and welfare of the other members, the continued cohesion of the single market . . . may be threatened.

Similarly, "if it is also accepted that pegged but adjustable exchange rates are fragile in the face of political unwillingness to realign promptly, and unstable in the face of speculative attacks on currencies seen as realignment candidates, the only way to guarantee the continued success of the single market may be to move rapidly on to EMU." The German banker quoted above also suggested "failure of the single currency project would put enormous upward pressure on the D-Mark, leading to sharp interest rate increases in several continental European countries, and regression into 'recurring competitive devaluations'. 'The final result, I fear, would be the renationalisation of economic policy in Europe,' said Mr Schmitz." (Gawith, 1996).

14. Such as the loss of the exchange-rate instrument, which will be discussed more below. Feldstein (1992), for example, in his story of an exporter who might look to his government to devalue in order to maintain the competitiveness of his exports to another country (in the face of a devaluation by a competing third country) overlooks the full implications of devaluation in a real world setting. The country that is being devalued "against," in other words, might want to have a say about the use of such a tool.

15. See De Grauwe (1992) on how reducing interest rates incorporating a risk premium could result in an increase in growth that would be more than temporary. That is, the country could be put on a permanently higher growth path, through the influence of dynamic economies of scale.

16. As in Andersen and Sørensen (1990).

17. Unless such risk is simply transferred to another part of the economy.

18. This, of course, comes closest to the German position. There is no particular consensus, however, among economists on the relationship between inflation and growth. It is possible that some positive rate of inflation is coincidental with the greatest rate of growth (see Bruno, 1995), but many would argue in return that maintaining a single rate of inflation at the optimal level for growth is very difficult. It would be better to aim for no or very low inflation in order to avoid an inflationary spiral that clearly would negatively influence investment and long-run allocation decisions.

19. See Bayoumi and Rose (1993) and Ingram (1973). Also see Amirkhalkhali and Dar (1990) on the degree of capital mobility in the EU.

20. Bofinger (1994, p. 41) suggests that

> in the case of the EC countries, empirical studies have shown that degree of production diversification is relatively high. According to calculations by Bini Smaghi and Vori (1993) the divergencies in the structure of manufacturing of EC countries amount to only half the size of divergencies that can be observed for the 12 U.S. Federal Reserve Districts. Therefore, it seems from the outset not very likely that the member countries of the EC could be affected by major idiosyncratic shocks.

21. See Goodhart (1995) and the sources noted there, including Eichengreen (1993). Also see Eichengreen (1989) and Thygesen (1987).

22. See also Gros and Thygesen (1992).

23. See Gerlach (1991) versus Laidler (1991).

24. The fact that Austria is a small country, especially open in trade to the large country with which it pegged, would not be one of these mitigating factors. In this way Austria's reaction should be in no way different from that of any country reacting to labor market conditions in the rest of the EU.

25. Another opinion is that an EU labor market will be more "transparent," meaning that workers will compare their wages with an EU rather than country or even regional standard. This could make it harder to achieve the kind of localized adjustments in wages necessary positively to affect employment. Some view recent trends in Germany as moving in this direction.

26. Sweeney (1991), on the other hand, looks to more shocks emanating from Eastern Europe affecting the EU states differentially. In terms of reaction, Bayoumi and Eichengreen (1993) find differential reaction to asymmetric shocks in Europe, with a core of states, generally coincidental with the group associated around the DM, more flexible in their reaction to such shocks (with implications for a two-speed Europe), probably related to the higher level of intra-industry trade existing within the core. They suggest in general, however, that European states adjust less quickly than U.S. regions to supply shocks, perhaps reflecting a larger degree of factor mobility in the United States.

27. See Bean (1992). Also, Kremers and Lane (1990) note that "a European central bank might be able to implement monetary control more effectively than the individual central banks."

28. A clear linkage important to the German case is the existence of balance-of-payments surpluses within a fixed-rate world, exacerbating demand and inflation from external imbalance. If the economy is in an over full employment position, domestic (monetary) policy is inadequate in dealing both with the surplus and potential inflation. See Kaufmann (1969) for an evaluation of the arguments around the 1961 German revaluation that remains strikingly pertinent, especially in representing the tensions between and positions of the underlying interest groups.

29. Kydland and Prescott (1977) and Barro and Gordon (1983) provide seminal contributions.

30. Tavlas (1993) adds the possibility of the government wishing to write off some of its outstanding debt as an inducement to inflate.

31. See Burdekin, et al. (1991) on the importance of political independence and a discussion on the value of mechanisms to support such independence.

32. See Goodhart (1995) on results from Masson and Taylor (1993) comparing the United States as a currency union on this point with the EC, finding that "there is certainly no presumption from the U.S. data that currency union makes convergence of living standards difficult." Again, it is not clear how much of this might have been due to factor mobility (perhaps influenced positively by currency union) and fiscal transfers.

33. See, however, Tsoukalis (1993).

34. See Bean (1992) and Grilli (1989) on these points.

Chapter 10

1. Caporaso and Keeler (1995, p. 43) suggest that "realism and neofunctionalism remain important and provide analytic categories that still organize much of the research."

2. Pentland (1973, pp. 75–76) says that

This is the basis for the functionalist critique of federal and confederal models, as well as of regional forms of integration, which may create, globally, deeper rifts than those they heal locally. If, therefore, we are to have regionalism at all, it must be functional, not territorial. In such terms, 'regions' are not entities like Western Europe or the Caribbean, but functional areas like railway transport or epidemic-control. For such fields the geographical scope of cooperation would be defined purely by their technological and human implications: railways, for example, might be planned on a continental scale, epidemic-control globally.

3. Caporaso and Keeler (1995, p. 31) use these very examples. For the functionalist

> Spillover referred to two different but related processes. The first, sectoral spillover, involved the expansion of integrative activities from one sector to another, e.g., from coal and steel to agriculture or from customs union to monetary policy. A second type of spillover involved increasing politicization of sectoral activity as, for example, when the coordination of monetary policies was replaced by a more centralized system of governance. Task expansion in this case requires a greater delegation of political authority by member states to international institutions.

4. As in Groom (1994, p. 115). "For the neofunctionalist the goal is the creation of a new state out of the integration of several states: neofunctionalism reinforces the state system in aspiring to beget more viable 'regional' states. There is no attempt to transcend the state system as in classical or traditional functionalism. The neofunctionalist strategy is merely a stratagem to give a new lease of life to the state system, not a device for its demise." Neofunctionalists, however, did not necessarily see it that way. Lindberg and Scheingold (1970, p. 7) suggest that "it might be argued that in the long run functionalism would necessarily undermine the nation-state. However, it posed no immediate—or even clear—threat [in postwar Europe]. Accordingly, in the European context, functionalism per se was an appealing path to those who wished to rebuild the nation-state and saw the primary obstacles as economic." They added that

> There was, in addition, a second brand of functionalism which we refer to as neofunctionalism. Neofunctionalism differs from traditional functionalism in that it establishes some prerequisites to effective problem-solving which involve a partial but direct threat to the autonomy of the nation-state. Specifically, it is argued that one must begin with a real delegation of decision-making authority to a supranational agency. In addition, it envisages a cumulative and expansive process whereby the supranational agency slowly extends its authority so as to progressively undermine the independence of the nation-state.

5. "The delegation of decision-making process to a new central organ." Lindberg (1994, p. 102) quotes Haas as saying that "Political integration is the process whereby political actors in several distinct national settings are persuaded to shift their loyalties, expectations and political activities toward a new center, whose institutions possess or demand jurisdiction over the preexisting national states. The end result of a process of political integration is a new political community, superimposed over the pre-existing ones."

6. Lindberg (1994, pp. 107–8) suggests that "The activities of the central institutions and non official elites may *create situations* [emphasis in original] that cannot be dealt with except by further central development and new central policies." Caporaso and Keeler (1995, p. 34) make the comparison with functionalism, in that the latter:

> self-consciously downplayed the importance of politics and the politician. By focusing on social and economic sectors, functionalism seemed to be saying that political actors could be 'finessed.' If concrete habits of cooperation could be put into place among countries by rival actors, governments would have to adjust policies and institutional frameworks. Neofunctionalists disagreed. They argued that a delegation of political power (however circumscribed) to a central authority was critical. Once in place, integration could proceed within this institutional framework; indeed the process of integration might outgrow the original framework and require institutional changes. Thus, for neofunctionalists supranational political elites were important catalysts to change.

7. Lindberg (1994, p. 107) again quotes Haas: "There is no dependable, cumulative process of precedent formation leading to ever more community-oriented organizational behavior, unless the task assigned to the institutions is inherently expansive, thus capable of overcoming the built-in autonomy of functional contexts and of surviving changes in the policy aims of member states."

8. As in Miles, Redmond and Schwok (1995).

9. See Bulmer (1994), Groom (1994), and Slater (1994).

10. As quoted in Caporaso and Keeler (1995, p. 35):

> The chief item in this lesson is the recognition that pragmatic-interest politics, concerned with economic welfare, has its own built-in limits. . . . Pragmatic interests, because they are pragmatic and not reinforced with deep ideological or philosophical commitments, are ephemeral. Just because they are weakly held they can be readily scrapped. And a political process that is built and projected from pragmatic interests, therefore, is bound to be a frail process susceptive to reversal.

11. See Caporaso and Keeler (1995, pp. 42–43).

12. Keohane and Hoffmann (1994, p. 253) find that, like the Treaty of Rome, the ratification of the SEA:

resulted less from a coherent burst of idealism than from a convergence of national interests around a new pattern of economic policymaking: not the Keynesian synthesis of the 1950s and 1960s but the neoliberal, deregulatory program of the 1980s. Reliance on 'mutual recognition' rather than harmonization reflected the decision to focus Community attention on removal of barriers rather than on means of economic intervention. This particular bargain illustrates the general point that the members of a regional organization must regard themselves as having a great deal in common, distinguishing themselves from outsiders.

13. Keohane and Hoffmann (1994, p. 251) reinforce that:

Part of the story of the Single European Act, therefore, is that governments decided to strike a bargain on deregulation which seemed to them to require, were it to be effective, reform of the decision-making system. Indeed, the Single European Act can even be seen as partly a way of completing arrangements for the enlargement of the Community to twelve members. A new form of spillover not from one economic sector to another but from one institutional dimension to another, took place. Under conditions of unanimous decisionmaking, expansion of the Community led to anticipation of institutional stalemate, and (because the key actors sought policy changes) created incentives for formal institutional change.

14. Overturf (1994a). Also, see Cameron (1992), who feels that:

In instituting a monetary regime that stabilized exchange rates and prices, the Community created the monetary foundation for a single internal market. By stabilizing exchange rates and prices, in an era after the collapse of the Bretton Woods system of fixed exchange rates when currencies were fluctuating and floating, the EMS facilitated trade and commerce among the member states of the Community. In a sense, the creation of the EMS, or something like it, represented a necessary precondition for the free flow of goods, services, and capital within the Community (pp. 47–48).

See also Woolley (1992).

15. In a similar vein see Eichengreen and Frieden (1995):

In this case, then, the Single European Act forced the issue. It required the removal of capital controls, which undermined the viability of the EMS and confronted the Community with the choice of reverting to floating or moving forward to monetary unification. Floating was incompatible with Europe's long-standing aversion to exchange-rate variability. Monetary unification was therefore a prerequisite for reaping the benefits of the product- and factor-market integration foreseen by the Single European Act (p. 273).

16. Goodman (1989) emphasizes the interaction between the strength of the financial community and the independence of the central bank.

17. Katseli (1989) documents the increase in effective power of the financial sector, and its concomitant attachment to stability, as represented by independent central banks.

18. Lake (1995, p. 129), referring to Keohane. See also Cohen (1995).

19. Keohane and Hoffmann (1994). On the political deficiency of the EU Richter (1993) finds (p. 188) that "the European Community is accepted as an efficient structure for solving problems of convergence, but it becomes more and more incomprehensible as a coherent political body and as a democratic system of political power." Similarly, he finds the EU an "invisible community" as viewed from the perspective of democratic ideals, a point not affected by the small steps taken on EPU. In sum he finds "The efficiency of an overall capitalist system represents a new, very loose form of collective identity for the territorially enlarged Community" (p. 193). Without questioning these views, it is interesting to note that, to the extent that they are valid, they can either be viewed along a full spectrum from representing control of the system by a small section of powerful financial and industrial elites to the classic traditional functionalist vision of the withering away of the need for nation-states.

20. See Sandholtz (1994).

21. Caporaso and Keeler (1995). See also Rhodes and Mazey (1995) for a careful delineation of terminology. Following more or less general practice, the term "realism" will apply without distinguishing between realism and neorealism. In this instance, the distinction seems less helpful and necessary as that between functionalism and neofunctionalism. Perhaps the reason realism is used so generally as the appropriate term—and one often finds realism and neorealism used interchangeably—is that they are very close and constitute almost a shared vision.

22. See Frieden and Lake (1991) and Mansfield (1994).

23. Similarly, "the extent to which process-level variables are said to supplement or dominate the effects of structural variables differs among critics of neorealism and other purely structural approaches. But they are all of the opinion that the elegance of structural theories is gained at the expense of explanatory power, and that adequate explanations of patterns of certain aspects of international relations cannot be developed in the absence of (at least some) reference to process-level variables" (Mansfield, 1994, p. 8). See also Krasner (1991).

24. See Moravcsik (1994), Woolley (1992 and 1993) and Coughlin, et al. (1991), as well as the discussion in Rhodes and Mazey (1995) on regime theory, with explicit reference to two-level games (Putnam).

25. For more on the French political problem of German economic power, and how best to try to control or at least effectively deal with a powerful Germany, see Le Gloannec (1992) and Overturf (1992).

26. There are, of course, possible answers to this, but their full consideration would move well beyond the scope of this chapter. One answer, however, the supposed "bargain" or trade at Maastricht, EMU for European acquiesce to reunification, betrays a misreading of all of the history prior to Maastricht, where Germany has hardly been a reluctant follower in moves toward EMU.

27. Eichengreen and Frieden (1995), p. 281, suggest "Germany had nothing to gain from monetary unification," while Sandholtz (1994, p. 283) finds that "on purely economic grounds, German motives for pursuing EMU would remain puzzling."

28. For a discussion and example, see Mansfield (1994) and Krasner (1991), respectively.

29. See, in further support, Guerrieri and Padoan (1989), who refer to new economic research efforts to delineate the dynamic gains from trade, especially as associated with economies of scale. They suggest (p. 15) that "in such a framework, government economic policies—industrial, trade and macroeconomic—aimed at influencing the productive structure and specialization of different countries play a much more relevant role than the one usually assigned to them in the traditional approach."

30. As in Rogowski (1989).

31. Eichengreen and Frieden (1995), Schmitter and Streeck (1994), Frieden (1991), and Gourevitch (1989). The last finds that there was in the postwar years something of a grand compromise (p. 270):

> the left accepted the market and property rights. The capitalists accepted trade unions and collective bargaining in a constitutionalist political framework, and the welfare state. Both groups supported agricultural programmes while the agricultural sector accepted support of industrial goals. All groups supported relatively open access to the international economy." Similarly (pp. 272–3), "the internationalists became the progressives, looking for labour's help to achieve an open trading system. Progressive business seems to have been characterized by high technology, an export orientation, and the manufacture of finished consumption goods; and it also included shipping and international commercial banking.

The labor-capital compromise was to be lost in the 1970s and 1980s under economic pressures and the need to deregulate and reduce costs, but without loss of power wielded by business interests. Goodman (1989) adds that the independence of the central bank (probably best not viewed as an exogenous variable), especially in Germany, undermined much of the political power one might associate with elections, political parties and labor. Also see Katseli (1989).

32. Again examining domestic interests, it has been proposed that there can be powerful interests that actually prefer fixed exchange rates over more variable rates that might provide some stimulus to export expansion through devaluation. These include importers, of course but, perhaps more importantly, the externally-oriented financial sector that benefits in the expansion of its international role from stability. See Katseli (1989).

33. See Le Gloannec (1992). The mid-1990s would witness a questioning of the viability of this linkage.

34. In economic parlance it was the "n–1st country," as in such a system only one country among the many participating (n countries) could independently set its

own policy. Again, any real devaluation that might occur for Germany in this model was only an extra marginal advantage, one that could easily be forfeited in periodic realignments in order to insure low inflation. In fact, the ideal would be no exchange rate changes at all, but this was only possible based upon perfect policy coordination.

35. Soon after his retirement from the Bundesbank, H. Schlesinger was asked after a speech how one could maintain a system of fixed exchange rates and independent monetary policies when capital was free to move. His answer was instructive; it was "Ah, that is the problem."

36. See Gowa (1994), Mansfield (1994), and the sources noted there.

37. Lake (1991) and Le Gloannec (1992). Katseli (1989) and Goodman (1989) argue for German macroeconomic power as exerted by the Bundesbank. See, however, Guerrieri and Padoan (1989).

38. Hoffmeyer (1996) notes that "the Germans resent others talking about the power which Germany has acquired. But irrespective of the incessant declarations by the country's politicians that power in Europe is not their aim, it is beyond question that the strength which the German economy has gained over many years is so substantial that it is a factor. When the Germans express an opinion or a wish on a political or economic issue they are listened to in a way that other countries are not."

39. See Kindleberger (1986) and Krasner (1991).

40. It is a part of the debate surrounding hegemonic stability whether or not a series of smaller states might, lacking a hegemon, agree to share the burdens imposed, as in Guerrieri and Padoan (1989). They look at Germany more as an oligopolistic leader than as a true hegemon, and define the conditions under which a system of oligopolistic interdependence might render integration possible. This in turn raises questions of state incentives, associated with the "prisoner's dilemma," which suggests that outcomes may be less than fully optimal given independent perceptions of the reactions of other players. See Gowa (1994).

41. The first of these points emphasizing countercyclical lending is less clear from the data, as net outflow slowed, for example, during the 1981–82 recession.

42. A criticism of hegemonic stability as a realist theory is that it does not seem to contain the exercise of power. Kaelberer (1995) posits, alternatively, that Germany was able to use its position as principal creditor in the EMS to force other members into realignments if they were otherwise impossible to achieve by mutual agreement. The incidents surrounding the 1992 crisis, where the Bundesbank seemed to support France without limit but did so in what has been described as a more tepid fashion for Italy and the United Kingdom, lend support to this view. More broadly, see also Lake (1995), Eichengreen (1995) and Krasner (1991).

43. Although Kaelberer (1995) is somewhat uncomfortable with the application of the term hegemon to Germany, he adds an important aspect of German leadership to the model, that of standard setting. Germany, that is, provided the model and the standard for growth and stability, and in this role it needed and needs to refuse to accept any other standard than its own. Other countries follow, and to the extent that they are satisfied and do not exit, policy conflict is avoided. See also Eichengreen (1995) on Britain and the United States providing a focal point for policy harmonization during their years as global hegemons. Le Gloannec (1992), incidentally,

adds "bribery" to the inducements to follow economic leadership, a point perhaps pertinent to the regional funding expected to accompany EMU.

44. Not unrelated, Goodman (1989) focuses on the importance of institutions for more medium-sized states, those that do not exactly fit the mold of a dominant state.

45. J. Walsh, in a letter to the author (May 19, 1995), underscores the reluctance of the Bundesbank to take on the role of hegemon by suggesting that the costs of German dominance of the EMS had been small for Germany, and when there was friction between external and internal objectives Germany would typically default toward the latter:

> The costs to Germany of participation in the ERM have been deliberately kept relatively small. When there has been a clear conflict between the domestic goal of low inflation and the international goal of stable exchange rates, the Bundesbank has chosen the former. Events in 1992–93 are only the latest and most dramatic example of this behavior. The Bundesbank has also had a relatively easy time of it with regard to intervention, rarely intervening 'intra-marginally' before the late 1980s, thereby forcing the burden of intervention on relatively weak currency countries with limited reserves.

It is, incidentally, another area of controversy in this area of the actual need for the hegemon to do much more than choose its own internal policy and let the rest of the world (in the case of global hegemons) follow suit. See, for example, Eichengreen (1995).

46. Hans Wrage, Deutsche Shell AG (retired), adds (in a letter to the author, dated February 22, 1994) that "in addition to rebuilding East Germany in the widest sense, there are structural problems in our West German industry, which will have to be solved. The social net is too extensive and is subject to misuse, unemployment is a long term problem and the budget deficits on a federal as well as a state and community level are exorbitant." He suggests that "basically the German industry is still strong, but without structural changes the future is bleak. Without a strong industrial backbone and continuing high exports we cannot maintain the strength of the DM, and we cannot extend leadership in monetary questions. Until we regain that strength EMU will have to wait as there seems to be nobody else in Europe who would be prepared or would be capable of taking over the role of the leading player." He adds in a later letter (February 2, 1996): "Personally I believe that EMU will come not necessarily for economic reasons but for overall political considerations, and there will be some leniency when it comes to the criteria."

References

Abraham, F. (1993), "Regional Adjustment and Wage Flexibility in the EC," paper presented at the CEPR conference in Vigo, Spain.

Abraham, F. and P. Van Rompuy (1992), "Regional Convergence in the European Monetary Union," paper presented at the North American Regional Science Association conference.

Amirkhalkhali, S. and A. Dar (1990), "On the Degree of Capital Mobility: An Empirical Analysis of OECD Countries," paper presented to the Eastern Economic Association conference in Lisbon, September.

Andersen, T. and J. Sørensen (1990), "Uncertain Exchange Rate Policies and Interest Rate Determination," unpublished.

Andrews, D. (1995), "European Monetary Diplomacy and the Rolling Crisis of 1992–1993," in C. Rhodes and S. Mazey, eds., *The State of the European Union, Volume 3*, Boulder, CO: Lynne Rienner.

Artis, M. and M. Taylor (1988), "Exchange rates, interest rates, capital controls and the European Monetary System: assessing the track record," in F. Giavazzi, S. Micossi and M. Miller, eds., *The European Monetary System*, Cambridge: Cambridge University.

Artus, P. and H. Bourguinat (1994), "The stability of the EMS," in A. Steinherr, ed., *30 Years of European Monetary Integration from the Werner Plan to EMU*, NY: Longman.

Baer, G. and T. Padoa-Schioppa (1989), "The Werner Report Revisited," backing paper to Delors Report (1989).

Barro, R. and D. Gordon (1983), "Rules, Discretion and Reputation in a Model of Monetary Policy," *Journal of Monetary Economics*, 12, 101–21.

Barzini, L. (1984), *The Europeans*, London: Penguin.

Basevi, G. (1988), "Liberalization of Capital Movements in the European Community: a Proposal, with Special Reference to the Case of Italy," *European Economy*, 36 (May), Belgium: Commission of the EC.

Bayoumi, T. and A. Rose (1993), "Domestic Savings and Intra-National Capital Flows," *European Economic Review*, 37 (August), 1197–1202.

Bayoumi, T. and B. Eichengreen (1993), "Shocking aspects of European monetary integration," in F. Torres and F. Giavazzi, eds., *Adjustment and growth in the European Monetary Union*, Cambridge: Cambridge University.

Bayoumi, T. and P. Masson (1994), "What Can the Fiscal Systems in the United States and Canada Tell Us about EMU," in P. Welfens, ed., *European Monetary Integration*, Berlin: Springer-Verlag.

Bean, C. (1992), "Economic and Monetary Union in Europe," *The Journal of Economic Perspectives*, 6, no. 4 (Fall), 31–52.

Beck, N. (1992), "An Institutional Analysis of the Proposed European Central Bank: A Political Scientist's Perspective," paper presented at the Western Economic Association meeting in San Francisco, July.

Bessembinder, H. (1991), "The Costs of Market Making: Evidence from Currency Markets," draft.

Bini Smaghi, L. and S. Vori (1993), "Rating the EU as an optimal currency area," *Banca d'Italia Temi di Discussione*, no. 187, January.

Bloomfield, A. (1973), "The Historical Setting," in L. Krause and W. Salant, eds., *European Monetary Unification and Its Meaning for the United States*, Washington, DC: Brookings Institution.

Bofinger, P. (1994), "Is Europe an optimum currency area?" in A. Steinherr, ed., *30 Years of European Monetary Integration from the Werner Plan to EMU*, NY: Longman.

Boyer, M. (1994), "Application of the Maastricht Treaty and the experience of a year of crisis in the European Monetary System," in A. Steinherr, ed., *30 Years of European Monetary Integration from the Werner Plan to EMU*, NY: Longman.

Brittan, L. (1991), (Vice-President of the Commission), speech to the Richmond Division Conservative Association, Commission Press Release, March 23.

Brittan, S. (1993), "Europe will still need a monetary system," *Financial Times*, 2 August, 10.

Bruno, M. (1995), "Inflation and Growth in an Integrated Approach," in P. Kenen, ed., *Understanding Interdependence: The Macroeconomics of the Open Economy*, Princeton, NJ: Princeton University.

Bulmer, S. (1994), "Domestic Politics and European Community Policy Making," in B. Nelsen and A Stubb, eds., *The European Union*, Boulder, CO: Lynne Rienner.

Burdekin, R., J. Westbrook and T. Willett (1991), "The Political Economy of Discretionary Monetary Policy: A Public Choice Analysis of Proposals for Reform," unpublished.

Caesar, R. (1988), "German Monetary Policy and the EMS," in D. Fair and C. de Boissieu, eds., *International Monetary and Financial Integration—The European Dimension*, Dordrecht: Martinus Nijhoff.

Cameron, D. (1992), "The 1992 Initiative: Causes and Consequences," in A. Sbragia, ed., *Euro-Politics*, Washington, DC: Brookings Institution.

Caporaso, J. and J. Keeler (1995), "The European Union and Regional Integration Theory," in C. Rhodes and S. Mazey, eds., *The State of the European Union, Volume 3*, Boulder, CO: Lynne Rienner.

Christie, H. (1989), "Comment" on Lomax (1989), in P. De Grauwe and T. Peters, eds., *The ECU and European Monetary Integration*, London: Macmillan.

Cohen, B. (1995), "The Triad and the Unholy Trinity: Problems of International Monetary Cooperation," in J. Frieden and D. Lake, eds., *International Political Economy*, 3rd edition, NY: St. Martin's.

Colchester, N. and D. Buchan (1990), *Europe Relaunched*, London: Hutchinson.

Collins, S. (1988), "Inflation and the European Monetary System," in F. Giavazzi, S. Micossi and M. Miller, eds., *The European Monetary System*, Cambridge: Cambridge University.

Copeland, L. (1989), *Exchange Rates and International Finance*, Workingham, UK: Addison-Wesley.

Costa, C. (1990), "EMU: The Benefits Outweigh the Costs," *European Affairs*, 4, no. 3 (Autumn), 22–7.

Coughlin, C., K. Chrystal and G. Wood (1991), "Protectionist Trade Policies: A Survey of Theory, Evidence, and Rationale," in J. Frieden and D. Lake, eds., *International Political Economy*, 2nd edition, NY: St. Martin's.

Craig, R. (1992), "Interest Rates, and the Incentive to Realign Prior to European Monetary Union," draft.

Crockett, A. (1994), "The role of convergence in the process of EMU," in A. Steinherr, ed., *30 Years of European Monetary Integration from the Werner Plan to EMU*, NY: Longman.

Cushman, D. (1986), "Has Exchange Risk Depressed International Trade? The Impact of Third Country Exchange Risk," *Journal of International Money and Finance*, 5, 361–79.

——. (1988), "U.S. Bilateral Trade Flows and Exchange Risk During the Floating Period," *Journal of International Economics*, May, 317–30.

Cutler, T., C. Haslam, J. Williams and K. Williams (1989), *1992 and the Struggle for Europe: A Critical Examination of the European Community*, Oxford: Berg.

Davidson, J. (1993), "Europe's flights of fantasy," *Financial Times*, 13 September, 30.

De Cecco, M. (1989), "The European Monetary System and national interests," in P. Guerrieri and P. Padoan, eds., *The Political Economy of European Integration*, Savage, MD: Barnes and Noble.

De Grauwe, P. (1992), *The Economics of Monetary Integration*, Oxford: Oxford University.

De Grauwe, P. and G. Tullio (1994), "The exchange rate changes of 1992 and inflation convergence in the EMS," in A. Steinherr, ed., *30 Years of European Monetary Integration from the Werner Plan to EMU*, NY: Longman.

De Grauwe, P. and G. Verfaille (1988), "Exchange Rate Variability, Misalignment, and the European Monetary System," in R. Marston, ed., *Misalignment of Exchange Rates: Effects on Trade and Industry*, Chicago: University of Chicago.

Delors Report (1989) (Committee for the Study of Economic and Monetary Union), *Report on Economic and Monetary Union in the European Community (with submitted collection of papers)*, Luxembourg: EC Official Publications, 1989.

Demopoulos, G. and K. Prodromidis (1994), "Fiscal Discipline in the European Monetary Union," *Atlantic Economic Journal*, 22, no. 3 (September), 1–7.

Dinan, D. (1994), *Ever Closer Union*, Boulder, CO: Lynne Rienner.

Directorate-General for Economic and Financial Affairs (1990), "One market, one money," *European Economy*, 44 (October), Belgium: Commission of the EC.

Driffill, J. (1988), "The stability and sustainability of the European Monetary System with perfect capital markets," in F. Giavazzi, S. Micossi and M. Miller, eds., *The European Monetary System*, Cambridge: Cambridge University.

EC Commission (1990a) (Final Proposal), "Economic and Monetary Union," August 21.

EC Commission (1990b) (Working Document), "Economic and Monetary Union: the Economic Rationale and Design of the System," March 20.

Economist (1991), "A German Idea of Europe," July 27, 50.

Edison, H. and M. Melvin (1990), "The Determinants and Implications of the Choice of an Exchange Rate System," in W. Haraf and T. Willett, eds., *Monetary Policy for a Global Economy,* Washington, DC: American Enterprise Institute.

EEC Commission (1962), *Memorandum of the Commission on the Action Programme of the Community for the Second Stage,* Brussels.

Eichengreen, B. (1989), "Is Europe an Optimum Currency Area?," paper presented at the conference on European Economic Integration and External Relations in Basel.

————. (1993), "Labor Markets and European Monetary Unification," in P. Masson and M. Taylor, eds., *Policy Issues in the Operation of Currency Unions,* Cambridge: Cambridge University.

————. (1995), "Hegemonic Stability Theories of the International Monetary System," in J. Frieden and D. Lake, eds., *International Political Economy,* 3rd edition, NY: St. Martin's.

Eichengreen, B. and J. Frieden (1995), "The Political Economy of European Monetary Unification: An Analytical Introduction," in J. Frieden and D. Lake, eds., *International Political Economy,* 3rd edition, NY: St. Martin's.

European Communities (1990), *Eurostat: Basic Statistics of the Community,* 27th edition, Luxembourg: Office for Official Publications of the European Community.

Feldstein, M. (1992), "The case against EMU," in *The Economist,* (June 13), 19–22.

Filc, W. (1994), "Credibility of German monetary policy on the road towards EMU," in A. Steinherr, ed., *30 Years of European Monetary Integration from the Werner Plan to EMU,* NY: Longman.

Folkerts-Landau, D. and D. Mathieson (1989), "The European Monetary System in the Context of the Integration of European Financial Markets," *Occasional Paper,* Washington, DC: International Monetary Fund.

Frieden, J. (1991), "Capital Politics: Creditors and the International Political Economy," in J. Frieden and D. Lake, eds., *International Political Economy,* 2nd edition, NY: St. Martin's.

Frieden, J. and D. Lake (1991), "Introduction," in J. Frieden and D. Lake, eds., *International Political Economy,* 2nd edition, NY: St. Martin's.

Froot, K. and K. Rogoff (1991), "The EMS, the EMU, and the Transition to a Common Currency," NBER Working Paper No. 3684, April.

Gawith, P. (1996), "Banker warns against 'stopping the Emu train'," *Financial Times,* February 9.

Gerlach, S. (1991), "Adjustable Pegs vs. Single Currencies: How valuable is the option to realign?" unpublished, July.

German Economists (1994), "EC currency union—an acid test for Europe," 1992 manifesto signed by sixty German economists, in A. Steinherr, ed., *30 Years of European Monetary Integration from the Werner Plan to EMU,* NY: Longman.

Giavazzi, F. and A. Giovannini (1987), "Models of the EMS: Is Europe a Greater Deutschmark Area?," in R. Bryant and R. Portes, eds., *Global Macroeconomics: Policy Conflict and Cooperation,* London: Macmillan.

Giavazzi, F. and A. Giovannini (1988), "The role of the exchange-rate regime in a disinflation: empirical evidence on the European Monetary System," in F. Giavazzi, S. Micossi and M. Miller, eds., *The European Monetary System,* Cambridge: Cambridge University.

Giavazzi, F. and L. Spaventa (1989), "The New EMS," paper presented at the conference on The European Monetary System in the 1990s, Athens.

Giavazzi, F. and M. Pagano (1988), "Capital Controls and the European Monetary System," in D. Fair and C. de Boissieu, eds., *International Monetary and Financial Integration—The European Dimension,* Dordrecht: Martinus Nijhoff.

Gibson, H. and E. Tsakalotos (1990), "Capital Flight and Financial Liberalization: A Study of Five European Countries," paper presented at the European Economic Association conference in Lisbon.

Gilibert, P. (1994), "Living dangerously: the lira and the pound in a floating world," in A. Steinherr, ed., *30 Years of European Monetary Integration from the Werner Plan to EMU,* NY: Longman.

Gillies, P. (1991), "East's Problems 'Rooted in the Ruins of Socialism'," *Die Welt,* 21 March, translated in *The German Tribune,* (March 31), 3.

Giovannini, A. (1994), "The debate on nominal convergence before and after the 1992 crisis," in A. Steinherr, ed., *30 Years of European Monetary Integration from the Werner Plan to EMU,* NY: Longman.

Giscard d'Estaing, V. (1994), "The year 2000: the European currency's first birthday," in A. Steinherr, ed., *30 Years of European Monetary Integration from the Werner Plan to EMU,* NY: Longman.

Glick, R. and M. Hutchinson (1992), "Budget Rules and Monetary Union in Europe," *FRBSF Weekly Letter,* no. 92–32, September 18.

Godeaux, J. (1989), "The working of the EMS: A personal assessment," backing paper to Delors Report (1989).

Goodhart, C. (1995), "The Political Economy of Monetary Union," in P. Kenen, ed., *Understanding Interdependence: The Macroeconomics of the Open Economy,* Princeton, NJ: Princeton University.

Goodman, J. (1989), "Monetary politics in France, Italy, and Germany: 1973–85," in P. Guerrieri and P. Padoan, eds., *The Political Economy of European Integration,* Savage, MD: Barnes and Noble.

Gourevitch, P. (1989), "The politics of economic policy choice in the post-war era," in P. Guerrieri and P. Padoan, eds., *The Political Economy of European Integration,* Savage, MD: Barnes and Noble.

Gowa, J. (1994), *Allies, Adversaries, and International Trade,* Princeton, NJ: Princeton University.

Grilli, V. (1989), "Seigniorage in Europe," in M. De Cecco and A. Giovannini, eds., *A European Central Bank?,* Cambridge: Cambridge University.

Groom, A. (1994), "Neofunctionalism: A Case of Mistaken Identity," in B. Nelsen and A Stubb, eds., *The European Union,* Boulder, CO: Lynne Rienner.

Gros, D. and A. Steinherr (1994), "In favour of EMU: a manifesto of European economists," in A. Steinherr, ed., *30 Years of European Monetary Integration from the Werner Plan to EMU*, NY: Longman.

Gros, D. and N. Thygesen (1992), *European Monetary Integration*, NY: St. Martin's.

Guerrieri, P. and P. Padoan (1989), "Integration, co-operation and adjustment policies," in P. Guerrieri and P. Padoan, eds., *The Political Economy of European Integration*, Savage, MD: Barnes and Noble.

Guitián, M. (1988), "The European Monetary System: A Balance Between Rules and Discretion," in *Policy Coordination in the European Monetary System*, Washington, DC: International Monetary Fund.

Harrop, J. (1989), *The Political Economy of Integration in the European Economy*, Hants, UK: Edward Elgar.

Hasse, R. (1988), "Costs and Benefits of Financial Integration in Europe," in D. Fair and C. de Boissieu, eds., *International Monetary and Financial Integration—The European Dimension*, Dordrecht: Martinus Nijhoff.

————. (1990), "A European Central Bank as an Instrument of European Monetary Integration," paper presented at the Western Economic Association conference in San Diego.

Henning, C. (1994), *Currencies and Politics in the United States, Germany, and Japan*, Washington, DC: Institute for International Economics.

Herz, B. and W. Röger (1992), "The EMS is a greater Deutschmark Area," *European Economic Review*, 36 (October), 1413–1425.

Hitiris, T. and A. Fervoyianni (1983), "Monetary Integration in the European Community," in J. Lodge, ed., *Institutions and Policies of the European Community*, London: Frances Pinter.

Hochreitner, E. and G. Winckler (1995), "The advantages of tying Austria's hands: The success of the hard currency strategy," *European Journal of Political Economy*, II, no. 1 (March), 83–111.

Hoffmeyer, E. (1996), "Bystanders at the infighting," *Financial Times*, February 9.

Huhne, C. (1989), "All Eyes are on Germany," *International Economy*, 3 (September/October), 18–20.

Hyde, A. (1991), "Toward a European Monetary Union," paper presented to the ECSA conference in Fairfax, VA.

Ingram, J. (1973), "The Case for European Monetary Integration," *Princeton Essays on International Finance*, no. 98 (April), Princeton, NJ: Princeton University.

Jenkins, R. (1990), "Thatcher: A Satisfactory Alternative to Delors?," *European Affairs*, 1/90, Spring.

Johnson, C. (1990), "A 10-Point Plan for European Monetary Union," *European Affairs*, 4, no. 2, 78–80.

Jozzo, A. (1989), "The Use of the ECU as an Invoicing Currency," in P. De Grauwe and T. Peters, eds., *The ECU and European Monetary Integration*, London: Macmillan.

Kaelberer, M. (1995), "Leadership and Monetary Cooperation," Chapter 5 in the author's dissertation, *Money and Power in Europe: The Political Economy of European Monetary Cooperation*, unpublished.

Katseli, L. (1989), "The political economy of macroeconomic policy in Europe," in P. Guerrieri and P. Padoan, eds., *The Political Economy of European Integration,* Savage, MD: Barnes and Noble.

Kaufmann, H. (1969), "A Debate Over Germany's Revaluation 1961," *Weltwirtschaftliches Archiv,* Band 103, Heft 2.

———. (1995), "The Importance of Being Independent: Central Bank Independence and the European System of Central Banks," in C. Rhodes and S. Mazey, eds., *The State of the European Union, Volume 3,* Boulder, CO: Lynne Rienner.

Kaufmann, H. and S. Overturf (1991), "Progress Within the European Monetary System," in L. Hurwitz and C. Lequesne, eds., *The State of the European Community,* Boulder, CO: Lynne Rienner.

Kenen, P. (1969), "The Theory of Optimum Currency Areas: An Eclectic View," in R. Mundell and A. Swoboda, eds., *Monetary Problems of the International Economy,* Chicago: University of Chicago.

———. (1988), "Reflections on the EMS experience," in F. Giavazzi, S. Micossi and M. Miller, eds., *The European Monetary System,* Cambridge: Cambridge University Press.

Keohane, R. and S. Hoffmann (1994), "Institutional Change in Europe in the 1980s," in B. Nelsen and A Stubb, eds., *The European Union,* Boulder, CO: Lynne Rienner.

Kindleberger, C. (1986), *The World in Depression, 1929–1939,* Berkeley, CA: University of California.

Krasner, S. (1991), "State Power and the Structure of International Trade," in J. Frieden and D. Lake, eds., *International Political Economy,* 2nd edition, NY: St. Martin's Press.

Kremers, J. and T. Lane (1990), "Economic and Monetary Integration and the Aggregate Demand for Money in the EMS," *IMF Staff Papers,* 37, no. 4 (December), 777–805.

Krugman, P. (1991), *Geography and Trade,* Cambridge, MA: MIT.

Kruse, D. (1980), *Monetary Integration in Western Europe: EMU, EMS and Beyond,* London: Butterworths.

Kydland, F. and E. Prescott (1977), "Rules Rather than Discretion: The Inconsistency of Optimal Plans," *Journal of Political Economy,* 85, 473–92.

Laidler, D. (1991), "One Market, One Money? Well, Maybe . . . Sometimes," in *Policy Implications of Trade and Currency Zones,* symposium sponsored by the Federal Reserve Bank of Kansas City, Jackson Hole, Wyoming, August.

Lake, D. (1991), "International Economic Structures and American Foreign Policy, 1887–1934," in J. Frieden and D. Lake, eds., *International Political Economy,* 2nd edition, NY: St. Martin's Press.

———. (1995), "British and American Hegemony Compared: Lessons for the Current Era of Decline," in J. Frieden and D. Lake, eds., *International Political Economy,* 3rd edition, NY: St. Martin's Press.

Le Gloannec, A. (1992), "The Implications of German Unification for Western Europe," in P. Stares, ed., *The New Germany and the New Europe,* Washington, DC: Brookings.

Lindberg, L. (1994), "Political Integration: Definitions and Hypotheses," in B. Nelsen and A Stubb, eds., *The European Union,* Boulder, CO: Lynne Rienner.

Lindberg, L. and S. Scheingold (1970), *Europe's Would-be Polity,* Englewood Cliffs, NJ: Prentice-Hall.

Lodge, J. (1989), "EC Policymaking: Institutional Considerations," in J. Lodge, ed., *The European Community and the Challenge of the Future,* London: Pinter.

Lomax, D. (1989), "The ECU as an Investment Currency," in P. De Grauwe and T. Peters, eds., *The ECU and European Monetary Integration,* London: Macmillan.

Ludlow, P. (1982), *The Making of the European Monetary System,* London: Butterworths.

Maastricht Treaty (Treaty on European Union) (1992), Council and Commission of the European Communities, Luxembourg: Office for Official Publications of the European Communities.

MacDonald, R. and M. Taylor (1990), "Exchange Rates, Policy Convergence and the European Monetary System," Discussion Paper Series, no. 444, September, London: Center for Economic Policy Research.

Machlup, F. (1977), *A History of Thought on European Integration,* NY: Praeger.

Mansfield, E. (1994), *Power, Trade, and War,* Princeton, NJ: Princeton University.

Marsh, P., I. Dawnay and D. Buchan (1991), "UK May Abandon 'Hard' ECU," *Financial Times,* May 13, 1, 18.

Masera, R. (1987), "An Increasing Role for the ECU: A Character in Search of a Script," *Essays in International Finance,* no. 167 (June), Princeton, NJ: Princeton.

Masson, P. and M. Taylor (1993), "Currency Unions: A Study of the Issues," in P. Masson and M. Taylor, eds., *Policy Issues in the Operation of Currency Unions,* Cambridge: Cambridge University.

Mastropasqua, C., S. Micossi and R. Rinaldi (1988), "Interventions, sterilisation and monetary policy in European Monetary System countries, 1979–87," in F. Giavazzi, S. Micossi and M. Miller, eds., *The European Monetary System,* Cambridge: Cambridge University.

Maystadt, P. (1994), "The role of the European Monetary Institute," in A. Steinherr, ed., *30 Years of European Monetary Integration from the Werner Plan to EMU,* NY: Longman.

McCulloch, R. (1983), "Unexpected Real Consequences of Floating Exchange Rates," *Essays in International Finance,* no. 153, August, Princeton, NJ: Princeton University.

McKinnon, R. (1963), "Optimum Currency Areas," *American Economic Review,* 51, 717–25.

Melitz, J. (1988), "Monetary discipline and cooperation in the European Monetary System," in F. Giavazzi, S. Micossi and M. Miller, eds., *The European Monetary System,* Cambridge: Cambridge University.

Melvin, M. and K. Tan (1991), "Foreign Exchange Market Bid-Ask Spreads and the Market Price of Social Unrest," paper presented at the Western Economic Association meeting in Seattle.

Miles, L., J. Redmond and R. Schwok (1995), "Integration Theory and the Enlargement of the European Union," in C. Rhodes and S. Mazey, eds., *The State of the European Union, Volume 3,* Boulder, CO: Lynne Rienner.

Mitrany, D. (1966), *A Working Peace System,* Chicago: Quadrangle Books.

Moravcsik, A. (1994), "Negotiating the Single European Act: National Interests and Conventional Statecraft in the European Community," in B. Nelsen and A Stubb, eds., *The European Union,* Boulder, CO: Lynne Rienner.

Mundell, R. (1961), "A Theory of Optimum Currency Areas," *American Economic Review,* 51, 657–65.

Norman, P. and L. Barber (1992), "The monetary tragedy of errors that led to currency chaos," *Financial Times,* December 11, 2.

Olsen, E. (1992), "Denmark on the Rocky Road from Maastricht via Edinburgh to Europe," unpublished.

Overturf, S. (1986), *The Economic Principles of European Integration,* NY: Praeger.

————. (1989), "The Real Impact of the European Monetary System," paper presented at the ECSA conference in Washington, DC.

————. (1992), "Forcing the Integration of Europe," *National Forum,* LXXII, no. 2, Spring, 26–28.

————. (1994a), "The Economics of the Renewed Integration Movement," *The Annals,* 531 (January), 84–93.

————. (1994b), "The European Community as an Optimum Currency Area," in P. Welfens, ed., *European Monetary Integration,* Berlin: Springer-Verlag.

Padoa-Schioppa, T. (1985), *Money, Economic Policy and Europe,* Brussels: EC Publications.

————. (1988), "The European Monetary System: A long-term view," in F. Giavazzi, S. Micossi and M. Miller, eds., *The European Monetary System,* Cambridge: Cambridge University.

————. (1989), "The ECU and the International Monetary System, A Panel Discussion," in P. De Grauwe and T. Peters, eds., *The ECU and European Monetary Integration,* London: Macmillan.

Papadia, F. and F. Saccomanni (1994), "From the Werner Plan to the Maastricht Treaty: Europe's stubborn quest for monetary union," in A. Steinherr, ed., *30 Years of European Monetary Integration from the Werner Plan to EMU,* NY: Longman.

Pelkmans, J. (1989), "Is convergence prompting fragmentation? The EMS and national protection in Germany, France and Italy," in P. Guerrieri and P. Padoan, eds., *The Political Economy of European Integration,* Savage, MD: Barnes and Noble.

Pentland, C. (1973), *International Theory and European Integration,* NY: The Free Press.

Peters, T. (1982), "EMU: Prospects and Retrospect," in M. Sumner and G. Zis, eds., *European Monetary Union: Progress and Prospects,* London: Macmillan.

Pinder, J. (1989), "The Single Market: a Step Towards European Union," in J. Lodge, ed., *The European Community and the Challenge of the Future,* London: Pinter.

Rey, J. and J. Michielsen (1988), "European Monetary Arrangements: Their Functioning and Future," in D. Fair and C. de Boissieu, eds., *International Monetary and Financial Integration—The European Dimension,* Dordrecht: Martinus Nijhoff.

Rhodes, C. and S. Mazey (1995), "Introduction: Integration in Theoretical Perspective," in C. Rhodes and S. Mazey, eds., *The State of the European Union, Volume 3*, Boulder, CO: Lynne Rienner.

Richter, E. (1993), "German Unification and European Integration: Points of Tension in Community Building," in H. Kurz, ed., *United Germany and the New Europe*, Brookfield, VT: Edward Elgar.

Rogoff, K. (1985), "Can Exchange Rate Predictability be Achieved Without Monetary Convergence? Evidence from the EMS," *European Economic Review*, June-July, 93–115.

Rogowski, R. (1989), *Commerce and Coalitions*, Princeton, NJ: Princeton University.

Rome Treaty (1957), (Treaty establishing the European Economic Community), Brussels: Secretariat of the Interim Committee for the Common Market and Euratom.

Russo, M. and G. Tullio (1988), "Monetary coordination within the European Monetary System: is there a rule," in F. Giavazzi, S. Micossi and M. Miller, eds., *The European Monetary System*, Cambridge: Cambridge University.

Sachs, J. and C. Wyplosz (1986), "The Economic Consequences of President Mitterrand," *Economic Policy*, 2 (April), 261–313.

Sandholtz, W. (1991), "The Politics of Monetary Union: Interests and Ideas," paper presented to the ECSA conference in Fairfax, VA.

———. (1993), "Monetary Bargains: The Treaty on EMU," in A. Cafruny and G. Rosenthal, *The State of the European Community, Volume 2*, Boulder, CO: Lynne Rienner.

———. (1994), "Choosing Union: Monetary Politics and Maastricht," in B. Nelsen and A Stubb, eds., *The European Union*, Boulder, CO: Lynne Rienner.

Sandholtz, W. and J. Zysman (1994), "1992: Recasting the European Bargain," in B. Nelsen and A Stubb, eds., *The European Union*, Boulder, CO: Lynne Rienner.

Schmitter, P. and W. Streeck (1994), "Organized Interests and the Europe of 1992," in B. Nelsen and A Stubb, eds., *The European Union*, Boulder, CO: Lynne Rienner.

Slater, M. (1994), "Political Elites, Popular Indifference and Community Building," in B. Nelsen and A Stubb, eds., *The European Union*, Boulder, CO: Lynne Rienner.

Smith, M. and W. Sandholtz (1995), "Institutions and Leadership: Germany, Maastricht, and the ERM Crisis," in C. Rhodes and S. Mazey, eds., *The State of the European Union, Volume 3*, Boulder, CO: Lynne Rienner.

Sommer, T. (1991), "Germany: United, But Not A World Power," *European Affairs*, 1 (February/March), 38–41.

Swann, D. (1988), *The Economics of the Common Market*, 6th edition, London: Penguin.

Sweeney, R. (1991), "Outlook for the European Monetary Union: The Message from Eastern Europe," *Contemporary Policy Issues*, 9, no. 4 (October).

Tavlas, G. (1993), "The Theory of Optimum Currency Areas Revisited," *Finance and Development*, 30, no. 2 (June), 32–35.

Taylor, P. (1989), "The New Dynamics of EC Integration in the 1980s," in J. Lodge, ed., *The European Community and the Challenge of the Future*, London: Pinter.

Thursby, J. and M. Thursby (1987), "Bilateral Trade Flows, the Linder Hypothesis, and Exchange Risk," *The Review of Economics and Statistics,* August, 488–95.

Thursby, M. and J. Thursby (1985), "The Uncertainty Effects of Floating Exchange Rates: Empirical Evidence on International Trade Flows," in S. Arndt, et al., eds., *Exchange Rates, Trade, and the U.S. Economy,* Cambridge, MA: Ballinger.

Thygesen, N. (1987), "Is the European Economic Community an Optimal Currency Area?" in R. Levich and A. Sommariva, eds., *The ECU Market,* Massachusetts: Heath.

———. (1988), "Introduction," in F. Giavazzi, S. Micossi and M. Miller, eds., *The European Monetary System,* Cambridge: Cambridge University Press.

———. (1989), "The Delors Report and European Economic and Monetary Union," *International Affairs.*

———. (1994a), "Monetary Arrangements," in C. Henning, E. Hochreiter and G. Hufbauer, eds., *Reviving the European Union,* Washington, DC: Institute for International Economics.

———. (1994b), "Reinforcing Stage Two in the EMU process," in A. Steinherr, ed., *30 Years of European Monetary Integration from the Werner Plan to EMU,* NY: Longman.

———. (1995), "The Prospects for EMU by 1999—and Reflection on Arrangements for the Outsiders," Economic Policy Research Unit, Copenhagen Business School.

Tietmeyer, H. (1994), "On the architecture of EMU," in A. Steinherr, ed., *30 Years of European Monetary Integration from the Werner Plan to EMU,* NY: Longman.

Tower, E. and T. Willett (1976), *The Theory of Optimum Currency Areas and Exchange-Rate Flexibility,* Special Papers in International Economics, no. 11, Princeton, NJ: Princeton University.

Tsoukalis, L. (1977), *The Politics and Economics of European Monetary Unification,* London: George Allen and Unwin.

———. (1993), *The New European Economy,* Oxford: Oxford University.

Ungerer, H. (1997), *A Concise History of European Monetary Integration: From EPU to EMU,* Westport, CT: Quorum.

Ungerer, H., O. Evans and P. Nyborg (1983), "The European Monetary System: The Experience, 1979–82," *Occasional Paper,* 19, Washington, DC: International Monetary Fund.

Ungerer, H., O. Evans, T. Mayer and P. Young (1986), "The European Monetary System: Recent Developments," *Occasional Paper,* 48, Washington, DC: International Monetary Fund.

Velis, J. (1995), "The Collapse of the EMS: Symptomatic of a Doomed EMU?" paper presented at the ECSA conference in Charleston, SC.

Viñals, J. (1990), "Spain's Capital Account Shock," Discussion Paper Series, no. 477 (November), London: Centre for Economic Policy Research.

Vona, S. and L. Bini Smaghi (1988), "Economic growth and exchange rates in the European Monetary System: their trade effects in a changing external environment," in F. Giavazzi, S. Micosi and M. Miller, eds., *The European Monetary System,* Cambridge: Cambridge University Press.

Weber, A. (1990), "EMU and Asymmetries and Adjustment Problems in the EMS: Some Empirical Evidence," Discussion Paper Series, no. 148 (August), London: Center for Economic Policy Research.

Welfens, P. (1994), "European Monetary Union: Post-Maastricht Perspectives on Monetary and Real Integration in Europe," in P. Welfens, ed., *European Monetary Integration*, Berlin: Springer-Verlag.

Werner Report (1970) (Werner Group), *Report to the Council and the Commission on the realisation by stages of Economic and Monetary Union in the Community*, Luxembourg: Council-Commission of the EC.

Wihlborg, C. and T. Willett (1991), "Optimum Currency Areas Revisited on the Transition Path to a Currency Union," in C. Wihlborg, M. Fratianni and T. Willett, eds., *Financial Regulation and Monetary Arrangements after 1992*, Amsterdam: Elsevier.

Williamson, J. (1983), *The Exchange Rate System*, Cambridge, MA: MIT.

Wood, G. (1988), "European Monetary Arrangements: their Functioning and Future," in D. Fair and C. de Boissieu, eds., *International Monetary and Financial Integration—The European Dimension*, Dordrecht: Martinus Nijhoff.

Woolley, J. (1992), "Policy Credibility and European Monetary Institutions," in A. Sbragia, ed., *Euro-Politics*, Washington, DC: Brookings.

———. (1993), "Linking Political and Monetary Union: The Maastricht Agenda and Domestic Politics," paper presented at the ECSA conference in Washington, DC.

Index